Success Stories

Dear Jyl,

I love your cookbooks! I just bought your newest addition, *Superfoods: Cook Your Way to Health*. I can't wait to start creating all the new recipes! For the past few years, I have enjoyed using all your cookbooks as a source of wonderful, healthy recipes. As a result, I have been able to maintain my weight. I am thirty-three years old; I began a diet *and* lifestyle change in May 1998 and have proceeded to lose seventy-six pounds! I have kept that weight off and love eating healthy. Your cookbooks offer so many choices in great tastes and wonderful ingredients. One of my favorites is your dessert cookbook. I can still have my cake and eat it, too! All your cookbooks contain recipes that are quick, delicious and very, very satisfying. Thank you for all of your efforts!!! Again, many thanks for your cookbooks . . . they are a staple in my kitchen! Keep up the "super" work!

—Mae Soleiman, Scarsdale, NY

Dear Jyl,

I received your book *Superfoods: Cook Your Way to Health* for my fortieth birthday from a friend. It is the best cookbook I have; at last count I had fifty-two books! I especially like the way your introduction was so full of great information. I love the simplicity of the recipes, the shopping lists and the nutritional information that is part of each recipe. It is a great book, and the best part about it is how much my family loves the recipes I make from it! I have made it a point to cook something from it almost every day since I received it. Have a great day!

—Paula Mesojedec, Streetsboro, OH

Dear Jyl,

I have ordered all of your cookbooks and absolutely love your recipes! They really help me plan my daily meals! Let me know when your new book comes out!

—Grace Bartholomew, Winchester, VA

Dear Jyl,

My New Year's resolution was to start an exercise and weight loss program. Within the past four months, I have lost thirty-four pounds. I belong to a weight-loss club and mentioned that I discovered a delicious date-bran muffin from your *Fat Free Living Super Cookbook*. Everyone asked that I bring the recipe to our next meeting. Well, I decided to take samples as well, and the entire group enjoyed them as much as I do. I also showed them my copy of your cookbook and many of them purchased it that week. Thank you so much for providing us with the tools necessary to continue on a weight-loss program while enjoying healthy and tasty meals. Every week I try several new recipes and have yet to be disappointed. Keep up the good work.

—Sherri Corle, Hague, VA

Dear Jyl,

I love your *Fat Free Living Family Cookbook* and *Roll Yourself Thin in 12 Minutes*. My husband's cholesterol was high, and since I started cooking from your books, he has lowered his cholesterol dramatically. Your cookbooks are great! Thank you so much!

—Sandra Atkinson, Littleton, CO

Dear Jyl,

My mother introduced me to your cookbooks, and I absolutely love them. I had two back-to-back pregnancies and have gained a considerable amount of weight. I recently purchased your family cookbook and enjoy making a lot of the different varieties of blender shakes. Thanks! P.S. I have lost twenty-six pounds, and I feel great!

—Tami Miller, Nevis, MN

Dear Jyl,

I wanted to take a minute this morning to thank you for all your cookbooks. Glad to see someone else has found the key to life . . . Fad diets are out. A healthy lifestyle is in! Keep up the good work.

—Pat Garrett, Belleview, FL

Dear Jyl,

I purchased your *Fat Free Living Super Cookbook* a few years ago and have made several of your terrific recipes. I have tried to get everyone I know to purchase this wonderful book. The recipes are not only delicious but contain ingredients that are readily available and easy to make. I have received many compliments, as well as surprises, from my family and friends when I tell them it is from my "fat-free" cookbook. They can't believe that fat free can be so easy and delicious. One of my favorite features of your cookbooks is the quick reference shopping list at the bottom of each page. This *so* handy! The nutritional information is wonderful for anyone watching their cholesterol, carbohydrates, etc. Having all this available along with the servings is a real time-saver.

Thanks for making fat-free eating so simple and good! Keep up the good work!

—Teresa Sedlacek, Chandler, AZ

Dear Jyl,

I now own five of your cookbooks, and we enjoy trying out new recipes from them every week. Every time we find a "keeper," I copy it into a small notebook that goes along with us when we travel. When we visit family around the country, I use the recipes to cook healthy dinners for all of us. We all love your recipes.

—Theresa Huggins, Aurora, MN

Dear Jyl,

I want to tell you the high regard I have for your books. Over the years I have collected a lot of books. I almost gave up hope of finding good low-fat books. I have every one you have written. I have a slight cholesterol and triglyceride problem. My weight is okay, but a few pounds less wouldn't hurt. I now feel I have the answer to both. Thanks for all the effort that went into your writing. Love the loads of recipes and choices.

—Ida Riegelmayer, Bedford, OH

Dear Jyl,

My sister bought your cookbook *Superfoods* from QVC. We started the two-week menu, and we love the food. Thank you for your time and your books. I never thought eating so healthy could taste so good!

—Anna Paris, Cambridge, MA

Dear Jyl,

I have all your cookbooks and just love them. My favorite is your latest, *Superfoods: Cook Your Way to Health*—especially the soups! I almost exclusively cook out of your books every night. For the holidays, I made the Minestrone Soup, and my entire family raved! The Tortilla Soup is also a big hit! When is your next cookbook coming out? Thanks for the great recipes!

—Melody Konte, Mill Valley, CA

COOK ONCE, EAT FOR A WEEK

Jyl Steinback

A Perigee Book

A Perigee Book
Published by The Berkley Publishing Group
A division of Penguin Putnam Inc.
375 Hudson Street
New York, New York 10014

ISBN 0-7394-3358-X

Printed in the United States of America

CONTENTS

ACKNOWLEDGMENTS

I want to thank all of you for helping me make the world a healthier place as you feed your families with all our recipes. I love your letters and e-mails. You make my day, and I appreciate all of your wonderful support and energy.

To all the wonderful success stories: You are amazing! You make my mission to create a healthier world so enjoyable and exciting. Thank you for your words of encouragement and fabulous support. Please keep those cards and letters coming (as my dad always says). (See contact information, page xiii.) I love them all! I truly enjoy working with each and every one of you. Thank you!

Gary—You are my best friend, mentor and lover. Together we grow strong. Thank you for "you" and for being a part of this exciting journey. We are a great team! I love you, Gar, with all my heart and soul!

Jamie—What a beautiful lady you are, from the inside out. I look so forward to seeing you each morning when you come into the exercise room before school. Every day, I look at you and think how lucky I am to have you as my daughter. Thank you for your special heart and wonderful love. You are a blessing in my life! I love you, Jam!

Scott—You are my sunshine! Your smiling eyes are electrifying, and you make my heart melt! I love the way you always express yourself with such energy and excitement. You are a gift in my life! I love you, Scott!

Mom and Dad—I say this every time but you are my best cheerleaders. I could not be where I am in life—mentally, physically or spiritually—if it weren't for both of you. Thank you for the gift of life, and as you know, I am loving every minute of it!

Jacie—You edited this whole book! You are fabulous! Thank you! You are an extraordinary sister! Thank you for your unconditional love all the time! I love you!

Jeff, Diane, Alex and Casey—I love you and I love being on QVC because I get to stay at your house and stay up all night talking. Your house and Vegas are the only two places I can stay up past 9 P.M. Thanks for everything! I love you!

Snooky and Harlan—Thank you for always being there and for all your wonderful support. I love you both very much!

Grandma—I love you!

I have been blessed in so many ways in life. Working with these extraordinary and creative people is at the top of my list. Thank you to each and every one of you for making this book possible!

Mikki—You are a miracle in progress! You are talented and creative beyond words. You are an extraordinary friend and partner. I thank you for your gentle kindness, loving heart and special friendship. All of your hard work helped me create and make *Cook Once, Eat for a Week* possible. Thanks, Mikki, for always being there!

Deb—I love working with you. This is our ninth book together. Your support is amazing, and you are an incredible nutritionist and special friend! Thank you so much, Deb! (Debra Kohl can be reached at 602-266-0324.)

El—You are part of the family by now. This is our sixth cover together and you have made them all fun. You work well with my family, and your photography is extraordinary. The front cover is spectacular. Thank you for everything. As always, you are the best. (Elliot Lincis can be reached at 602-923-1858.)

Linda Ship, you did wonders to my face and hair. An instant face-lift and I love it, with all of your wonderful make-up and creative talents. Thanks a million.

John Duff—It was great having you in sunny Arizona for our family photo cover shoot. Your special touch and wonderful humor helped make *Cook Once, Eat for a Week* perfect and relaxed for all of us. Thank you so much for always going that extra mile to make everything extraordinary.

Jeanette Egan—What a blessing you are and a fabulous editor. Thank you for all your detail touches in helping design our beautiful center island for our cover photo. Thank you for all your support.

INTRODUCTION

Cook Once, Eat for a Week is a fabulous book for the "busy mom" who wants to feed her family healthy meals without spending hours in the kitchen. We have added easy-to-read shopping lists; subtitles that classify preparation, cooking, storage and reheating methods; health and cooking tips; a mix-and-match menu plan; and, for the first time ever, a substitution and equivalent chart that can be used to meet your personal taste. Don't like trout or almonds? We provide a list of alternates. It also solves those last-minute cooking emergencies when you're in the middle of preparing a cake for dessert and discover you're out of powdered sugar! What to do? The substitutions and equivalents charts come to the rescue without you having to run to the store! My favorite part is being able to cook once and provide fun, exciting and delicious meals all week long.

As America's Healthiest Mom, I've played every starring role—housekeeper, chef, chauffeur, teacher, doctor, nurse, psychologist, police patrol, planner and entertainer. How do I juggle multiple roles, maintain a happy and healthy home and keep my sanity intact?

One meal plan with
Recipes my family loves.
Grocery lists with food and packing supplies such as
All kinds of wrap for
No-leak, seal-tight, safety-proof storage.
Individual servings stored in
Ziploc and vacuum-pack bags or containers (variety of sizes, shapes and colors)
Accurately labeled with instructions to
Thaw, reheat and serve.
Instant mixes, soups, marinades and an
Open mind to experience something
New and exciting to save time, energy and money with a positive focus on health!

The concept of the book is simple: Plan, prep and cook ahead for simple, convenient meal planning. Each recipe includes information for preparation, cooking and storing directly under each title. Having a holiday party? Select recipes that can be prepared ahead, frozen and baked later. Want to cook this morning for tonight's dinner? Select recipes you can prepare, refrigerate and serve later. Get the idea? It's simple, quick and convenient.

Learning the lingo . . .

- **Prep—Chill:** Prepare recipe and refrigerate, and it's ready to serve when you are. Check chart (page xviii), for safe refrigerated storage times.
- **Prep—Chill—Bake:** Prepare recipe, refrigerate and bake when ready to serve. Many of these recipes can also be frozen before or after cooking (read recipe for specific instructions).
- **Prep—Bake—Refrigerate or Freeze:** Prepare recipe, bake and refrigerate or freeze according to instructions. Follow tips for safe storage, seal-tight containers and reheating.
- **Prep—Cook—Refrigerate or Freeze:** Prepare recipe, cook on stovetop or microwave oven and refrigerate or freeze. This applies mostly to soups, stews and skillet dishes.

Cook Once, Eat for a Week includes a nutritionally balanced variety of recipes from appetizers to desserts—main dishes for meat lovers and vegetarians and simple sides to complete your meals. Each chapter includes helpful information on the following topics:

- **Guidelines for safe food-handling and storage.**
- **To freeze or not to freeze** . . . That's always the question! From hot to cold and cold to hot—the easiest and safest methods for taking your meal from freezer to table (packing, thawing and reheating tips).
- **Timesavers save time!** Simple tips for those who love shortcuts!
- **Seasonings and spice for everything nice!** Spark up any recipe with a variety of seasonings and spices—be daring, bold and innovative as *you* create the flavors your family loves!
- **Everything old is new again!** Don't get rid of leftovers . . . make them work for you!
- And just when you thought it couldn't get any better than that, there is your best guide to **substitutions and equivalents** along with the perfect **mix-and-match menus** for simple meal planning!

Important:

- *Recipes in this book include recommended cooking/baking times that have been successfully tested in our kitchens, BUT oven temperatures can vary and altitude levels will affect cooking times. Check dishes a few minutes before the indicated time and adjust cooking times according to your equipment (oven, microwave, stovetop).*
- *All the recipes call for cooking spray to be used on dishes, pans and cookie sheets. Cooking spray is not included in the ingredient list unless it is to be applied to food, but should be a staple in your kitchen.*
- *In most cases, optional ingredients or ingredients not required for recipe preparation are not included in the nutritional information or shopping list. Plan accordingly once you decide what you want to accompany the particular recipe (i.e., vegetable crudités, crackers, salsa, cheese).*
- *Be creative! Adapt recipes to individual preferences. If you or your family are not excited about a particular ingredient in the recipe such as onions or chiles, omit or substitute with ingredient of your choice and prepare as directed.*
- *For any questions regarding serving sizes, equivalents and substitutions, refer to the complete guide (page 249).*

Jyl Steinback, 15202 N. 50th Place, Scottsdale, AZ 85254
1-866-LIVE-FIT
e-mail: **Jyl@AmericasHealthiestMom.com**
website: AmericasHealthiestMom.com

THINGS EVERY COOK
NEEDS TO KNOW

General Food Safety

- Wash your hands often, especially before and after handling raw food.
- Keep raw meats and poultry separate from other foods.
- Use separate cutting boards for raw meats and poultry.
- Cook foods to proper internal temperatures: ground meats to 160°F; ground poultry to 165°F; beef, veal and lamb steaks, roasts and chops may be cooked to 145°F; all cuts of fresh pork to at least 160°F; whole poultry should reach 180°F in the thigh, 170°F in the breast.
- For rapid cooling, divide cooked foods into small, shallow containers to store in refrigerator or freezer until serving.
- Refrigerate cooked foods at temperatures below 40°F.
- The USDA recommends keeping hot foods hot (above 140°F) and cold foods cold (below 40°F).
- Throw away any foods kept at temperatures between 41 to 139°F for more than 2 hours, because at these temperatures, any bacteria present can double every 20 to 30 minutes.
- Most leftovers are safe in the refrigerator for 3 to 4 days. They are safe indefinitely in the freezer but are best if used within 2 to 4 months. All leftovers should be reheated to 165°F.
- Do not taste food until it has reached a safe internal temperature.
- Never partially cook food you plan to finish cooking later. This will increase the risk of bacterial growth on the food. Bacteria are killed when foods reach a safe internal temperature.
- It is safe to reduce oven temperature by 25°F when using a convection oven. Check the manufacturer's directions for additional information.
- Safe microwaving tips:
  - Stir or rotate food halfway through cooking time to eliminate cold spots and guarantee more even cooking.
  - Cover food with microwave-safe wrap.
  - Foods can be partially cooked in the microwave *only* if the food is immediately finished cooking by baking, broiling, grilling or stir-frying.
  - Follow recipe instructions for "standing times" as foods finish cooking once removed from microwave.

For more food safety tips, contact Food and Safety Information:
USDA's Meat and Poultry Hotline
1-800-535-4555

10 A.M. to 4 P.M. Eastern time, Monday through Friday, with
recorded messages available 24 hours a day.
FDA's Food Information and Seafood Hotline
1-800-332-4010
Recorded message and fax service available 24 hours a day.
Partnership for Food Safety Education Website
www.fightbac.org

Keeping Foods Fresh

- Freeze foods at peak quality; they will taste better than foods frozen after several days of refrigeration.
- Immediately freeze foods you don't plan to use within 1 to 2 days.
- Slightly undercook prepared foods; they will finish cooking when reheated.
- Most casseroles can be prepared and refrigerated up to 24 hours in advance. Add 15 to 20 minutes to cooking time if casseroles are chilled.
- To test egg freshness: Immerse egg into a pan of salted, cool water. If the egg sinks, it's fresh; if it rises to the surface, throw it away.
- Most canned foods, when properly stored at normal room temperatures, will stay good for several years.
  - Low-acid canned goods, including canned meat/poultry; soups and stews (without tomato base); pasta products; vegetables: 2 to 5 years
  - High-acid canned goods, including tomato products, fruits and foods in vinegar-based sauce or dressing: 12 to 18 months
  - Canned meat and poultry: 2 to 5 years

Best Freezing Supplies

- Heavy-duty aluminum foil, plastic wrap, plastic freezer bags and vacuum-packed FoodSaver® bags
- Food-grade plastic containers made of moisture- and vapor-resistant material
- Freezer-to-microwave or freezer-to-oven containers in a variety of sizes:
  - Quart containers hold 4 to 6 servings.
  - Pint containers hold 2 to 3 servings.
- Select containers with wide top openings so food can be easily removed without thawing.
- Foods can be frozen in supermarket wrappings if they are used within a month or two. For longer storage, overwrap packages with moisture- and vapor-resistant materials.

To Freeze or Not to Freeze . . .
Foods That Don't Freeze Well

BAKED GOODS
- cake icings made with egg whites
- cream fillings
- custards
- meringues
- puddings
- unbaked biscuits or muffins

CONDIMENTS
- mayonnaise

DAIRY/EGGS
- buttermilk
- cottage, cream and ricotta cheeses
- eggs, whole or cooked egg whites
- heavy cream (won't whip after freezing)
- milk-based sauces
- pasteurized whipping cream
- sour cream
- whipped butter or margarine
- yogurt

FRUITS
- raw apples
- melons

PREPARED FOODS
- battered foods
- bread crumb toppings
- foods made with gelatin
- fried foods (other than french fries and onion rings)
- fruit jelly inside sandwiches
- gravies or fat-based sauces
- hard-cooked egg whites
- luncheon meats
- pastas and grains in cooked recipes will become softer (undercook for best results)
- soups/stews thickened with cornstarch and flour
- soups/stews made with potatoes
- stuffing inside turkey
- tube cans of rolls, biscuits or pizza dough

SEASONINGS
- extracts and flavorings
- dried herbs

VEGETABLES, RAW
- cabbage
- celery
- cucumber
- potatoes
- radishes
- salad greens
- tomatoes

Safe Storage Times for Refrigerated or Frozen Foods

Product	Refrigeration (40°F or less)	Freezer (0°F)
BAKED GOODS		
• Unbaked bread		1 month
• Baked, unfrosted cake (angel food, chiffon, sponge or cheesecake)		2–3 months
• Baked, unfrosted chocolate, pound, white or yellow cake		4–6 months
BEVERAGES		
• Citrus fruit and homemade frozen juices	6 days	6 months
• Fruit juice concentrates		12 months
CASSEROLES		
• Meat, fish or poultry	3–4 days	2–3 months
CONDIMENTS		
• Mayonnaise, commercial, opened	2 months	DO NOT FREEZE
• Hard cheese	2–3 weeks	4 months (thaw in refrigerator)
DAIRY		
• Hard cheese	2–3 weeks	4 months (thaw in refrigerator) 4–8 months in FoodSaver® bag
• Soft cheese	5 days	DO NOT FREEZE
• Butter		6–9 months
• Cream		2 months (thaw in refrigerator; heavy cream will not whip after freezing)
• Fresh eggs in shell	3–5 weeks	DO NOT FREEZE
• Raw egg whites and yolks	2–4 days	12 months
• Hard-cooked eggs	7 days	DO NOT FREEZE
• Pasteurized egg substitute, unopened	10 days	

Product	Refrigeration (40°F or less)	Freezer (0°F)
• Pasteurized egg substitute, opened	3 days	
• Cooked egg dishes	3–4 days	12 months
• Margarine	4–5 months	1 month (thaw in
• Milk	7 days	refrigerator; best if used for cooking and baking)
• Buttermilk, sour cream or yogurt	7 days	DO NOT FREEZE
FISH		
• Bluefish, perch, mackerel or salmon	1–2 days	2–3 months
• Breaded fish		3 months
• Cod, flounder, haddock or sole		6 months
• Shellfish, cooked		3 months
• Shellfish, uncooked		3–6 months
FROZEN FOODS		
• Ice cream, ice milk, sherbet		2 months
• TV dinners, frozen casseroles		3–4 months
FRUITS		
• Apples	1–3 weeks	DO NOT FREEZE
• Berries, cherries, peaches, pears, pineapple, etc.	1–2 days	12 months
• Fresh, uncut limes	1 month	
• Fresh, cut limes (in plastic bag)	5 days	
• Melons	7 days	DO NOT FREEZE
• Strawberries	3 days	12 months
MEAT		
• Ground beef, raw	1–2 days	2–3 months
• Hot dogs, unopened	2 weeks	1–2 months
• Hot dogs, opened package	1 week	1–2 months
• Luncheon meat, unopened	2 weeks	1–2 months
• Luncheon meat, opened	3–5 days	1–2 months
• Steaks or chops, uncooked	2–3 days	4–6 months
• Cooked meat and meat casseroles	3–4 days	2–3 months

THINGS EVERY COOK NEEDS TO KNOW

Product	Refrigeration (40°F or less)	Freezer (0°F)
POULTRY		
• Chicken, whole or cut up, uncooked	1–2 days	3 months
• Cooked	3–4 days	3–4 months
• Cooked casseroles	3–4 days	4–6 months
SOUPS/STEWS		
• Vegetable or meat	3–4 days	2–3 months
VEGETABLES		
• Home frozen		10 months
• Fresh: asparagus, corn in husks, beans (green or wax), mushrooms, shredded cabbage, leaf and bib lettuce, salad greens, tomatoes (ripe) or cabbage	1–2 days	All vegetables: 1–2 years in vacuum-packed FoodSaver® bags
• Head lettuce (washed and drained), unshelled peas, lima beans and or spinach	3–5 days	
• Beets, cabbage, carrots, celery and radishes	7–14 days	
• Purchased frozen packages (cartons, plastic bags or boil-in bags)		8 months
OTHER FOODS		
• Gravy, broth	1–2 days	
• Canned fruits, opened	7 days	
• Canned vegetables, opened	2–3 days	
• Puddings or custards, opened	1–2 days	
• Pizza	3–4 days	1–2 months
• Stuffing, cooked	3–4 days	1 month
• Prepared deli salads (chicken, egg, tuna, macaroni or potato)	3–5 days	DO NOT FREEZE
• Unopened vacuum-packed dinners with USDA seal	2 weeks	

Freeze-Safe Tips

- Freezer temperatures should never go above 0°F; fluctuating temperatures can affect the quality of frozen foods.

- Supermarket wrappings are safe for most foods frozen 1 to 2 months, but for best quality, overwrap packages with heavy-duty freezer materials or store in plastic freezer bags.
- Cool foods quickly before packaging. Don't let food stand at room temperature longer than 30 minutes before freezing.
- Freeze food as soon as it is cooled to room temperature (or refrigerate in shallow containers uncovered until cooled, then package and freeze).
- Label all foods with recipe name, date, number of servings, thawing and reheating directions and "use-by" date.
- Do not overload your freezer with new foods; add no more than 2 to 3 pounds of food per cubic foot of freezer capacity so air can circulate for proper freezing.
- Leave space between packages so air can circulate around them.
- If you are unsure about the quality of certain foods after freezing, freeze a small amount first and test for quality after thawing and reheating.
- Frozen raw foods that have been cooked can be refrozen (i.e., fresh chicken → packaged and frozen → thawed → cooked → frozen → thawed → reheated).
- You can refreeze unused portions of cooked foods that have previously been frozen and thawed in the refrigerator.
- Seal containers with as little air as possible **unless** freezing liquid or semiliquid foods that expand when frozen. Leave a 1½-inch space below the rim to allow for expansion.
- When freezing casserole dishes or containers with empty space between the food and lid, fill "dead spaces" with crumpled wax paper.
- Store food in 1-gallon freezer bags; press out all the air and seal tightly so bags can be stacked on top of each other.
- Do not freeze tomato-based or other acidic foods in aluminum baking pans, or cover them with aluminum foil.

How to Prevent Freezer Burn
- Freezer burn occurs when foods are frozen for an extended period of time or not properly wrapped and sealed. Even though these foods do not pose any health risks, the freezer-burned areas will be dried out and tasteless. For best results, cut away freezer-burned portions before or after cooking.
- When wrapping foods for freezing, get as much air out as possible so moisture cannot get in. Vacuum-packing in FoodSaver® bags removes the air and keeps moisture out so foods can be frozen longer without freezer burn.

- Use moisture- and vapor-resistant packaging that can be tightly sealed.

Thawing Foods Safely
- NEVER defrost perishable foods (meat, poultry, fish/seafood, dairy, eggs) outdoors, in a cold room in the house or on the kitchen counter.
- Refrigerate meat/poultry/seafood or casseroles 24 to 48 hours or until completely thawed. Foods thawed in the refrigerator can usually be safely refrozen without changing taste or quality.
  - Allow 8 hours per pound of meat.
  - Allow 4 hours per pound of poultry.
  - Allow 6 hours per pound of fruit or vegetables.
- For fast thawing, place frozen packages in a watertight, sealed bag and cover with cold water. Change water every 30 minutes until food is completely thawed.
- In microwave oven:
  - Remove food from store wrapping (foam trays or plastic wrap) that may release chemicals into foods.
  - Allow 6 to 8 minutes per pound of food when thawing in microwave on low heat. Once food is defrosted, reheat on high heat.
- Precooked foods low in moisture content (breads, cakes, cookies) can be thawed at room temperature.
- Precooked foods higher in moisture content and/or containing dairy or egg products should be thawed in the refrigerator.

Reheating
- Reheat all previously cooked food to an internal temperature of at least 165°F. The food must reach this temperature within 2 hours. If the food will not reach this temperature within 2 hours, reheat it in small batches to shorten the reheating time.
- Use a clean meat thermometer to check internal food temperatures.
- Reheating frozen food without thawing:
  - Bake at 300 to 350°F for almost double the original cooking time.
  - Cooking frozen foods at higher temperatures does not result in quicker cooking. Higher temperatures will cook the outside before the inside is completely thawed.
- Microwave reheating:
  - Cook until foods are steaming and hot (at least 165°F).
  - Cover foods with microwave-safe wrap; vent to prevent steam buildup.
  - Stir foods from the outside in to encourage even heating.
  - CAUTION: Be careful when opening microwaved plastic bags as steam can build up and cause burns when bags are opened.

- When microwaving food in a FoodSaver® bag, be sure to snip off a corner for venting.

Leftovers
- Leftovers should be refrigerated as soon as possible.
- Cut meat into slices (3 inches thick or less).
- Store leftovers in small, shallow containers to hasten cooling.
- Remove all the stuffing from turkey, chicken or meat and store separately.

What "Use-By" and "Sell-By" Labels Really Mean
- Use-By: Food is no longer acceptable for consumption and should not be purchased or used after the given date.
- Date of Pack or Manufacture: This date refers to when the food was packed or processed for sale. Freeze food that will not be used within 3 to 5 days of purchase.
- Freshness, Pull- or Sell-By: This refers to the last day that a particular food should be sold, but can be safely used for 1 week past the "sell-by" date (i.e., dairy and fresh bakery products).
- Use Before or Best if Used By: This refers to the date at which food may begin to lose quality but can still be used safely (i.e., frozen foods, cereals, canned food, pasta, rice).

Top Timesavers
- Fresh-cut and packaged, canned or frozen vegetables and fruits
- Jarred minced garlic or garlic powder instead of fresh garlic cloves
- Bottled marinades
- Shredded cheese
- Precooked chicken breast tenders, slices or cuts

BASIC BEGINNINGS

Safe Food-Handling and Storage
- Make dips at least a day ahead of time so flavors have time to develop.
- Do not leave food out for more than 2 hours. Keep extra platters in the refrigerator and replace as needed without fuss.

To Freeze or Not to Freeze
- Get more pop in your popcorn: Freeze kernels and pop while still frozen.
- Flash-freeze small individual foods (meatballs, wontons, mini pizzas, burritos, cheese puffs). Line a baking sheet with waxed paper. Arrange the items in a single layer. Place baking sheet, uncovered, in the freezer for 2 to 3 hours. Remove from freezer, wrap food properly and freeze in storage bags. Small items can be placed directly into freezer bags; larger items should be individually wrapped before storing in freezer bag.

Shortcuts with the Same Results (in Less Time)
- Freeze cheese 30 minutes before shredding for easy preparation.

Always Room for Improvement
- For perfect meatballs: Shape meat mixture into a log, cut into slices and roll into balls or pat meat into a square and cut into cubes that can be rolled into uniform-size meatballs.
- Recrisp stale crackers: Spread crackers on a foil-lined baking sheet. Bake in 300°F oven for 5 minutes. Cool completely and seal in airtight container, plastic bag or FoodSaver® canister.

Party Planning Tips
- Plan five to six appetizers per person per hour.
- Include a variety of textures, flavors and colors.
- Select as many make-ahead appetizers as possible. This will eliminate stress and let you enjoy your own party.

Asian-Style Meatballs

Prep—Bake—Refrigerate or Freeze ◆ Serves: 6

1 lb. Laura's lean ground beef*
½ cup bread crumbs
¼ cup egg substitute
¼ cup nonfat beef broth
¼ cup + ⅔ cup water, divided
½ cup canned water chestnuts, finely chopped

½ cup diced celery
2 tbsp. prepared horseradish
⅔ cup apricot jam
½ tsp. garlic powder
½ cup low-sodium soy sauce
1 tbsp. lemon juice

Preheat oven to 350°F. Line baking sheet with foil and spray with cooking spray. Combine ground beef, bread crumbs, egg substitute, beef broth, ¼ cup water, water chestnuts, celery and horseradish in medium bowl; mix until ingredients are blended. Form mixture into small balls and arrange in a single layer on baking sheet. Bake 25 to 30 minutes, until lightly browned. Combine remaining ingredients in saucepan and bring to a boil over high heat. Cook, stirring constantly, 2 to 3 minutes. Meatballs can be cooled to room temperature, refrigerated and reheated or frozen. Store sauce in separate container. To serve: Defrost sauce and pour into saucepan. Bring to a boil over medium-high heat. Add meatballs; reduce heat to low, cover and simmer until meatballs are heated through.

Shopping List:

PRODUCE	PACKAGED/CANNED	4 oz. low-sodium soy
1 small bunch celery	14½-oz. can nonfat	sauce
Lemon juice	beef broth	
	6-oz. can sliced water	SPICES
DAIRY	chestnuts	Garlic powder
Egg substitute	Bread crumbs	
MEAT	CONDIMENTS	
1 lb. Laura's lean	6 oz. apricot jam	
ground beef	Prepared horseradish	

NUTRITION PER SERVING Calories 236 • Fat 1 g • Carbohydrates 41 g • Protein 21 g • Cholesterol 174 mg • Dietary Fiber 2 g • Sodium 261 mg
EXCHANGES 2½ very lean meat • 2 other carb • 2 vegetable
CARB CHOICES 3

*All recipes calling for superlean ground beef were prepared using Laura's Lean Beef, which is 4% fat ground round. 1800 ITS-LEAN or www.laurasleanbeef.com

4

Baked Crabmeat Dip in Bread Bowl

Prep—Chill—Bake

• Serves: 6

1 round loaf sourdough bread,
  unsliced
12-oz. can crabmeat, drained
1 cup nonfat sour cream
½ cup nonfat mayonnaise

2 tbsp. minced celery
2 tbsp. minced onion
2 tbsp. white wine
½ tsp. dried dill

Carefully cut top off of sourdough bread. Scoop out bread from inside, leaving ¼-inch shell. Slice bread into 1½- to 2-inch cubes and keep fresh in plastic bag. Combine remaining ingredients in bowl and mix well. Spoon crabmeat mixture into bread shell; wrap in foil and refrigerate until ready to serve. Preheat oven to 350°F. Bake crab dip (keep wrapped in foil) 40 to 45 minutes, until bubbly hot. Remove foil and heat 3 to 5 minutes, until bread crust is crisp and dip is bubbly hot. Serve dip with bread cubes.

Shopping List:

PRODUCE	PACKAGED/CANNED	CONDIMENTS
1 bunch celery	Unsliced round loaf	Nonfat mayonnaise
1 small onion	sourdough bread	
	12-oz. can crabmeat (do	SPICES
DAIRY	not use imitation	Dried dill
8 oz. nonfat sour cream	crab)	
	White wine	BREAD
		1 round loaf

NUTRITION PER SERVING Calories 321 • Fat 3.6 g • Carbohydrates 48 g • Protein 15.5 g • Cholesterol 57 mg • Dietary Fiber 2 g • Sodium 892 mg
EXCHANGES 1 other carb • 2 starch • 1 lean meat
CARB CHOICES 3

Can you believe the savings? Simply substituting nonfat sour cream and nonfat mayonnaise for regular varieties saves 289 calories and 25 grams of fat per serving!

California Roll

Prep—Chill   • Serves: 4

½ cup canned crabmeat   ½ cup shredded carrots
1½ tsp. nonfat mayonnaise   Wasabi or Sushi Dipping Sauce (page
2 sheets nori (dried seaweed)   26)
2 cups Sushi Rice (page 27)

Combine crabmeat and mayonnaise in small cup; mix well. Spray nonstick skillet with cooking spray and heat over medium-high heat. Put nori sheets in pan, one at a time, and cook until crisp, about 1 minute. Place a nori sheet on bamboo mat (available at specially cookware shops and Asian markets) or towel; spread about ¾ to 1 cup Sushi Rice on each nori sheet, leaving ½-inch border. Arrange shredded carrots and crabmeat mixture lengthwise down center of rice. Roll up bamboo mat or towel and press firmly; remove carefully. Wrap sushi roll in plastic wrap and refrigerate up to one day before serving. When ready to serve, cut sushi roll into bite-size pieces and serve with wasabi or Sushi Dipping Sauce.

Shopping List:

PRODUCE	CONDIMENTS
Shredded carrots	Nonfat mayonnaise
	Wasabi or Sushi
PACKAGED	Dipping Sauce
Short grain rice	ingredients (optional)
6-oz. can crabmeat	
Nori sheets	

NUTRITION PER SERVING Calories 185 • Fat .5 g • Carbohydrates 37 g • Protein 6 g • Cholesterol 17 mg • Dietary Fiber 1 g • Sodium 394 mg
EXCHANGES 1 vegetable • 2 starch • ½ very lean meat
CARB CHOICES 2

Wasabi, the popular condiment served with sushi, has been acclaimed as a superfood, because it contains compounds that help prevent certain cancers and blood clots.

Chicken-Chile Tortilla Rollups

Prep—Chill

♦ Serves: 8

¼ cup minced, cooked chicken breast cuts
¼ cup nonfat cream cheese, softened
1 tbsp. + 1 tsp. chopped black olives

1 tbsp. + 1 tsp. minced fresh onion
1 tbsp. + 1 tsp. chopped green chiles
4 low-fat flour tortillas
1 cup salsa

Combine chicken, cream cheese, olives, onion and chile in small bowl; mix until all ingredients are blended. Divide mixture and spread on tortillas, covering the entire surface. Roll tortillas jelly-roll style; wrap in plastic wrap and refrigerate several hours or overnight. When ready to serve, slice each roll into 6 to 8 slices and serve with salsa.

Shopping List:

PRODUCE	MEAT	
1 small onion	6-oz. pkg. cooked chicken breast cuts	4-oz. can chopped green chiles
DAIRY		Low-fat flour tortillas
3-oz. pkg. nonfat cream cheese	**PACKAGED/CANNED**	8 oz. salsa
	4-oz can chopped black olives	

NUTRITION PER SERVING Calories 97 • Fat .5 g • Carbohydrates 18 g • Protein 4 g • Cholesterol 3 mg • Dietary Fiber 2 g • Sodium 449 mg
EXCHANGES ½ starch • ½ other carb
CARB CHOICES 1

Tortilla sales in the United States reached the $4.4 billion mark in 2000 and are expected to hit $5.7 billion in sales by 2002. The Tortilla Industry Association estimates that Americans consumed approximately 85 billion tortillas in 2000 (not including tortilla chips).

Chicken Lettuce Wraps

Prep—Chill—Reheat

• Serves: 4

2 cups low-fat chicken breast tenders, cooked and chopped
1 cup chopped jicama
2 cups canned mung bean sprouts, rinsed and drained

1 cup shredded carrots
¼ cup chopped green onions
¼ cup low-sodium teriyaki sauce
Iceberg lettuce leaves

Combine chicken, jicama, bean sprouts, carrots, green onions and teriyaki sauce in medium bowl; mix well. Spray large skillet with cooking spray and heat over medium-high heat. Add chicken mixture to skillet and cook, stirring frequently, until heated through, 2 to 3 minutes. Serve with large lettuce leaves or divide mixture among leaves, wrap and serve. To reheat: Microwave chicken mixture 1 to 1½ minutes, until heated through. These can also be served cold.

Shopping List:

PRODUCE	MEAT	PACKAGED
1 small bunch green onions	1 lb. low-fat chicken tenders or	16-oz. can mung bean sprouts
1 large carrot	18 oz. Louis Rich chicken breast cuts	
1 small jicama		CONDIMENTS
Iceberg lettuce		4 oz. low-sodium teriyaki sauce

NUTRITION PER SERVING Calories 187 • Fat 2.5 g • Carbohydrates 21 g • Protein 22 g • Cholesterol 46 mg • Dietary Fiber 4 g • Sodium 1,327 mg
EXCHANGES 3 very lean meat • 2 vegetable • 1 other carb
CARB CHOICES 2

Chicken, a rich source of easily absorbed iron and zinc, helps prevent anemia, a leading cause of fatigue in women.

Chicken Spread

Prep—Chill   ◆ Serves: 6

3 cups shredded, cooked low-fat
   chicken breast
8-oz pkg. nonfat cream cheese
½ cup minced green onions
¾ cup minced celery

½ cup minced red bell pepper
¾ tsp. Mrs. Dash seasoning
Lahvosh, low-fat crackers or pita
   crisps (not included in nutritional
   information)

Combine all ingredients except lahvosh in medium bowl and mix well. Cover and refrigerate up to 2 days. Serve with lahvosh, low-fat crackers or pita crisps.

Shopping List:

PRODUCE	MEAT	PACKAGED
1 small bunch green onions	1 lb. low-fat chicken tenders or 18 oz.	Lahvosh, low-fat crackers or pita crisps
1 small bunch celery	Louis Rich chicken breast cuts	
1 red bell pepper		SPICES
DAIRY		Mrs. Dash seasoning
8-oz. pkg. nonfat cream cheese		

NUTRITION PER SERVING Calories 136 • Fat 1.9 g • Carbohydrates 4 g • Protein 22 g • Cholesterol 46 mg • Dietary Fiber <1 g • Sodium 880 mg
EXCHANGES 3 very lean meat • 1 vegetable
CARB CHOICES 0

In 2000, the National Chicken Council reported that the average American consumes 81 pounds of chicken per year.

Cowboy Caviar

Prep—Chill   ◆ Serves: 4

1½ lbs. eggplant
¾ tsp. garlic powder
6 tbsp. vegetable broth, divided
1 cup chopped onion
1 tsp. minced garlic
¾ cup chopped green bell pepper

1 cup canned diced tomatoes with
  roasted garlic, drained well
2 tbsp. tomato paste
1 tsp. lemon juice
1 tsp. red wine vinegar
Pepper to taste

Preheat oven to 400°F. Line baking sheet with foil and spray with cooking spray. Cut eggplant into 1-inch slices and arrange on baking sheet. Sprinkle eggplant with garlic powder and spray lightly with cooking spray. Bake 30 to 40 minutes, until soft. Cool slightly; peel and chop eggplant. Spray large nonstick skillet with cooking spray; add 3 tablespoons broth and heat over medium-high heat. Cook onion and garlic until softened. Add bell pepper, and cook 1 to 2 minutes. Add chopped eggplant and additional vegetable broth (if needed); stir in diced tomatoes, tomato paste, lemon juice, red wine vinegar and pepper. Remove from heat and mix well. Transfer eggplant mixture to bowl or container; cover and refrigerate up to 5 days. Serve with crackers, pita crisps or cucumber slices.

Shopping List:

PRODUCE	6oz. can tomato paste	SPICES
1½ lbs. eggplant	14½-oz. can diced	Minced garlic
1 large green pepper	tomatoes with	Garlic powder
1 small onion	roasted garlic	Pepper
Lemon juice		
	CONDIMENTS	OTHER
PACKAGED/CANNED	Red wine	Pita crisp crackers
14½-oz. can vegetable	vinegar	Cucumber slices
broth		(optional)

NUTRITION PER SERVING Calories 79 • Fat .6 g • Carbohydrates 18 g • Protein 3 g • Cholesterol 0 mg • Dietary Fiber 2 g • Sodium 326 mg
EXCHANGES 3 vegetable
CARB CHOICES 1

Timesaving tip: Purchase frozen bell pepper strips or chopped peppers at the supermarket salad bar.

Crab Crisps

Prep—Chill—Bake ♦ Serves: 8

8 oz. surimi seafood chunks, thinly
   sliced
½ cup diced red bell pepper
2 to 3 tbsp. nonfat mayonnaise
1 tsp. dried parsley
2 tbsp. chopped green onions

1 tbsp. lemon juice
1 tbsp. Dijon mustard
2 tsp. grated nonfat Parmesan cheese
4 to 5 drops Tabasco sauce
16 slices Italian bread, cut in half

Combine all ingredients except bread slices in bowl and mix well. Cover with plastic wrap and refrigerate until ready to serve. Preheat broiler on high heat. Line baking sheet with foil and spray with cooking spray. Spread 1 tbsp. mixture on each bread slice and arrange in single layer on baking sheet. Broil crab crisps 4 inches from heat for 4 to 5 minutes, until lightly browned.

Shopping List:

PRODUCE	MEAT	SPICES
1 small red bell pepper	8 oz. surimi seafood	Dried parsley
1 small bunch green	chunks	
onions		BREAD
Lemon juice		1-lb. loaf Italian bread
	CONDIMENTS	
DAIRY	Nonfat mayonnaise	
Grated nonfat	Dijon mustard	
Parmesan cheese	Tabasco sauce	

NUTRITION PER SERVING Calories 82 • Fat .6 g • Carbohydrates 14 g • Protein 4 g • Cholesterol 6 mg • Dietary Fiber 1 g • Sodium 372 mg
EXCHANGES ½ very lean meat • ½ starch • ½ other carb
CARB CHOICES 1

Monitor salt intake; sodium can damage the heart by raising blood pressure. The average American consumes 6,000 mg of sodium each day—almost three times the suggested intake.

11

Crackers with Sweet Tomato Relish

Prep—Chill   ◆ Serves: 6

2 tbsp. nonfat chicken broth
1 cup chopped onion
2 (28-oz.) cans chopped tomatoes,
   drained well
½ cup red wine vinegar

⅓ cup packed brown sugar
¼ tsp. pepper
Assorted low-fat crackers, pita crisps
   or flatbreads (not included in
   nutritional information)

Pour chicken broth into large saucepan and heat over medium-high heat. Add onion and cook, stirring occasionally, until tender and transparent. Add tomatoes, vinegar, brown sugar and pepper to onion; bring to a boil over high heat. Reduce heat to medium-high (so mixture doesn't boil over) and continue cooking, stirring occasionally, until mixture thickens, 25 to 30 minutes. Remove from heat and cool to room temperature. Pour mixture into bowl, cover and refrigerate up to 2 days. Serve with assorted low-fat crackers, pita crisps or flatbreads.

Shopping List:

PRODUCE	Nonfat chicken broth	OTHER
1 large onion	Red wine vinegar	Assorted crackers,
	Brown sugar	pita crisps or
PACKAGED		flatbreads
2 (28-oz.) cans chopped	SPICES	
tomatoes	Pepper	

NUTRITION PER SERVING Calories 96 • Fat 0 • Carbohydrates 25 g • Protein 2 g • Cholesterol 0 mg • Dietary Fiber 1 g • Sodium 1,065 mg
EXCHANGES 2 vegetable • 1 other carb
CARB CHOICES 1

Tomatoes' high vitamin C content enhances the absorption of iron.

Crunchy Veggie Bites

Prep—Bake—Freeze ◆ Serves: 8

1½ lbs. broccoli florets (about 5 cups)
2 lbs. cauliflower florets (about 4½ cups)
1 cup egg substitute
¼ cup evaporated skim milk

1½ cups cornflake crumbs
½ cup grated nonfat Parmesan cheese
¾ tsp. garlic powder
¼ tsp. pepper

Preheat oven to 475°F. Line baking sheet(s) with foil and spray with cooking spray. Place broccoli in microwave-safe dish; add several tablespoons water, cover and microwave 4 to 7 minutes, just until tender-crisp. Repeat with cauliflower. Drain well. Combine egg substitute and evaporated skim milk in medium bowl and mix well. Combine cornflake crumbs, Parmesan cheese, garlic powder and pepper on paper plate or plastic bag and toss until well mixed. Dip vegetables in egg mixture; roll in crumb mixture until coated. Arrange vegetables in single layer on baking sheet(s) and spray lightly with cooking spray. Bake 15 to 20 minutes, until crisp and browned. Vegetables can be frozen; thaw in refrigerator for several hours and reheat in 500°F oven 7 to 8 minutes, until heated through.

Shopping List:

PRODUCE	DAIRY	PACKAGED
1½ lbs. broccoli florets	5-oz. can evaporated	Cornflake crumbs
2 lb. cauliflower florets	skim milk	
	2 oz. grated nonfat	SPICES
	Parmesan cheese	Garlic powder
	8 oz. egg substitute	Pepper

NUTRITION PER SERVING Calories 146 • Fat .5 g • Carbohydrates 26 g • Protein 11 g • Cholesterol <1 mg • Dietary Fiber 5 g • Sodium 314 mg
EXCHANGES 1 starch • 2 vegetable • ½ very lean meat
CARB CHOICES 2

Six broccoli florets provide a day's worth of vitamin C and 20 percent of the daily value for vitamin A in the form of beta-carotene.

13

Cucumber Sushi Rolls

Prep—Chill   ◆ Serves: 4

2 sheets nori (dried seaweed)   Wasabi or Sushi Dipping Sauce (page
2 cups Sushi Rice (page 27)   26)
1 small cucumber, cut into
    matchsticks

Spray nonstick skillet with cooking spray and heat over medium-high heat.
Put nori sheets, one at a time, in pan and cook until crisp, about 1 minute.
Place a nori sheet on a bamboo mat (available at specialty cookware shops
and Asian markets) or towel; spread ¾ to 1 cup Sushi Rice on each nori
sheet, leaving ½-inch border. Arrange cucumber sticks lengthwise down
center of rice. Roll up bamboo mat or towel and press firmly; remove
carefully. Wrap sushi roll in plastic wrap and refrigerate up to 1 day before
serving. When ready to serve, cut sushi roll into bite-size pieces and serve
with wasabi or Sushi Dipping Sauce.

Shopping List:

PRODUCE	PACKAGED	CONDIMENTS
1 small cucumber	Short-grain rice	Wasabi or Sushi
	Nori sheets	Dipping Sauce
		ingredients (optional)

NUTRITION PER SERVING Calories 171 • Fat .2 g • Carbohydrates 38 g •
Protein 3 g • Cholesterol 0 mg • Dietary Fiber 1 g • Sodium 293 mg
EXCHANGES 2 starch • 1 vegetable
CARB CHOICES 3

*According to findings reported by the 2000 International Chemical Congress
of Pacific Basin Societies, wasabi may contribute to the prevention of tooth
decay, because it contains isotbiocyanates that may inhibit the growth of
certain bacteria associated with tooth decay.*

Garlic Cheese Spread

Prep—Chill   • Serves: 4

¼ cup chopped green onions
½ cup fresh parsley, chopped
¾ tsp. garlic powder
8-oz. pkg. nonfat cream cheese,
    softened
3 tbsp. chopped pimiento
2 tbsp. lemon juice

1 tsp. Worcestershire sauce
⅛ tsp. cayenne pepper
¼ tsp. dried basil
¼ tsp. black pepper
Cut-up vegetables, low-fat crackers
    or baked chips (not included in
    nutritional information)

Combine all ingredients except cut-up vegetables or crackers in food processor or blender and process until smooth and creamy. Spoon cheese mixture into bowl and cover with plastic wrap; refrigerate up to 1 week. Serve with vegetables, low-fat crackers or baked chips.

Shopping List:

PRODUCE	CONDIMENTS	OTHER
1 small bunch green onions	Worcestershire sauce	Low-fat crackers or baked chips
1 small bunch parsley	Pimiento	(optional)
Lemon juice		
Cut-up vegetables	SPICES	
	Garlic powder	
DAIRY	Cayenne pepper	
8-oz. pkg. nonfat cream cheese	Dried basil	
	Black pepper	

NUTRITION PER SERVING Calories 59 • Fat .1 g • Carbohydrates 7 g • Protein 9 g • Cholesterol 0 mg • Dietary Fiber <1 g • Sodium 417 mg
EXCHANGES ½ other carb
CARB CHOICES 0

According to ancient Greek herbal lore, black pepper was once used as an aphrodisiac due to its heat-producing powers.

Japanese Tuna Salad Rolls

Prep—Chill   • Serves: 4

½ cup canned tuna in water, drained
1½ tsp. nonfat mayonnaise
½ tsp. onion powder
1½ tsp. minced celery
2 sheets nori (dried seaweed)

2 cups Sushi Rice (page 27)
2 lettuce leaves
Wasabi or Sushi Dipping Sauce (page 26)

Combine tuna, mayonnaise, onion powder and celery in a small cup; mix well. Spray nonstick skillet with cooking spray and heat over medium-high heat. Put nori sheets in pan, one at a time, and cook until crisp, about 1 minute. Place nori sheet on bamboo mat (available at specialty cookware shops and Asian markets) or towel; spread ¾ to 1 cup sushi rice on each nori sheet, leaving ½-inch border. Place one lettuce leaf on each nori sheet. Spread tuna mixture down center of lettuce leaf. Roll up bamboo mat or towel and press firmly; remove carefully. Wrap sushi roll in plastic wrap and refrigerate up to 1 day before serving. When ready to serve, cut sushi roll into bite-size pieces and serve with wasabi or Sushi Dipping Sauce.

Shopping List:

PRODUCE	Short-grain rice	Dipping Sauce
Lettuce	Nori sheets	ingredients
Celery		
	CONDIMENTS	SPICES
PACKAGED	Nonfat mayonnaise	Onion powder
6-oz. can tuna packed	Wasabi or Sushi	
in water		

NUTRITION PER SERVING Calories 220 • Fat .4 g • Carbohydrates 36 g • Protein 16 g • Cholesterol 8 mg • Dietary Fiber <1 g • Sodium 458 mg
EXCHANGES 2 starch • 1½ very lean meat
CARB CHOICES 2

What makes sushi, sushi? The two essential ingredients are nori (thin sheets of edible dried seaweed) and sticky rice, a short-grained rice seasoned with rice vinegar, sugar and salt.

Melba Cheese Puffs

Prep—Chill—Bake

• Serves: 6

1½ cups nonfat mayonnaise
1½ cups grated nonfat Parmesan cheese
¾ cup chopped green onions
1½ tbsp. skim milk
Melba toast

Combine all ingredients except melba toast, and mix until completely blended. Cover and refrigerate up to 3 days. When ready to serve, preheat broiler on high heat. Line baking sheet with foil and spray with nonfat cooking spray. Arrange melba toast in single layer; top each cracker with a spoonful of cheese mixture. Broil 1 to 2 minutes, until lightly browned.

Shopping List:

PRODUCE	CONDIMENTS
1 small bunch green onions	12 oz. nonfat mayonnaise

DAIRY	OTHER
6-oz. grated nonfat Parmesan cheese	Melba toast (flavor of choice)
Skim milk	

NUTRITION PER SERVING Calories 154 • Fat 3 g • Carbohydrates 4 g • Protein 26 g • Cholesterol 57 mg • Dietary Fiber <1 g • Sodium 317 mg
EXCHANGES 3½ very lean meat • 1 vegetable
CARB CHOICES 0

A simple substitution of nonfat mayonnaise for regular saves 89 calories and 11 grams of fat per tablespoon!

Pita Crisp Crackers

Prep—Bake—Freeze   • Serves: 8

6 whole pita breads
Cooking spray
Seasonings of choice (see below)

Preheat oven to 350°F. Line baking sheet(s) with foil and spray with cooking spray. Cut pitas into 8 wedges; split pieces (12 to 16 wedges per pita). Arrange pita wedges in single layer on baking sheet(s). Spray lightly with cooking spray; sprinkle with 1 to 2 tablespoons seasonings of choice. Bake 10 to 15 minutes, until crisp and golden brown. Pita wedges can be served immediately or cooled to room temperature and stored in tightly sealed freezer bags. To reheat: Thaw crisps and reheat in 300°F oven 3 to 5 minutes, until crisp.

Shopping List:

SPICES	lahvosh or low-fat
See note below	flour tortillas if
	desired)
BREAD	
1 package pita pocket	**OTHER**
breads (or soft	Cooking spray

NUTRITION PER SERVING Calories 79 • Fat .4 g • Carbohydrates 15 g • Protein 3 g • Cholesterol 0 mg • Dietary Fiber <1 g • Sodium 161 mg
EXCHANGES 1 starch
CARB CHOICES 1

Choose from a variety of flavors for pita crisps: Italian—sprinkle with Italian seasoning; Southwest—sprinkle with cumin and cayenne pepper; garlic—sprinkle with garlic powder.

Savory Salmon Dip

Prep—Chill   • Serves: 6

8-oz. pkg. nonfat cream cheese,   Assorted crackers, crudités or
  softened   pumpernickel bread slices (not
7½-oz. can salmon, well drained   included in nutritional
¼ cup nonfat sour cream   information)
1 tbsp. minced green onion

Combine all ingredients except crackers, crudités or pumpernickel slices in medium bowl; blend with electric mixer until creamy and smooth. Cover and refrigerate at least 1 hour or up to 1 day ahead. Serve with assorted crackers, crudités or pumpernickel bread slices.

Shopping List:

PRODUCE	DAIRY	CANNED
1 small bunch green onions	8-oz. pkg. nonfat cream cheese	7½-oz. can salmon
	Nonfat sour cream	

NUTRITION PER SERVING Calories 88 • Fat 2.1g • Carbohydrates 3 g • Protein 13 g • Cholesterol 20 mg • Dietary Fiber 0 g • Sodium 470 mg
EXCHANGES 2 very lean meat
CARB CHOICES 0

Salmon is a good source of riboflavin (vitamin B$_2$), the energy vitamin that helps relieve stress and fatigue and improve mood.

Seafood Stuffed Mushrooms

Prep—Chill—Bake   ◆ Serves: 6

7-oz. can crabmeat, drained
1½ tbsp. chopped green onion
1½ tbsp. minced celery
¼ tsp. dried thyme
¼ tsp. dried basil
Pepper to taste

¼ cup nonfat mayonnaise
½ cup grated nonfat Parmesan
   cheese, divided
1 lb. large brown mushrooms,
   cleaned, stems and gills removed
½ tsp. paprika

Spray shallow baking dish with cooking spray. Combine crabmeat, green onion, celery, thyme, basil and pepper in small bowl; mix well. Stir in mayonnaise and ¼ cup Parmesan cheese; mix until ingredients are blended. Fill mushroom cups with crabmeat filling and arrange in single layer in baking dish; sprinkle with remaining Parmesan cheese and paprika. Cover with plastic wrap and refrigerate up to 1 day. Preheat oven to 350°F. Bake stuffed mushroom caps 12 to 15 minutes, until lightly browned.

Shopping List:

PRODUCE	DAIRY	CONDIMENTS
1 lb. large brown mushrooms	Grated nonfat Parmesan cheese	Nonfat mayonnaise
Green onions		SPICES
Celery	CANNED	Dried thyme
	7-oz. can crabmeat (do not use imitation crab)	Dried basil
		Paprika
		Pepper

NUTRITION PER SERVING Calories 81 • Fat 1.1 g • Carbohydrates 8 g • Protein 10 g • Cholesterol 33 mg • Dietary Fiber <1 g • Sodium 299 mg
EXCHANGES 1 vegetable • 1 very lean meat • ½ other carb
CARB CHOICES 1

Most of the compounds found in mushrooms are classified as HDPs (host defense potentiators), compounds that help the body regulate the development of lymphoid stem cells and other important defense responses.

Shrimp Lettuce Wraps with Spicy Sauce

Prep—Chill ◆ Serves: 4

1 lb. cooked shrimp, chopped
2 cups canned mung bean sprouts, rinsed and drained
¾ cup chopped water chestnuts
1 cup very thinly sliced jicama
1 cup very thinly sliced red bell pepper

½ cup sugar
½ cup sherry vinegar
¼ tsp. crushed red pepper
1 tsp. low-sodium soy sauce
½ tsp. garlic powder
Iceberg lettuce leaves

Combine shrimp, bean sprouts, water chestnuts, jicama and bell pepper in large mixing bowl; mix well. Combine sugar, sherry vinegar, crushed red pepper, soy sauce and garlic powder in small bowl and mix until blended. Add 2 to 3 tablespoons to shrimp mixture; mix until coated. Cover shrimp mixture and remaining sauce; refrigerate up to 1 day. Serve with large lettuce leaves or wrap before serving. Serve hot or cold with remaining sauce.

Shopping List:

PRODUCE	PACKAGED	CONDIMENTS
1 small jicama	6-oz. can sliced water chestnuts	Sherry vinegar
1 large red bell pepper	16-oz. can mung bean sprouts	Low-sodium soy sauce
Iceberg lettuce	Sugar	
		SPICES
MEAT		Garlic powder
1 lb. cooked shrimp		Crushed red pepper

NUTRITION PER SERVING Calories 236 • Fat 1 g • Carbohydrates 41 g • Protein 21 g • Cholesterol 174 mg • Dietary Fiber 2 g • Sodium 261 mg
EXCHANGES 2½ very lean meat • 2 other carb • 2 vegetable
CARB CHOICES 3

According to a National Restaurant Association survey, shrimp is the top seafood ordered in restaurants, followed by salmon and swordfish.

Spicy Hummus

Prep—Chill   ♦ Serves: 6

15½-oz. can garbanzo beans, drained
  and rinsed
2 tbsp. vegetable broth
2 tbsp. water
4-oz. can chopped medium to hot
  green chiles

¼ tsp. garlic powder
1 tbsp. tahini
¼ cup lemon juice
Low-fat crackers, pita crisps or baked
  tortilla chips (not included in
  nutritional information)

Combine garbanzo beans, vegetable broth, water, chiles, garlic powder, tahini and lemon juice in food processor or blender; mix until smooth and creamy (if too thick, add a little more water). Transfer to bowl, cover and refrigerate up to 3 days. Serve with low-fat crackers, pita crisps or baked tortilla chips.

Shopping List:

CANNED	CONDIMENTS
15½-oz. can garbanzo beans	Lemon juice
4-oz. can chopped green chiles	Tahini
Vegetable broth	**SPICES**
	Garlic powder

NUTRITION PER SERVING Calories 97 • Fat 2.6 g • Carbohydrates 15 g • Protein 4 g • Cholesterol 0 •Dietary Fiber 4 g • Sodium 530 mg
EXCHANGES 1 starch • ½ fat
CARB CHOICES 1

The capsaicin found in chile peppers has been found to be an anticoagulant, contributing to reduced risk of heart attacks and strokes caused by blood clots.

Spinach-Chicken Rollups

Prep—Chill ♦ Serves: 6

8-oz. pkg. nonfat cream cheese,
  softened
3 tbsp. chopped green onion
1½ cups cooked chicken breast cuts
2 tbsp. nonfat sour cream
1 tsp. dried dill

4 (10-inch) low-fat flour tortillas
1½ cups fresh spinach
Nonfat ranch salad dressing or salsa
  (not included in nutritional
  information)

Combine cream cheese, onion, chicken, sour cream and dill in medium bowl; mix until blended. Spread ¼ cup filling on each tortilla; place spinach leaves on top, leaving about ½-inch border. Roll tortillas tightly and wrap in plastic wrap. Refrigerate at least 1 hour before serving. Slice and serve with nonfat ranch dip or salsa.

Shopping List:

PRODUCE	MEAT	OTHER
1 small bunch green onions	6-oz. pkg. cooked chicken breast cuts	Nonfat ranch salad dressing or salsa (optional)
⅓ to ½ lb. fresh spinach		
	SPICES	
	Dried dill	
DAIRY		
8-oz. pkg. nonfat cream cheese	BREAD	
Nonfat sour cream	19-oz. pkg. 10-inch low-fat flour tortillas	

NUTRITION PER SERVING Calories 120 • Fat 2 g • Carbohydrates 15 g • Protein 11 g • Cholesterol 11 mg • Dietary Fiber 1 g • Sodium 258 mg
EXCHANGES 1½ meat • ½ starch • 1 vegetable
CARB CHOICES 1

Chicken and all meats contain a complete array of amino acids to fuel the growth of new skin cells.

Stuffed Cucumbers

Prep—Chill   • Serves: 4

½ cup nonfat cream cheese, softened
½ cup nonfat sour cream
4 tbsp. diced red onion, divided
1 tsp. dried dill

½ tsp. lemon extract
2 large cucumbers, cut into 1-inch-
    thick slices

Combine cream cheese, sour cream, 2 tablespoons red onion, dill and
lemon extract in bowl; beat with electric mixer until blended. Scoop holes
in centers of cucumber slices. Spoon 1 teaspoon cream cheese mixture into
center of cucumber; garnish with remaining red onion. Cover and refrigerate several hours before serving.

Shopping List:

PRODUCE	DAIRY	SPICES
2 large cucumbers	4 oz. nonfat cream	Dried dill
1 small red onion	cheese	Lemon extract
	4 oz. nonfat sour cream	

NUTRITION PER SERVING Calories 61 • Fat <1 g • Carbohydrates 10 g •
Protein 4 g • Cholesterol 1 mg • Dietary Fiber 2 g • Sodium 48 mg
EXCHANGES 2 vegetable
CARB CHOICES 1

Did you know that cucumbers and pumpkins are related to one another?

Super Bowl Taco Dip

Prep—Chill—Bake   • Serves: 8

2 (16-oz.) cans nonfat refried beans
4-oz. can chopped green chiles
¼ tsp. chili powder
1 lb. Laura's extra-lean ground beef
  (see Note, p. 4)
½ tsp. garlic powder
1½ tsp. onion powder

1 cup shredded nonfat cheddar
  cheese
½ cup shredded reduced-fat cheddar
  cheese
1¼ cups chunky salsa
12 oz. baked tortilla chips

Preheat oven to 350°F. Spray 9 × 13-inch baking dish with cooking spray. Combine beans, chiles and chili powder in medium bowl; mix until ingredients are blended. Spread bean mixture in bottom of baking dish. Spray nonstick skillet with cooking spray and heat over medium-high heat. Add ground beef, breaking into small pieces; season with garlic powder and onion powder. Cook over medium heat, stirring frequently, until meat is browned and cooked through. Remove from heat; cool 5 minutes and spread meat mixture on top of beans. Combine cheeses in plastic bag; shake until mixed. Spread salsa on top of beef; sprinkle cheese mixture over top. Taco dip can be covered with plastic or foil and refrigerated up to 24 hours. Bake 25 to 30 minutes, until mixture is bubbly hot and cheese is lightly browned. Serve with baked tortilla chips.

Shopping List:

DAIRY	MEAT	12-oz. jar chunky salsa
4 oz. shredded nonfat cheddar cheese	1 lb. Laura's extra-lean ground beef	12 oz. baked tortilla chips
2 oz. reduced-fat shredded cheddar cheese	**PACKAGED/CANNED** 2 (16-oz.) cans nonfat refried beans 4-oz. can chopped green chiles	**SPICES** Chili powder Garlic powder Onion powder

NUTRITION PER SERVING Calories 409 • Fat 4.7 g • Carbohydrates 62 g • Protein 29 g • Cholesterol 32 mg • Dietary Fiber 4 g • Sodium 1,412 mg
EXCHANGES 3½ starch • 2 lean meat • ½ other carb
CARB CHOICES 4

Can you believe the savings? One serving of Taco Bell's Nachos Beef Supreme would set you back 450 calories and 24 grams of fat—50 percent of the calories are from fat!

Sushi Dipping Sauce

Prep — Chill   ◆ Serves: 8

1 cup rice vinegar
½ cup vegetable broth
¼ cup miso
¼ cup sugar
1 tsp. powdered wasabi

Combine all ingredients in blender; puree until all ingredients are blended smooth. Pour into covered dish and refrigerate until ready to serve with sushi rolls.

Shopping List:

PACKAGED/CANNED	CONDIMENTS
Vegetable broth	Rice vinegar
Miso	Powdered wasabi
Sugar	

NUTRITION PER SERVING Calories 46 • Fat .6 g • Carbohydrates 10 g • Protein 1 g • Cholesterol 0 mg • Dietary Fiber <1 g • Sodium 363 mg
EXCHANGES ½ other carb
CARB CHOICES 1

Don't get discouraged with less than perfectly formed sushi; it takes 10 years of training for an apprentice to become a sushi chef in Japan.

Sushi Rice

Prep—Chill   • Serves: 6

1½ cups short-grain rice (Japanese-style rice)
1½ cups water
⅓ cup rice vinegar
2 tbsp. sugar
1 tsp. salt

Combine rice and water in medium saucepan; bring to a boil over high heat. Boil 45 to 60 seconds; reduce heat to low, cover and simmer 20 minutes. Remove from heat and let rice stand 10 minutes. Combine vinegar, sugar and salt in small saucepan; bring to a boil and cook until sugar and salt are completely dissolved. Spread hot rice onto large platter or bowl; pour vinegar mixture over rice and fold carefully without smashing rice. When rice is cooled, it can be used to prepare Japanese Tuna Salad Rolls (page 16) or Cucumber Sushi Rolls (page 14). Makes 3 cups rice.

Shopping List:

PACKAGED	CONDIMENTS
Short-grain rice	Rice vinegar
Sugar	
	SPICES
	Salt

NUTRITION PER SERVING Calories 192 • Fat .2 g • Carbohydrates 43 g • Protein 3 g • Cholesterol 0 mg • Dietary Fiber <1 g • Sodium 358 mg
EXCHANGES 3 starch
CARB CHOICES 3

For best results, do not use instant, converted or brown rice to prepare sushi rice.

Vegetable Lettuce Wraps

Prep—Chill
♦ Serves: 4

½ cup rice vinegar
½ cup sugar
½ tsp. crushed red pepper
1¼ tsp. garlic powder
2 cups canned mung bean sprouts,
   rinsed and drained

2 cups shredded Chinese cabbage
1 cup very thinly sliced jicama
½ cup chopped canned water
   chestnuts
Iceberg lettuce leaves
Soy sauce or teriyaki sauce (not
   included in nutritional
   information)

Combine rice vinegar, sugar, crushed red pepper and garlic powder in large bowl and mix until sugar is dissolved and ingredients are blended. Add remaining ingredients except lettuce leaves and toss until coated. Cover and refrigerate up to 24 hours. Remove from refrigerator 1 hour before serving; toss several times to keep mixture moist. Serve with lettuce leaves or wrap and serve with soy sauce, teriyaki sauce, etc.

Shopping List:

PRODUCE	PACKAGED	CONDIMENTS
1 small jicama	6-oz. can sliced water	Rice vinegar
½ lb. Chinese cabbage	chestnuts	Soy sauce or teriyaki
Iceberg lettuce	16-oz. can mung bean	sauce
	sprouts	
	Sugar	SPICES
		Crushed red pepper
		Garlic powder

NUTRITION PER SERVING Calories 147 • Fat <1 g • Carbohydrates 41 g • Protein 3 g • Cholesterol 0 mg • Dietary Fiber 2 g • Sodium 23 mg
EXCHANGES 2 vegetable • 2 other carbs
CARB CHOICES 3

Did you know that cabbage is 91 percent water?

MORNING TO MIDDAY MEALS

❖

Safe Food-Handling and Storage

- Whole raw eggs:
  - Should always be kept cold to prevent bacterial growth.
  - Should be refrigerated as soon as possible after purchase.
  - Should be stored in the carton rather than in the egg tray on the side of the refrigerator door.
  - Should *not* be washed before storing; they will spoil more quickly.
  - Should be used within 3 to 5 weeks.
- Leftover egg yolks or whites should be used within 4 days.
- Hard-cooked eggs can be safely stored in the refrigerator for 7 to 10 days.

To Freeze or Not to Freeze

- Breads: In general, the lower the moisture level in breads, the more successfully they will freeze.
  - If wrapped carefully, fresh bread may be frozen for several months without losing quality. (If frozen in a FoodSaver® bag, bread will keep 1 to 3 years.)
  - Whole loaves of bread keep moisture longer and freeze better than sliced breads.
  - Bread will stay fresher longer if frozen or kept at room temperature. Refrigerating bread causes it to become stale faster and may cause molding.
  - Yeast bread or pizza dough can be frozen 1 to 2 months before baking. For best results, add a little extra yeast when preparing the dough.
- Fruit:
  - Use completely thawed fruits immediately.
  - Partially thawed fruit can be refrozen, but some quality may be lost.
- Eggs: Can be frozen under the following conditions:
  - Whole eggs can be safely frozen if the yolks and whites are beaten together before freezing.
  - Egg whites can be frozen alone; freeze in ice cube trays for easy removal. Use 1 cube as 1 egg white.
  - Freeze yolks by stirring in 1 teaspoon sugar or ½ teaspoon salt per six egg yolks.
  - Use separated frozen eggs within 1 year.

From Stovetop to Refrigerator or Freezer and Back Again

- Breads and other baked goods can be thawed at room temperature. They can be refrozen, but may be slightly drier when thawed the second time.

Shortcuts with the Same Results (in Less Time)

- The easiest lunches are last night's leftovers.
- Use packaged egg whites or pasteurized egg substitutes for quick meals.
- Instant oatmeal, cream-of-wheat or other hot cereals can be prepared in less time than regular cooked cereals.
- Prepare egg white omelettes the night before. Blend egg whites, a little water or skim milk, vegetables and cheese (if desired) in a microwave-safe dish. Cover and refrigerate overnight. In the morning, microwave on High 2 to 3 minutes per egg white until cooked through.
- Cut bagels in half before freezing for faster defrosting and toasting.

Always Room for Improvement

- Seasonings and spices:
  - Breads: coriander, cumin, caraway, dill, anise, fennel, rosemary
  - Eggs: chives, dill, anise, basil, chervil, coriander, cumin, marjoram, parsley, rosemary, sage, tarragon
  - Salads: basil, chervil, chives, coriander, cumin, dill, parsley, tarragon, thyme
- Pancakes:
  - Squeeze pancake batter onto hot skillet with a turkey baster for perfectly shaped pancakes.
  - Adding a little sugar to pancake batter will ensure even browning.
  - For lighter pancakes, substitute apple cider or club soda for milk.
- Oatmeal: Perk up oatmeal by toasting oats on a baking sheet in 350°F oven 5 to 8 minutes; prepare as directed.

Everything Old Is New Again!

- Make bread crumbs by processing leftover bread (bagels, rolls, baguettes, sandwich bread or pitas) in food processor. Store in freezer-safe containers or bags and remove as needed for breading meat, poultry, fish or seafood. Thaw before using to prepare recipes.
- Reconstitute hard raisins or currants. Place fruits in a saucepan and cover with cold water. Bring water to a boil, remove from heat and let stand 5 minutes. Drain and use as needed.
- Freshen stale rolls: Seal rolls in a brown paper bag, sprinkle the outside with water and heat 10 to 15 minutes in 350°F oven or spray lightly with cold water and microwave on Low for 30 seconds.

Apple-Nut Zucchini Bread

Prep—Bake—Freeze   • Serves: 24 slices

2 cups all-purpose flour
2 cups whole-wheat flour
2 tsp. baking soda
1 tsp. baking powder
2 tsp. ground cinnamon
½ tsp. ground nutmeg
1 cup egg substitute
2 large egg whites

14-oz. can crushed pineapple in juice, undrained
1½ cups granulated sugar
1½ cups packed brown sugar
1 tbsp. vanilla extract
2 cups shredded zucchini
1 cup shredded apple
1 cup chopped walnuts

Preheat oven to 350°F. Spray 3 (8 × 4-inch) loaf pans with cooking spray. Combine flours, baking soda, baking powder, cinnamon and nutmeg in large bowl; mix well. Combine egg substitute and egg whites in medium bowl; beat with electric mixer until frothy. Pour egg mixture into flour mixture. Add pineapple, sugars and vanilla; mix well. Fold in zucchini, apple and walnuts. Divide batter among loaf pans. Bake 45 to 55 minutes, until toothpick inserted in center comes out clean. Cool 10 minutes; remove bread from loaf pans and cool completely before slicing. Bread can be frozen whole or sliced; thaw at room temperature or microwave individual pieces 10 to 15 seconds each.

Shopping List:

PRODUCE	CANNED	BAKING
2 medium zucchinis	14-oz. can crushed	All-purpose flour
1 medium apple	pineapple in juice	Whole-wheat flour
		Baking soda
	SPICES	Baking powder
DAIRY	Ground cinnamon	Sugar
8 oz. egg substitute	Ground nutmeg	Brown sugar
2 large eggs	Vanilla extract	Chopped walnuts

NUTRITION PER SERVING Calories 210 • Fat 2.2 g • Carbohydrates 45 g • Protein 5 g • Cholesterol 0 mg • Dietary Fiber 2 g • Sodium 106 mg
EXCHANGES 3 other carbs
CARB CHOICES 3

Eating just 8 to 11 walnuts each day can lower LDL (bad) cholesterol levels by 11 percent or more.

Bacon 'n' Eggs Brunch

Prep—Chill—Bake   • Serves: 6

4 slices whole-wheat low-fat bread,
  crusts removed
1 cup egg substitute
4 large egg whites
1½ cups skim milk
¼ tsp. pepper
½ tsp. Mrs. Dash seasoning

¾ cup shredded nonfat cheddar
  cheese, divided
¾ cup low-fat bacon crumbles
  (i.e., McCormick)
⅓ cup sliced mushrooms (optional)
½ cup frozen low-fat hash brown
  potatoes, thawed

Spray a 9-inch-square baking dish with cooking spray. Arrange bread slices on bottom of dish. Combine egg substitute, egg whites, skim milk, pepper, Mrs. Dash seasoning, ½ cup cheese, bacon crumbles and mushrooms, if using, in medium bowl; mix well. Pour mixture over bread slices. Top with hash brown potatoes and sprinkle with remaining ¼ cup cheese. Cover and refrigerate overnight. Preheat oven to 350°F. Bake, uncovered, 40 to 45 minutes, until knife inserted in center comes out clean.

Shopping List:

PRODUCE	8 oz. egg substitute	SPICES
3 oz. mushrooms	4 large eggs	Mrs. Dash seasoning
(optional)		Pepper
	PACKAGED	
DAIRY	3 (1.3-oz.) pkgs.	**FROZEN**
Skim milk	McCormick bacon	18-oz. pkg. frozen low-
3 oz. shredded nonfat	crumbles	fat hash brown
cheddar cheese	1 loaf whole-wheat	potatoes
	bread	

NUTRITION PER SERVING Calories 178 • Fat 3.9 g • Carbohydrates 18 g • Protein 18 g • Cholesterol 1 mg • Dietary Fiber 2 g • Sodium 702 mg
EXCHANGES ½ starch • ½ milk • 1½ very lean meat • ½ fat
CARB CHOICES 1

Egg whites contain a significant amount of sulfur, an antioxidant that promotes healthy nerve and muscle function.

Baked French Toast

Prep—Chill—Bake   • Serves: 8

1 cup lite maple syrup
1 lb. loaf French bread, cut into
  2-inch-thick slices
¾ cup egg substitute
3 large egg whites

1½ cups skim milk
2 tsp. vanilla extract
¾ tsp. ground cinnamon
¼ tsp. ground nutmeg

Spray large baking dish with cooking spray. Pour syrup in bottom of dish. Arrange bread slices on top of syrup. Combine egg substitute, egg whites, skim milk, vanilla extract, cinnamon and nutmeg in a medium bowl and mix until blended. Pour mixture over bread slices, generously soaking bread. Cover with plastic wrap and refrigerate overnight. To prepare and serve: Preheat oven to 350°F. Bake French toast casserole 40 to 45 minutes, until golden brown. Serve with additional syrup, powdered sugar or cinnamon-sugar mixture if desired.

Shopping List:

DAIRY	SPICES	OTHER
12 oz. skim milk	Ground cinnamon	12 oz. lite maple syrup
3 large eggs	Ground nutmeg	Powdered sugar and/or
6 oz. egg substitute	Vanilla extract	cinnamon (optional)
	BREAD	
	1 lb. loaf French bread	

NUTRITION PER SERVING Calories 305 • Fat 2.3 g • Carbohydrates 62 g • Protein 10 g • Cholesterol 1 mg • Dietary Fiber 1 g • Sodium 428 mg
EXCHANGES 3 starch • ½ lean meat
CARB CHOICES 0

One more good reason not to skip breakfast: Those who eat breakfast are up to 10 pounds slimmer than those who go hungry before noon.

Banana Bran Bread

¼ cup egg substitute
2 large egg whites
1½ cups mashed ripe bananas
¼ cup applesauce
1 cup oat or wheat bran
¼ cup granulated sugar
⅓ cup packed brown sugar
½ tsp. vanilla extract
¾ cup whole-wheat flour

¾ cup all-purpose flour
2½ tsp. baking powder
½ tsp. baking soda
½ tsp. ground cinnamon
½ cup chopped dates
Nonfat cream cheese or preserves
(not included in nutritional
information)

Preheat oven to 350°F. Spray 8 × 4-inch loaf pan with cooking spray. Combine egg substitute, egg whites, bananas, applesauce, bran, sugars and vanilla extract in medium bowl; mix until blended. Gradually add flours, baking powder, baking soda and cinnamon to egg mixture; mix just until ingredients are blended. Fold in dates. Spoon batter into loaf pan and bake 45 to 60 minutes, until toothpick inserted in center comes out clean. Cool slightly; remove from loaf pan and cool to room temperature. Slice cooled bread into single-size servings; wrap and refrigerate or freeze until ready to serve. After thawing or refrigerating, microwave 15 to 20 seconds or wrap in foil and heat in 350°F oven 10 to 15 minutes. Top with nonfat cream cheese or your favorite preserves.

Shopping List:

PRODUCE	PACKAGED	BAKING
4 to 5 medium bananas	6-oz. pkg. chopped dates	Whole-wheat flour
		All-purpose flour
DAIRY	4 oz. applesauce	Sugar
Egg substitute	Bran	Brown sugar
2 large eggs	Nonfat cream cheese or preserves	Baking powder
		Baking soda
	SPICES	
	Ground cinnamon	
	Vanilla extract	

NUTRITION PER SERVING Calories 272 • Fat 1 g • Carbohydrates 65 g • Protein 6 g • Cholesterol 0 mg • Dietary Fiber 6 g • Sodium 240 mg
EXCHANGES 4 other carbs
CARB CHOICES 4

Dates are one of the few fruits that don't contain any vitamin C.

Blueberry Cornbread

Prep—Bake—Freeze

♦ Serves: 8

½ cup egg substitute
2 large egg whites
¾ cup sugar
¼ cup applesauce
½ cup nonfat vanilla yogurt
2 tbsp. orange juice

1 cup yellow cornmeal
½ cup all-purpose flour
1¼ tsp. baking powder
½ tsp. baking soda
1½ cups blueberries

Preheat oven to 350°F. Spray 8- or 9-inch-square baking dish with cooking spray. Combine egg substitute, egg whites, sugar, applesauce, yogurt and orange juice in medium bowl; mix until blended smooth. Combine cornmeal, flour, baking powder and baking soda in plastic bag; shake until ingredients are mixed. Gradually add flour mixture to egg mixture; mix until blended. Fold in blueberries. Spoon batter into prepared baking dish and bake 23 to 25 minutes, until toothpick inserted in center comes out clean. Cool to room temperature. Cut cornbread into squares; wrap in freezer wrap and store in freezer bag. To serve, remove as many squares as needed. Microwave 30 to 45 seconds per square on Low and serve with honey or preserves if desired.

Shopping List:

PRODUCE	BAKING	OTHER
¾ lb. blueberries	Yellow cornmeal	4 oz. applesauce
	Flour	Orange juice
DAIRY	Sugar	Honey or preserves
4 oz. nonfat vanilla	Baking powder	(optional)
yogurt	Baking soda	
2 large eggs		
4 oz. egg substitute		

NUTRITION PER SERVING Calories 199 • Fat .5 g • Carbohydrates 45 g • Protein 5 g • Cholesterol <1 mg • Dietary Fiber 2 g • Sodium 148 mg
EXCHANGES 3 other carbs
CARB CHOICES 3

Blueberries contain high levels of anthocyanin, an antioxidant that prevents cell damage in the body.

Bow-Tie Chicken 'n' Bean Pasta Salad

Prep—Chill　　　　　　　　　　　　　　　　　◆ Serves: 6

6 oz. bow-tie pasta
3 cups cooked chicken breast cuts
14-oz. can (1½ cups) white beans,
　drained and rinsed

1 cup cherry tomatoes, halved
1 tsp. dried basil
2 tsp. dried parsley
¾ cup nonfat Italian salad dressing

Cook pasta according to package directions; drain well and place in large bowl. While pasta is still warm, add remaining ingredients and toss until mixed. Cover and refrigerate up to 2 days.

Shopping List:

PRODUCE	or 1 lb. boneless	CONDIMENTS
Cherry tomatoes	chicken	6 oz. nonfat Italian salad dressing
MEAT	**PACKAGED/CANNED**	**SPICES**
3 (6-oz.) pkgs. cooked chicken breast cuts	14-oz. can white beans	Dried basil
	6-oz. pkg. bow-tie pasta	Dried parsley

NUTRITION PER SERVING Calories 309 • Fat 2.6 g • Carbohydrates 41g • Protein 25 g • Cholesterol 45 mg • Dietary Fiber <1 g • Sodium 791 mg
EXCHANGES 3 very lean meat • 1½ starch • 1 other carb • 1 vegetable
CARB CHOICES 3

The Food and Drug Administration (FDA) now requires that enriched grain products such as pasta contain added folic acid, which may protect against heart disease.

Sidebar: MORNING TO MIDDAY MEALS

38

Buttermilk Banana Muffins

Prep—Bake—Freeze

3 ripe bananas, mashed
½ cup granulated sugar
½ cup packed brown sugar
¼ cup egg substitute
¾ cup cinnamon-flavored
 applesauce
2 cups all-purpose flour

1 tsp. ground cinnamon
1 tsp. baking soda
1 tsp. baking powder
3 tbsp. nonfat buttermilk
2 tbsp. vanilla extract
2 tbsp. cinnamon-sugar mixture

Preheat oven to 325°F. Lightly spray 12 muffin cups with cooking spray. Combine bananas, sugars, egg substitute and applesauce in large mixing bowl; blend until smooth and creamy. Gradually add flour, cinnamon, baking soda and baking powder; mix just until blended. Add buttermilk and vanilla extract and blend well. Fill muffin cups two-thirds full. Bake 20 to 25 minutes, until lightly browned. Remove from oven; cool 10 to 15 minutes; sprinkle tops with cinnamon-sugar mixture. Cool to room temperature before refrigerating or freezing. Muffins can be thawed and microwaved 15 to 20 seconds.

Shopping List:

PRODUCE	SPICES	Brown sugar
3 bananas	Ground cinnamon	Baking soda
	Vanilla extract	Baking powder
DAIRY		
Nonfat buttermilk	BAKING	OTHER
4 oz. egg substitute	Flour	6 oz. cinnamon-flavored
	Sugar	applesauce

NUTRITION PER SERVING Calories 197 • Fat .4 g • Carbohydrates 45 g • Protein 3 g • Cholesterol <1 mg • Dietary Fiber 1 g • Sodium 111 mg
EXCHANGES 3 other carbs
CARB CHOICES 3

Bananas are a great source of fiber, which may lower LDL (bad) cholesterol by one-third and raise HDL (good) cholesterol levels by 30 percent.

Chicken 'n' Broccoli Quiche Muffins

Prep—Bake—Freeze   • Serves: 6

1½ cups skim milk
⅜ cup water
¾ cup egg substitute
3 large egg whites
1½ cups all-purpose flour
¾ cup grated nonfat Parmesan cheese

½ cup chopped cooked chicken
  breast cuts
½ cup frozen chopped broccoli,
  thawed and drained
¼ tsp. garlic powder
⅛ tsp. pepper

Preheat oven to 425°F. Spray 6 large muffin cups with cooking spray. Combine all ingredients in medium bowl and mix well. Divide batter among muffin cups and bake 25 to 30 minutes, until set. Remove from oven and let stand 5 minutes before serving. To freeze: Cool muffins to room temperature. Wrap individually in freezer-safe wrap and place in plastic freezer bag. To serve: Thaw in refrigerator several hours and reheat in microwave 1 to 2 minutes or thaw in microwave 1 to 2 minutes on Low and reheat 1 to 1½ minutes on High.

Shopping List:

DAIRY	MEAT	FROZEN
12 oz. skim milk	6-oz. pkg. cooked	10-oz. pkg. frozen
Grated nonfat	chicken breast cuts	chopped broccoli
Parmesan cheese		
6 oz. egg substitute	SPICES	OTHER
3 large eggs	Garlic powder	Flour
	Pepper	

NUTRITION PER SERVING Calories 209 • Fat 1 g • Carbohydrates 33 g •
Protein 17 g • Cholesterol 10 mg • Dietary Fiber 1 g • Sodium 210 mg
EXCHANGES 2 very lean meat • 2 other carbs
CARB CHOICES 2

Broccoli, a superstar among antioxidant-rich vegetables, provides 200 percent of the daily value for vitamin C and 90 percent of the daily value for vitamin A.

Cinnamon Whole-Wheat Pancakes
with Chunky Applesauce

Prep—Cook—Refrigerate or Freeze ・Serves: 6

1 cup all-purpose flour
1 cup whole-wheat flour
1 tsp. baking powder
1½ tsp. ground cinnamon
¼ tsp. ground nutmeg
¼ cup egg substitute

¼ cup packed brown sugar
1½ cups skim milk
1½ cups chunky-style
    applesauce
2 tbsp. cinnamon-sugar mixture

Combine flours, baking powder, cinnamon and nutmeg in medium bowl; mix well. Combine egg substitute, brown sugar and skim milk in covered container; shake until ingredients are blended. Gradually pour mixture into dry ingredients and mix until combined (do not overbeat). If batter is too thick, add a little more milk. Spray large nonstick skillet or griddle with cooking spray and heat over medium-high heat. Scoop batter with ¼ cup measuring cup and pour into hot skillet. Cook over medium heat until bubbles start to form on top; flip pancake and cook 1 to 2 minutes, until lightly browned on both sides. Place chunky-style applesauce in microwave-safe bowl; sprinkle with cinnamon-sugar mixture and mix well. Cover and heat on High 1 to 1½ minutes, until warmed. Serve with pancakes. Pancakes can be wrapped and refrigerated or frozen; heat applesauce just before serving pancakes.

Shopping List:

DAIRY	SPICES	BAKING
12 oz. skim milk	Cinnamon	All-purpose flour
Egg substitute	Nutmeg	Whole-wheat flour
	Cinnamon-sugar	Brown sugar
PACKAGED	mixture	Baking powder
12-oz. chunky-style		
applesauce		

NUTRITION PER SERVING Calories 267 • Fat .8 g • Carbohydrates 59 g • Protein 8 g • Cholesterol 1 mg • Dietary Fiber 4 g • Sodium 106 mg
EXCHANGES 4 other carbs
CARB CHOICES 4

Applesauce provides the same goodness of whole apples, especially when made with unpeeled apples.

41

Cranberry Scones

2 cups all-purpose flour
⅓ cup sugar
1 tbsp. baking powder
1 tsp. baking soda
½ tsp. ground ginger

2 tsp. grated orange peel
1¼ cups nonfat sour cream
6 oz. dried cranberries
¼ cup powdered sugar
½ tsp. water

Preheat oven to 375°F. Line baking sheet with foil and spray with nonfat cooking spray. Combine flour, sugar, baking powder, baking soda, ginger and orange peel in medium bowl; mix until blended. Stir in sour cream (if batter is too thick, add a few drops of skim milk). Fold in cranberries. Pat dough onto floured surface to ½-inch thickness. Cut out circles with 2-inch-round cutter or top of glass dipped in flour. Arrange scones on baking sheet and bake 15 to 20 minutes, until golden brown. Cool scones 10 minutes while preparing glaze: Combine powdered sugar and water in small cup and mix until smooth. Drizzle over scones. Serve immediately or freeze and reheat in microwave or oven. Wrap scones individually for quick thawing.

Shopping List

DAIRY	SPICES	Powdered sugar
10 oz. nonfat sour cream	Ground ginger	Baking powder
		Baking soda
	BAKING	Orange peel or extract
PACKAGED	Flour	
6 oz. dried cranberries	Sugar	

NUTRITION PER SERVING Calories 334 • Fat .4 g • Carbohydrates 74 g • Protein 8 g • Cholesterol 0 mg • Dietary Fiber 3 g • Sodium 226 mg
EXCHANGES 1 fruit • 3 starch
CARB CHOICES 5

Scones with your coffee, why not indulge? Coffee sometimes gets a bad rap, but no studies have conclusively linked coffee to cancer, heart disease or other major diseases.

Dress-It-Up Caesar-Style Salad Dressing

Prep — Chill

½ cup nonfat cottage cheese
⅔ cup plain nonfat yogurt
3 tbsp. grated nonfat Parmesan
  cheese
1 tbsp. balsamic vinegar

1 tbsp. lemon juice
1 tsp. anchovy paste
1 tsp. Dijon mustard
1 tsp. Worcestershire sauce
½ tsp. garlic powder

Combine all ingredients in food processor or blender; process until smooth and creamy. Pour into jar or covered bowl and refrigerate until ready to serve or up to 1 week. For last-minute meals: Serve with prepackaged romaine, cooked chicken strips or shrimp and a variety of vegetables from the grocery salad bar. Add nonfat croutons or sourdough roll for complete meal.

Shopping List:

DAIRY	PACKAGED	Dijon mustard
4 oz. nonfat cottage cheese	Anchovy paste	Worcestershire sauce
6 oz. plain nonfat yogurt	**CONDIMENTS**	**SPICES**
Grated nonfat Parmesan cheese	Balsamic vinegar	Garlic powder
	Lemon juice	

NUTRITION PER SERVING Calories 31 • Fat .2 g • Carbohydrates 4 g • Protein 3 • Cholesterol 1 mg • Dietary Fiber 0 g • Sodium 103 mg
EXCHANGES ⅓ other carb
CARB CHOICES 0

Plain low-fat or nonfat yogurt is as nutritious as nonfat (skim) milk; it's high in protein, calcium, magnesium, riboflavin and vitamins B_6 and B_{12}.

Egg White Frittata

Prep—Chill—Bake

◆ Serves: 4

8 large egg whites
4 cups frozen vegetables of your
   choice, thawed and drained
¼ tsp. garlic powder

1 tbsp. chopped dry-packed sun-dried
   tomatoes
½ tsp. Mrs. Dash seasoning
Pepper to taste

Spray 11-inch glass pie pan with cooking spray. Beat egg whites in medium bowl until frothy, about 1 minute. Add vegetables, garlic powder, sun-dried tomatoes, Mrs. Dash seasoning and pepper; mix until all ingredients are combined. Pour mixture into pie pan. Frittata can be covered with plastic wrap, refrigerated and baked the next morning, or baked, covered, refrigerated up to 3 days and reheated. When ready to serve: Preheat oven to 350°F. Bake 15 to 20 minutes, until egg whites are set. Remove from oven and serve with chopped green onions or salsa, or sprinkle with low-fat cheese if desired.

Shopping List:

DAIRY 8 large eggs	**SPICES** Garlic powder Mrs. Dash seasoning Pepper	(broccoli, spinach, cauliflower, peppers)

PACKAGED
Sun-dried tomatoes, dry
   packed
	FROZEN
	2 (16-oz.) pkg. frozen
	   vegetables of choice
		OTHER
		Green onions, salsa or
		   low-fat cheese
		   (optional)

NUTRITION PER SERVING Calories 146 • Fat .3 g • Carbohydrates 26 g •
Protein 12 g • Cholesterol 0 mg • Dietary Fiber 7 g • Sodium 176 mg
EXCHANGES 1 very lean meat • 5 vegetable
CARB CHOICES 2

Egg whites have certainly improved their reputation since the seventeenth century, when they were used as a popular form of "laundry detergent" in England.

Freeze-and-Serve Oatmeal

Prep—Freeze—Reheat   • Serves: 6

3 cups water
1 cup apple juice
1½ tsp. ground cinnamon
1 cup old-fashioned rolled oats (do
   not use quick-cooking oats)

¼ cup raisins
¼ cup maple syrup
Sliced peaches, berries or bananas for
   topping

Combine water, apple juice and cinnamon in 2-quart saucepan; bring to a
boil over high heat. Stir in oats and raisins; return to boil over high heat.
Reduce heat to low, cover and simmer 25 to 30 minutes. Remove pan from
heat and let stand, covered, 5 minutes to thicken. Stir in syrup and top
with fruits of choice.

Oatmeal can be frozen in individual-size servings and reheated in microwave; add fruit topping just before serving.

Shopping List:

PACKAGED	SPICES	FRUITS
Old-fashioned rolled oats	Ground cinnamon	Fresh, canned or frozen fruit
6-oz. pkg. raisins	**BEVERAGES**	
4 oz. maple syrup	8 oz. apple juice	

NUTRITION PER SERVING Calories 177 • Fat 1.9 g • Carbohydrates 37 g •
Protein 5 g • Cholesterol 0 mg • Dietary Fiber 4 g • Sodium 16 mg
EXCHANGES 1 starch • 1 fruit • ½ other carb
CARB CHOICES 2

*Raisins can cut the risk of colon cancer. They contain dietary fiber and
tartaric acid, which helps speed food and waste through the digestive system
as well as reduce levels of bile acids that promote tumor growth.*

Fruit 'n' Chicken Salad Stuffed Pitas

Prep—Chill ◆ Serves: 6

2 cups cooked low-fat chicken cubes
½ cup chopped celery
½ cup chopped canned water
    chestnuts
2 tbsp. chopped red bell pepper
8-oz. can pineapple chunks in juice,
    undrained

1 cup red or green seedless grapes
⅔ cup nonfat ranch salad dressing
6 whole-wheat pita breads, cut in half
Lettuce leaves

Combine all ingredients except pita bread and lettuce in large bowl; mix until ingredients are blended. Cover and refrigerate up to 3 days. Just before serving, line pitas with lettuce; add chicken salad, wrap and take for a perfect on-the-go lunch.

Shopping List:

PRODUCE
1 small bunch celery
1 small red bell pepper
½ lb. seedless grapes
    (red or green)
Lettuce

MEAT
¾ lb. boneless, skinless
    chicken or 2 (6-oz.)
    pkgs. cooked chicken
    breast cuts

CANNED
8-oz. can pineapple
    chunks in juice

6-oz. can water
    chestnuts

CONDIMENTS
8 oz. nonfat ranch salad
    dressing

BREAD
Whole-wheat pita bread

NUTRITION PER SERVING Calories 252 • Fat 2.7 g • Carbohydrates 39 g • Protein 17 g • Cholesterol 35 mg • Dietary Fiber 1 g • Sodium 490 mg
EXCHANGES 1 starch • 1 fruit • 1 vegetable • 2 very lean meat
CARB CHOICES 0

Grapes contain ellagic acid, a substance that may kill certain cancer-causing compounds in the body.

Jumbo Oatmeal Muffins

Prep—Bake—Freeze   • Serves: 6

½ cup whole-wheat flour
½ cup all-purpose flour
1 tsp. baking powder
½ tsp. ground cinnamon
1 cup rolled oats
⅓ cup packed brown sugar

3 tbsp. cinnamon-flavored applesauce
1 cup skim milk
1 tsp. vanilla extract
2 large egg whites
2 tbsp. egg substitute

Preheat oven to 400°F. Spray 6 large muffin cups with cooking spray. Combine flours, baking powder, cinnamon and oats in medium bowl and mix well. In a separate bowl, combine brown sugar, applesauce, skim milk, vanilla extract, egg whites and egg substitute; mix ingredients until completely blended. Quickly add liquid ingredients to flour mixture and mix until just blended. Divide mixture among muffin cups; bake 18 to 20 minutes, until toothpick inserted in center comes out clean. Cool slightly; remove from muffin pan. If freezing, cool muffins completely and wrap individually in freezer wrap. Store in plastic freezer bags. To reheat: Microwave on High 45 to 60 seconds until heated through. Variation: Fold in raisins, chopped apples, dates or other fruit to muffin batter.

Shopping List:

DAIRY	PACKAGED	BAKING
8 oz. skim milk	Rolled oats	All-purpose flour
2 large eggs	Cinnamon applesauce	Whole-wheat flour
Egg substitute		Brown sugar
	SPICES	Baking powder
	Cinnamon	
	Vanilla	

NUTRITION PER SERVING Calories 244 • Fat 2 g • Carbohydrates 48 g • Protein 9 g • Cholesterol 0 mg • Dietary Fiber 5 g • Sodium 94 mg
EXCHANGES 3 other carbs
CARB CHOICES 3

Oats contain beta-glucan, a soluble fiber that is a sure winner in the fight against cholesterol.

Make Ahead 'n' Marinate Garden Vegetable Salad

Prep—Chill ◆ Serves: 6

MORNING TO
MIDDAY MEALS

1 cup nonfat Italian salad dressing
⅓ cup balsamic vinegar
⅓ cup honey
2 cups broccoli florets
1½ cups cauliflower florets
2½ cups sliced mushrooms
1 medium red onion, cut into
  1-inch chunks

6 oz. grape tomatoes (optional)
1 small zucchini, cut into ½-inch
  chunks
1 large red bell pepper, cut into
  1-inch chunks
Nonfat cheddar cheese chunks *or*
  grated nonfat Parmesan cheese

Combine salad dressing, vinegar and honey in blender; blend until smooth. Combine remaining ingredients except cheese, if using, in large bowl and toss lightly. Pour dressing over vegetables and toss until well coated. Cover and refrigerate at least 2 hours or overnight. If desired, just before serving, add cheddar cheese chunks or sprinkle with nonfat Parmesan cheese.

Shopping List:

PRODUCE	DAIRY	CONDIMENTS/OTHER
½ lb. broccoli florets	Nonfat cheddar or	8 oz. nonfat Italian salad
½ lb. cauliflower florets	grated nonfat	dressing
1 red onion	Parmesan cheese	Balsamic vinegar
6 oz. grape tomatoes	(optional)	Honey
1 small zucchini		
1 large red bell pepper		
8 oz. sliced mushrooms		

NUTRITION PER SERVING Calories 113 • Fat .4 g • Carbohydrates 26 g • Protein 3 g • Cholesterol 0 mg • Dietary Fiber 3 g • Sodium 171 mg
EXCHANGES 4 vegetable • ½ other carb
CARB CHOICES 2

Honey contains pinocembrin, an antioxidant not found in any other product.

Curried Chicken Salad

Prep—Chill

• Serves: 6

1 cup nonfat mayonnaise
¼ cup mango chutney
1 tbsp. curry powder
¼ tsp. pepper
3 cups chopped, cooked chicken
  breast

¾ cup chopped green onions
¾ cup chopped celery
3 tbsp. chopped walnuts
2 small apples, diced
½ cup dried cranberries

Combine mayonnaise, chutney, curry powder and pepper in blender or food processor and puree until smooth. Combine remaining ingredients in bowl and toss until mixed. Pour dressing over chicken salad and toss to coat. Cover and refrigerate up to 2 days.

Shopping List:

PRODUCE	MEAT	CONDIMENTS
1 small bunch green onions	¾ lb. boneless, skinless chicken breast	8 oz. nonfat mayonnaise
1 small bunch celery		4 oz. mango chutney
2 small apples	PACKAGED	SPICES
	Dried cranberries	Curry powder
	Chopped walnuts	Pepper

NUTRITION PER SERVING Calories 248 • Fat 4.8 g • Carbohydrates 31 g • Protein 21 g • Cholesterol 53 mg • Dietary Fiber 3 g • Sodium 350 mg
EXCHANGES 2 very lean meat • 1 fat • 1 fruit • 1 vegetable • ½ other carb
CARB CHOICES 2

Timesaving tip: Substitute three 6-ounce packages cooked chicken breast cuts for boneless chicken and eliminate "cooking and chopping." One package contains 1⅓ cups chicken cubes.

Morning Glory Muffins

Prep—Bake—Freeze

1 cup vanilla or coconut nonfat
   yogurt
¼ cup granulated sugar
½ cup packed brown sugar
¼ cup egg substitute
2 tbsp. applesauce
1½ tsp. vanilla extract
½ cup crushed pineapple in juice,
   drained

1 cup whole-wheat flour
1 cup all-purpose flour
1 tbsp. baking powder
1 tsp. ground cinnamon
½ cup shredded carrots
⅓ cup raisins
¼ cup chopped walnuts

Preheat oven to 375°F. Spray 12 muffin cups with cooking spray. Combine yogurt, sugars, egg substitute, applesauce, vanilla extract and pineapple in medium bowl; mix until sugars are dissolved and mixture is blended. In separate bowl, combine flours, baking powder and cinnamon; mix well. Gradually add flour mixture to yogurt mixture, blending just until ingredients are moistened. Fold in carrots, raisins and walnuts. Fill each muffin cup two-thirds full; bake 20 to 25 minutes, until toothpick inserted in centers comes out clean. Cool 5 to 10 minutes before removing from muffin pan. Cool to room temperature before freezing. Wrap muffins separately in freezer wrap and place muffins in freezer bag. To reheat: Microwave on High for 1 to 2 minutes until heated through.

Shopping List:

PRODUCE
1 carrot

DAIRY
8-oz. container nonfat
   yogurt
Egg substitute

PACKAGED
4 oz. crushed pineapple
   in juice
Applesauce
Raisins
Chopped walnuts

SPICES
Ground cinnamon
Vanilla extract

BAKING
Whole-wheat flour
All-purpose flour
Sugar
Brown sugar
Baking powder

NUTRITION PER SERVING Calories 171 • Fat 1.8 g • Carbohydrates 36 g • Protein 4 g • Cholesterol <1 g • Dietary Fiber 2 g • Sodium 106 mg
EXCHANGES 2 other carbs
CARB CHOICES 2

Did you know that one 8-ounce container of yogurt provides 50 percent of your daily bone-building needs?

Morning-to-Midday Muffins

Prep—Bake—Freeze   • Serves: 12

1 cup all-purpose flour
1 cup whole-wheat flour
1 tsp. baking soda
¼ cup granulated sugar
½ cup packed brown sugar

½ cup egg substitute
¾ tsp. vanilla extract
1 cup vanilla nonfat yogurt
3 tbsp. skim milk

Preheat oven to 350°F. Spray 12 muffin cups with cooking spray. Combine flours and baking soda in large bowl; mix well. Add sugars to flour mixture; stir in egg substitute, vanilla extract and yogurt until ingredients are moistened and blended. Gradually add skim milk as needed until batter is not too thick. Fill muffin cups two-thirds full; bake 20 to 25 minutes, until toothpick inserted in centers comes out clean. Cool to room temperature; wrap muffins individually in freezer wrap and store in plastic freezer bag in freezer. Reheat muffins in microwave oven on High 45 to 75 seconds. Vary muffin recipes by adding: ¾ cup raisins, dried cranberries or other dried fruits; 1 to 2 tablespoon chopped walnuts; 1 cup fresh or frozen berries or ½ cup baking chips (chocolate, peanut butter, cinnamon or butterscotch).

Shopping List:

DAIRY	SPICES	Sugar
8-oz. container vanilla	Vanilla extract	Brown sugar
nonfat yogurt		Baking soda
4 oz. egg substitute	BAKING	
Skim milk	All-purpose flour	
	Whole-wheat flour	

NUTRITION PER SERVING Calories 135 • Fat .2 g • Carbohydrates 30 g • Protein 4 g • Cholesterol <1 mg • Dietary Fiber 2 g • Sodium 99 mg
EXCHANGES 2 other carbs
CARB CHOICES 2

On average, Americans consume only one serving of whole grains daily. Whole-grain foods give the nutritional benefits of the entire grain— vitamins, minerals, dietary fiber and phytochemicals.

Orange Almond Granola

Prep—Bake—Store up to 1 month   • Serves: 8

2 cups old-fashioned rolled oats
⅓ cup frozen juice concentrate of
   your choice, thawed
2 tbsp. brown sugar

1 tbsp. ground cinnamon
1 tsp. almond extract
1 cup dried cranberries
1 cup golden raisins

Preheat oven to 300°F. Line baking sheet with foil and spray with cooking spray. Combine oats, juice concentrate, brown sugar, cinnamon and almond extract in large bowl; mix well. Spread mixture onto baking sheet; bake 40 to 45 minutes, stirring once or twice. Cool slightly; mix in cranberries and raisins. Cool completely and store in airtight container for up to one month.

Shopping List:

PACKAGED	SPICES	FROZEN
Old-fashioned rolled oats	Ground cinnamon	6-oz. can frozen juice concentrate (flavor of choice)
6 oz. dried cranberries	Almond extract	
6 oz. golden raisins		
	BAKING	
	Brown sugar	

NUTRITION PER SERVING Calories 220 • Fat 1.4 g • Carbohydrates 50 g • Protein 4 g • Cholesterol 0 mg • Dietary Fiber 2 g • Sodium 5 mg
EXCHANGES 1 starch • 2 fruit • ½ other carb
CARB CHOICES 3

Studies show that 1 cup cooked oat bran or 1½ cups oatmeal daily can lower serum cholesterol by 5 percent.

Peanut Butter 'n' Raisin Muffins

Prep—Bake—Freeze   • Serves: 12

⅔ cup mashed ripe bananas
¼ cup reduced-fat peanut butter
¼ cup egg substitute
1 cup skim milk
¾ tsp. vanilla extract

½ cup granulated sugar
¼ cup packed brown sugar
2 cups all-purpose flour
2 tsp. baking powder
¾ cup raisins

Preheat oven to 350°F. Spray 12 muffin cups with cooking spray. Combine bananas, peanut butter, egg substitute, milk, vanilla extract and sugars in large bowl; beat with electric mixer until blended, smooth and creamy. Add flour and baking powder; mix until ingredients are blended. Fold in raisins. Fill muffin cups two-thirds full; bake 25 to 30 minutes, until toothpick inserted in centers comes out clean. Cool muffins; remove from pan and cool completely. Wrap individually in plastic wrap and store in freezer bag. To reheat: Warm in microwave oven on High 45 to 60 seconds.

Shopping List:

PRODUCE	PACKAGED	BAKING
2 bananas	Reduced-fat peanut butter	Flour
		Sugar
DAIRY	Raisins	Brown sugar
Egg substitute		Baking powder
8 oz. skim milk		Vanilla extract

NUTRITION PER SERVING Calories 210 • Fat 2.3 g • Carbohydrates 44 g • Protein 5 g • Cholesterol <1 mg • Dietary Fiber 2 g • Sodium 107 mg
EXCHANGES 3 other carb
CARB CHOICES 3

Don't know what to do with brown bananas? Peel and freeze in a single layer on a cookie sheet. Once frozen, place bananas in a plastic freezer bag. Use in any recipes that call for mashed bananas. They are an excellent and healthy addition to shakes or smoothies.

Pocket Full of Veggies

1 cup canned corn, drained
1 large tomato, diced
⅔ cup chopped green onions
1 cup broccoli florets, diced
1 cup cauliflower florets, diced
¾ cup diced jicama
1 large carrot, diced

1 tsp. Mrs. Dash seasoning
1 tsp. celery seeds
½ tsp. dried basil
½ cup nonfat Thousand Island
  salad dressing
6 whole pita pockets, cut in half
6 tbsp. sprouts (optional)

Combine all ingredients except pita bread and sprouts in large bowl; toss until mixed. Cover and refrigerate overnight. Fill pita pockets with vegetable filling and top with 1 tablespoon sprouts, if using.

Shopping List:

PRODUCE	CANNED	SPICES
1 large tomato	11-oz. can corn kernels	Mrs. Dash seasoning
1 large carrot	(no salt added)	Celery seed
1 bunch green onions		Dried basil
¼ lb. broccoli	**CONDIMENTS**	
¼ lb. cauliflower	4 oz. nonfat Thousand	**BREAD**
4 to 5 oz. jicama	Island salad dressing	6 pita pockets
Sprouts (optional)		

NUTRITION PER SERVING calories 194 • Fat 1.1 g • Carbohydrates 42 g • Protein 7 g • Cholesterol 0 mg • Dietary Fiber 4 g • Sodium 489 mg
EXCHANGES 1 starch • 3 vegetable • 1 other carb
CARB CHOICES 3

Timesaving tip: Purchase precut veggies packaged in the fresh produce section of supermarket or pick up ingredients at the supermarket salad bar.

Pumpkin Power Bread

• Serves: 8

1 cup whole-wheat flour
¾ cup all-purpose flour
1 tsp. baking soda
2 tsp. ground allspice
½ cup chopped dried apricots

1¾ to 2 cups canned pumpkin
½ to ¾ cup crushed pineapple in
   juice, drained
½ cup egg substitute
1 cup sugar

Preheat oven to 350°F. Spray 9 × 5-inch loaf pan with cooking spray. Combine flours, baking soda, allspice and apricots in bowl or plastic bag; stir or shake until mixed. Combine pumpkin, pineapple, egg substitute and sugar in large bowl; mix with electric mixer until smooth. Gradually add flour mixture and stir with a wooden spoon (do not use electric mixer) until all ingredients are mixed. Spoon batter into loaf pan; bake 40 to 50 minutes, until toothpick inserted in center comes out clean. Cool completely before slicing. Pumpkin bread can be refrigerated or frozen; reheat in microwave on High about 15 seconds per thawed slice or 30 to 45 seconds for frozen slices.

Shopping List:

DAIRY	8-oz. can crushed	BAKING
4 oz. egg substitute	pineapple in juice	Whole-wheat flour
	Dried apricots	All-purpose flour
PACKAGED/CANNED		Sugar
15-oz. can pumpkin	SPICES	Baking soda
	Allspice	

NUTRITION PER SERVING Calories 238 • Fat .6 g • Carbohydrates 56 g • Protein 5 g • Cholesterol 0 mg • Dietary Fiber 4 g • Sodium 128 mg
EXCHANGES 4 other carbs
CARB CHOICES 4

Slice fruit and nut breads while partially frozen to prevent crumbling.

Sausage-Egg Muffins

Prep—Bake—Chill • Serves: 6

¼ lb. Morningstar Farms Crumbles (textured soy protein)
¼ cup chopped green bell pepper
¼ cup chopped green onions
1 cup egg substitute
2 large egg whites
¼ cup chopped tomato, drained well
¾ cup shredded nonfat cheddar cheese

Preheat oven to 350°F. Spray 6 large muffin cups with cooking spray. Spray nonstick skillet with cooking spray; add Morningstar Farms Crumbles, bell pepper and green onions to skillet. Cook, stirring frequently, until pepper and onions are softened and crumbles are browned. Remove skillet from heat. Combine egg substitute, egg whites and tomato in medium bowl; add vegetable mixture and ¼ cup cheese. Stir until ingredients are combined. Divide mixture among muffin cups and sprinkle with remaining cheese. Bake 20 to 25 minutes, until eggs are set and muffins are lightly browned. Refrigerate egg muffins and heat in microwave on High 1 to 2 minutes for a quick on-the-go breakfast, lunch or snack.

Shopping List:

PRODUCE	DAIRY	FROZEN
1 small green bell pepper	3 oz. shredded nonfat cheddar cheese	Morningstar Farms Crumbles (textured soy or vegetable protein)
1 small bunch green onions	8 oz. egg substitute	
1 small tomato	2 large eggs	

NUTRITION PER SERVING Calories 71 • Fat 0 g • Carbohydrates 4 g • Protein 12 g • Cholesterol 0 mg • Dietary Fiber 1 g • Sodium 318 mg
EXCHANGES 1½ very lean meat • 1 vegetable
CARB CHOICES 0

Eggs are loaded with vitamin A, folic acid and lutein, an antioxidant that may prevent macular degeneration, a leading cause of blindness.

Spicy Turkey-Pepper Rolls

Prep—Chill   • Serves: 6

12 large romaine lettuce leaves	1½ cups sliced roasted red peppers,
2 tbsp. Dijon mustard	drained
2 tbsp. nonfat mayonnaise	2 tbsp. Italian seasoning
¾ lb. thin low-fat deli turkey slices	¾ tsp. pepper

Separate lettuce leaves and place cup-side up on work surface. Combine Dijon mustard and mayonnaise in small cup; mix until completely blended. Spread each lettuce leaf with mayo-mustard mix; divide turkey and roasted red pepper slices among lettuce leaves. Sprinkle with Italian seasoning and pepper. Roll lettuce leaves (starting at root end) and secure with a toothpick. Wrap individual "lettuce sandwiches" in plastic wrap and refrigerate up to 2 days.

Shopping List:

PRODUCE	PACKAGED	SPICES
1 to 2 heads romaine lettuce	16-oz. jar roasted red peppers	Italian seasoning Pepper
MEAT	**CONDIMENTS**	
¾ lb. thin low-fat deli turkey slices	Dijon mustard Nonfat mayonnaise	

NUTRITION PER SERVING Calories 139 • Fat 2.7 g • Carbohydrates 11 g • Protein 18 g • Cholesterol 39 mg • Dietary Fiber 1 g • Sodium 152 mg
EXCHANGES 2 vegetable • 2 very lean meat
CARB CHOICES 1

Red peppers contain three times the recommended daily requirement for vitamin C, which is responsible for boosting iron absorption and strengthening the immune system.

Tropical Blend Muesli

Prep—Chill • Serves: 6

2 cups quick-cooking rolled oats
¾ cup diced dried apricots
1 cup water
¾ cup orange juice

¼ cup chopped almonds
¼ cup chopped dates
¼ cup coconut flakes

Combine all ingredients in medium bowl and mix well. Cover and refrigerate overnight. Mix lightly before serving.

Shopping List:

PACKAGED	BEVERAGES
Dried apricots	6 oz. orange juice
Chopped dates	
Chopped almonds	BREAKFAST FOODS
Coconut flakes	1 lb. quick-cooking oats

NUTRITION PER SERVING Calories 220 • Fat 5.8 g • Carbohydrates 38 g • Protein 6 g • Cholesterol 0 mg • Dietary Fiber 4 g • Sodium 4.5 mg
EXCHANGES 1 starch • 1½ fruit • 1 fat
CARB CHOICES 3

Eating oatmeal can reduce blood cholesterol levels and the risk of heart disease. Why be concerned? Every 1 percent rise in blood cholesterol increases the risk of heart disease by 2 percent.

MORNING TO MIDDAY MEALS

Turkey Rollups

Prep—Chill

2 (8-oz.) pkgs. nonfat cream cheese, softened
3 whole green onions, finely chopped
1-oz. pkg. dry nonfat ranch salad dressing mix

6 low-fat flour tortillas *or* soft lahvosh
½ lb. low-fat turkey breast, roast beef, chicken or ham slices
6 whole iceberg lettuce leaves

Combine cream cheese, green onions and ranch mix; blend ingredients until mixed. Divide cream cheese mixture among tortillas, spreading an even layer on each tortilla. Place a lettuce leaf on each tortilla and top with 3 or 4 slices turkey breast. Roll tortilla tightly in plastic wrap and refrigerate up to 2 days. Great for on-the-go lunches or snacks!

Shopping List:

PRODUCE	MEAT	CONDIMENTS
1 small bunch green onions	½ lb. low-fat turkey breast slices (roast beef, ham or chicken can be substituted)	1-oz. pkg. dry ranch salad dressing mix
1 head iceberg lettuce		**BREAD**
DAIRY		19-oz. pkg. low-fat flour tortillas or soft lahvosh
2 (8-oz.) pkgs. nonfat cream cheese		

NUTRITION PER SERVING Calories 203 • Fat .8 g • Carbohydrates 14 g • Protein 33 g • Cholesterol 63 mg • Dietary Fiber <1 g • Sodium 866 mg
EXCHANGES 1 starch • 4 very lean meat
CARB CHOICES 1

Buyers beware! For real savings, make the switch to nonfat cream cheese. Reap all the benefits without the added calories and fat—70 calories and 10 grams of fat per ounce.

Whole-Wheat Raisin Bars

Prep—Bake—Refrigerate or Freeze   • Serves: 12

2½ cups whole-wheat flour
1 tsp. baking powder
1 tsp. baking soda
1½ tsp. ground cinnamon
½ cup egg substitute
¾ cup packed brown sugar

1 cup vanilla nonfat yogurt
1 tsp. vanilla extract
½ cup skim milk
1½ cups raisins
2 tbsp. chopped walnuts
Cinnamon-sugar mixture

Preheat oven to 350°F. Spray 9 × 13-inch baking dish with cooking spray. Combine flour, baking powder, baking soda and cinnamon in large bowl; mix well. Combine egg substitute, brown sugar, yogurt, vanilla extract and skim milk in separate bowl; mix until blended smooth. Add to flour mixture and mix until all ingredients are completely blended. Pour half the batter into baking dish; sprinkle with raisins and walnuts; top with remaining batter and spread evenly. Bake 25 to 30 minutes, until lightly browned and toothpick inserted in center comes out clean. Cool 15 to 20 minutes; sprinkle lightly with cinnamon-sugar mixture and cut into squares. Wrap squares in plastic wrap and freeze in plastic freezer bag. Thaw at room temperature before serving or defrost in microwave oven on Low heat 45 to 60 seconds.

Shopping List:

DAIRY	PACKAGED	BAKING
8 oz. vanilla nonfat yogurt	Raisins	Whole-wheat flour
4 oz. egg substitute	Chopped walnuts	Brown sugar
4 oz. skim milk		Baking powder
	SPICES	Baking soda
	Ground cinnamon	Cinnamon-sugar
	Vanilla extract	mixture or sugar

NUTRITION PER SERVING Calories 216 • Fat 1.3 g • Carbohydrates 48 g • Protein 6 g • Cholesterol <1 mg • Dietary Fiber 4 g • Sodium 134 mg
EXCHANGES 3 other carbs
CARB CHOICES 3

Harvard researchers have reported that women who eat more whole grains reduce their risk of diabetes. Whole grains provide more fiber and micronutrients such as folic acid, magnesium and vitamin E.

VIRTUOUS VEGETARIAN MEALS

❖

Safe Food-Handling and Storage

- Wash fruits and vegetables with cool tap water before use. Thick-skinned produce may be scrubbed with a brush. Do not use soap.
- Do not store vegetables and fruits in sealed plastic bags; they will stay fresh longer if you leave the bag open, allowing the foods to breathe.
- Dried pasta, rice, cereals and dried beans should be stored in a cool, dry place in an airtight container. Pasta and rice will keep for up to 2 years. Most cereals will keep for 6 to 12 months; dried beans and unopened canned goods for 12 months. Once package is opened, store foods in an airtight container.
- Fresh pastas will keep 3 to 7 days in the refrigerator or up to 30 days in the freezer.
- Store grains in airtight containers; they will keep at room temperature for up to 6 months.
- Cooked rice can be refrigerated for up to 1 week.
- Cooked pasta can be refrigerated for 3 to 5 days.
- Leftover cooked fresh vegetables can be refrigerated for 3 to 4 days.
- Leftover stuffing can be refrigerated for 1 to 2 days.

To Freeze or Not to Freeze

- Do *not* use foil to wrap high-acidic foods (i.e., tomatoes). Acid reacts with the aluminum foil and affects the flavor. Cover the food with plastic wrap before wrapping in foil to prevent any reaction during storage. Remove the foil and plastic wrap before heating.
- Cooked vegetables, pastas and grains become soft when frozen and reheated. For best results, slightly undercook these foods before freezing.

Shortcuts with the Same Results (in Less Time)

- Separate frozen vegetables by placing them in a colander in the sink and pouring boiling water over the top. Add to casseroles or other dishes to complete cooking.
- If pasta is being used in a dish that requires further cooking, under-cook the pasta. Cut cooking time by one-third. For example, if the package recommends cooking for 12 to 15 minutes, cook the pasta 8 to 10 minutes.

Always Room for Improvement

- Seasonings and spices for vegetables: basil, chives, cilantro, dill, marjoram, mint, oregano, parsley, rosemary, sage, savory, tarragon, thyme
- Seal small amounts of ingredients (i.e., rice, barley, lentils, raisins) in plastic sandwich bags. Place bags in a large airtight container.
- Do not add oil to pasta cooking water; the sauce will slide off the pasta.

Everything Old Is New Again!

- Leftover beans:
  - Mash with nonfat yogurt, season with favorite spices and serve as dip.
  - Add to salads or soups.
  - Mash beans and freeze in ice cube trays. When "cubes" are frozen, repackage and store in plastic freezer bags. Add the cubes to soup, stews or sauces.
  - Serve leftover beans in tortillas with chopped lettuce, green onions, tomatoes, salsa and shredded cheese.
- Leftover rice:
  - Combine with leftover vegetables and/or meat, fish or poultry; add some broth to moisten and bake or microwave until heated through.
  - Use to prepare fried rice.
- Leftover mashed potatoes:
  - Add chopped onion and shredded cheese to mashed potatoes. Bake in 350°F oven until heated through.
  - Form mashed potatoes into balls. Roll in a mixture of cornflake crumbs, garlic powder and Parmesan cheese. Arrange potato balls in a single layer on a foil-lined baking sheet sprayed with cooking spray; broil until lightly browned and crisp.
- Leftover noodles:
  - Add diced vegetables, Parmesan cheese and nonfat Italian salad dressing for cold pasta salad.
  - Add to stir-fries. Cook leftover noodles in hot broth for 1 to 2 minutes; remove, set aside and add to skillet at the end just to heat through.

Baked Eggplant 'n' Cheese Sandwiches

Prep—Chill—Bake or Prep—Bake—Chill   • Serves: 4

2 medium eggplants, peeled and
  sliced
1 ½ tsp. garlic powder
2 cups nonfat pasta sauce

2 cups nonfat ricotta cheese
1 ½ cups shredded nonfat mozzarella
  cheese
½ cup grated nonfat Parmesan cheese

Preheat broiler on high heat. Line baking sheet(s) with foil and spray with cooking spray. Arrange eggplant slices on baking sheet(s); sprinkle with garlic powder and spray lightly with cooking spray. Cook eggplant 5 minutes per side until lightly browned and tender. Preheat oven to 350°F. Spray 9 × 13-inch baking dish with cooking spray. Pour 1 cup pasta sauce into baking dish; arrange half the eggplant slices on top of sauce. Place 1 to 2 tablespoons ricotta cheese on each eggplant slice and top with remaining eggplant slices. Cover with remaining sauce; sprinkle with mozzarella and Parmesan cheeses. Eggplant can be covered, refrigerated and baked later, or baked 25 to 30 minutes, until cheese is lightly browned and casserole is heated through.

Shopping List:

PRODUCE	Grated nonfat	SPICES
2 eggplants	Parmesan cheese	Garlic powder
DAIRY	**PACKAGED**	**OTHER**
15-oz. container nonfat	16-oz. jar nonfat pasta	Nonfat cooking spray
ricotta cheese	sauce	
6 oz. shredded nonfat		
mozzarella cheese		

NUTRITION PER SERVING Calories 259 • Fat .2 g • Carbohydrates 25 g • Protein 38 g • Cholesterol 20 mg • Dietary Fiber 3 g • Sodium 985 mg
EXCHANGES 1 other carb • 2 vegetable • 4 very lean meat
CARB CHOICES 2

For better eggplant casseroles, select fat, rounded eggplants; they tend to be juicier and better suited for baking than long, slender ones.

Baked Rigatoni

Prep—Bake—Freeze or Prep—Freeze—Bake ♦ Serves: 12

½ cup egg substitute
2 cups nonfat ricotta cheese
¾ cup grated nonfat Parmesan cheese
1 tbsp. dried parsley
6½ cups nonfat pasta sauce

2 tsp. Italian seasoning
1 tsp. garlic powder
16 oz. rigatoni, cooked and drained
3 cups nonfat shredded mozzarella cheese

Preheat oven to 375°F (if baking after preparation). Spray 9 × 13-inch baking dish with cooking spray. Combine egg substitute, ricotta cheese, Parmesan cheese and parsley in medium bowl; mix until completely blended. Combine pasta sauce, Italian seasoning and garlic powder. Pour 2 cups pasta sauce in bottom of baking dish; top with half the cooked pasta, half the cheese mixture (drop by tablespoons) and 1 cup mozzarella cheese. Repeat with 2 cups sauce, remaining pasta, remaining cheese mixture and 1 cup mozzarella cheese. Top with remaining pasta sauce and mozzarella cheese.

Spray large foil sheet with cooking spray; cover baking dish. Pasta can be refrigerated at this point and baked later, or bake, covered, 60 to 70 minutes; uncover and bake 5 to 10 minutes, until lightly browned. Remove from oven and let stand at room temperature 5 minutes before serving. If planning to freeze casserole: Cool to room temperature. Slice into individual servings if desired, wrap in freezer wrap and store in plastic freezer bag. Frozen pasta meals can be baked directly from freezer (wrap in foil and heat in 350°F oven 20 to 25 minutes) or thawed in microwave and baked in 350°F oven 10 to 15 minutes.

Shopping List:

DAIRY
4 oz. egg substitute
15-oz. container nonfat
  ricotta cheese
3 oz. grated nonfat
  Parmesan cheese

¾ lb. shredded nonfat
  mozzarella cheese

PACKAGED
16-oz. pkg. rigatoni
2 (28-oz.) jars nonfat
  pasta sauce

SPICES
Italian seasoning
Garlic powder
Dried parsley

NUTRITION PER SERVING Calories 275 • Fat .6 g • Carbohydrates 41 g • Protein 23 g • Cholesterol 6 mg • Dietary Fiber 0 g • Sodium 710 mg
EXCHANGES 2 very lean meat • 2 starch • 2 vegetable
CARB CHOICES 3

Timesaving tip: Double the recipe and freeze half for another meal. You and your family will appreciate it!

Bean Burgers with Creamy Mustard Sauce

Prep—Cook—Chill   • Serves: 6

3 cups canned red kidney beans, mashed
½ cup chopped green bell pepper
1 tbsp. chopped green onion
½ cup egg substitute
2 tbsp. low-sodium soy sauce
½ cup bread crumbs

2 tsp. Mrs. Dash seasoning
½ tsp. garlic powder
½ cup nonfat sour cream
½ cup plain nonfat yogurt
2 tbsp. spicy mustard
½ tsp. dried dill

Combine beans, bell pepper, green onion, egg substitute, soy sauce, bread crumbs, Mrs. Dash seasoning and garlic powder in medium bowl; mix well. Spray large nonstick skillet with cooking spray and heat over medium-high heat. With a large spoon, scoop portions of bean mixture into skillet and press to flatten into 2- to 3-inch patties. Cook until browned on both sides, 4 to 5 minutes per side. Combine sour cream, yogurt, mustard and dill in small bowl; mix until blended. Cover and refrigerate several hours before serving. Wrap bean burgers in foil; cover and refrigerate until ready to serve. Reheat bean patties (wrapped in foil) in 350°F oven 10 to 15 minutes. Serve with mustard sauce, lettuce, tomatoes and onions in pita pocket breads.

Shopping List:

PRODUCE	PACKAGED CANNED	SPICES
1 green bell pepper	2 (15-oz.) cans red	Dried dill
1 green onion	kidney beans	Garlic powder
	Bread crumbs	Mrs. Dash seasoning
DAIRY		
4 oz. egg substitute	**CONDIMENTS**	**BREAD**
4 oz. nonfat sour cream	Low-sodium soy sauce	Pita bread
4 oz. plain nonfat yogurt	Spicy mustard	

NUTRITION PER SERVING Calories 190 • Fat 1.3 g • Carbohydrates 32 g • Protein 13 g • Cholesterol <1 mg • Dietary Fiber 7 g • Sodium 801 mg
EXCHANGES 1½ starch • ½ other carb
CARB CHOICES 2

Legumes are nutritional superfoods. One cup contains 200 to 250 calories, 14 to 20 grams of protein, 6 to 8 grams of fiber and fewer than 2 grams of fat, along with a multitude of vitamins and minerals.

Brown Rice with Black-Eyed Peas

Prep—Cook—Chill ◆ Serves: 6

1 to 4 tbsp. vegetable broth
1 cup chopped onion
¾ tsp. garlic powder
16-oz. can diced tomatoes, undrained
½ tsp. dried basil

¼ tsp. dried thyme
3 cups cooked brown rice
16-oz. can black-eyed peas, rinsed
    and drained
Pepper to taste

VIRTUOUS VEGETARIAN MEALS

Spray large nonstick skillet with cooking spray; add 1 tablespoon vegetable broth and heat over medium-high heat. Add onion; cook, stirring frequently, until softened and transparent. Sprinkle garlic powder over onion and cook 1 to 2 minutes. Add tomatoes, basil and thyme. Cook over medium heat 5 to 7 minutes until heated through. Add cooked rice and black-eyed peas; season with pepper. Cover and cook over low heat 12 to 15 minutes. Spray microwave-safe casserole dish with cooking spray; spoon rice mixture into dish, cover and refrigerate until ready to serve. Just before heating, add remaining vegetable broth (a tablespoon at a time) until casserole is moistened. Heat in microwave on High 8 to 10 minutes for whole casserole or 1 to 2 minutes for individual servings, until heated throughout.

Shopping List:

PRODUCE	16-oz. can black-eyed	Dried thyme
1 large onion	peas	Pepper
	Brown rice	
PACKAGED/CANNED		
Vegetable broth	SPICES	
16-oz. can diced	Garlic powder	
tomatoes	Dried basil	

NUTRITION PER SERVING Calories 194 • Fat 1.4 g • Carbohydrates 39 g •
Protein 7 g • Cholesterol 0 mg • Dietary Fiber 1 g • Sodium 359 mg
EXCHANGES 2 starch • 2 vegetable
CARB CHOICES 3

Black-eyed peas are digested slowly and serve as a good appetite suppressant while providing hefty amounts of anemia-fighting iron and nerve-soothing B vitamins.

Carrot-Zucchini Kugel

Prep—Bake—Freeze   • Serves: 6

1 tbsp. vegetable broth	1 cup egg substitute
2½ cups shredded zucchini	2 to 3 tbsp. matzo meal
2½ cups shredded carrots	½ tsp. Italian seasoning
1 medium potato, peeled and grated	⅛ tsp. pepper
1½ tsp. onion powder	¼ tsp. Mrs. Dash seasoning

Preheat oven to 350°F. Spray 9 × 13-inch baking dish with cooking spray. Pour 1 tbsp. vegetable broth into pan; place in oven 3 to 5 minutes to heat. Combine zucchini, carrots, potato, onion powder, ¾ cup egg substitute, 2 tbsp. matzo meal, Italian seasoning, pepper and Mrs. Dash seasoning; mix until thick and smooth. If needed, add additional egg substitute and/or matzo meal to reach desired texture. Pour mixture into baking dish; spray lightly with cooking spray. Bake 45 to 60 minutes, until golden brown. Cool to room temperature; kugel can be cut into individual servings, wrapped in freezer wrap and stored in freezer up to 2 months. To reheat: Microwave on High 1 to 3 minutes, until heated through. Kugel can be served hot or cold; garnish with nonfat sour cream if desired.

Shopping List:

PRODUCE	PACKAGED/CANNED	SPICES
1 lb. zucchini	Nonfat vegetable broth	Italian seasoning
3 large carrots	Matzo meal (cracker	Onion powder
1 medium potato	meal can be	Mrs. Dash seasoning
	substituted)	Pepper
DAIRY		
8 oz. egg substitute		

NUTRITION PER SERVING Calories 94 • Fat .3 g • Carbohydrates 19 g • Protein 5 g • Cholesterol 0 mg • Dietary Fiber 3 g • Sodium 66 mg
EXCHANGES 1 starch • 1 vegetable
CARB CHOICES 1

Zucchini, a member of the summer squash family, is loaded with potassium and only has 15 calories per serving.

Cook-It-Later Lasagna for Lazy Chefs

Prep—Freeze—Bake or Prep—Bake—Freeze • Serves: 8

4 cups nonfat pasta sauce
1 tsp. Italian seasoning
¾ tsp. garlic powder
12 oz. lasagna noodles, uncooked

2 cups nonfat ricotta cheese
3 cups shredded nonfat mozzarella
  cheese

VIRTUOUS VEGETARIAN MEALS

Spray 2 (9-inch-square) baking dishes with cooking spray. Combine pasta sauce, Italian seasoning and garlic powder; mix well. Pour 1 cup sauce in bottom of each baking dish. Layer ¼ lasagna noodles, ricotta cheese, mozzarella cheese and sauce in each pan; repeat layers. Cover with foil and freeze. At least 1 day before serving: place lasagna in refrigerator (do not microwave) until completely thawed. Preheat oven to 350°F. Bake lasagna, covered, 45 to 50 minutes; remove foil and bake 10 to 15 minutes, until lightly browned. Let stand at room temperature 5 to 10 minutes, until cheese sets. Lasagna can also be baked, frozen and reheated if desired.

Shopping List:

DAIRY	PACKAGED	SPICES
15-oz. container nonfat ricotta cheese	12-oz. pkg. lasagna noodles	Italian seasoning Garlic powder
¾ lb. shredded nonfat mozzarella cheese	32-oz. jar nonfat pasta sauce	

NUTRITION PER SERVING Calories 312 • Fat .6 g • Carbohydrates 43 g • Protein 29 g • Cholesterol 10 mg • Dietary Fiber 1 g • Sodium 775 mg
EXCHANGES 3 very lean meat • 2 starch • 2 vegetable
CARB CHOICES 3

The freezer can become your best friend for planning, preparing and cooking meals; store frozen meals at 0°F or below and use within 3 months for best quality.

Cornbread

1 cup self-rising flour
1⅓ cups cornmeal
2 tbsp. egg substitute
1½ tbsp. sugar
1 cup skim milk

¾ cup canned corn kernels, drained well
1 tbsp. chopped green chiles, drained well

Preheat oven to 400°F. Spray 6 large or 12 regular muffin cups with cooking spray. Combine self-rising flour and cornmeal in plastic bag; shake until blended. Combine egg substitute, sugar and milk in medium bowl; beat until completely blended and sugar is dissolved. Gradually add flour mixture to egg mixture; mix until ingredients are blended. Fold in corn kernels and green chiles. Divide batter among muffin cups; bake 15 to 20 minutes (regular) or 20 to 25 minutes (large) until toothpick inserted in centers comes out clean. Muffins can be refrigerated or frozen; thaw and heat in microwave on High 15 to 20 seconds per muffin. A perfect side dish with chili, soup or stew.

VIRTUOUS VEGETARIAN MEALS

Shopping List:

DAIRY	CANNED	BAKING
8 oz. skim milk	8-oz. can corn kernels	¼ lb. self-rising flour
4 oz. egg substitute	4-oz. can chopped green chiles	½ lb. cornmeal
		Sugar

NUTRITION PER SERVING Calories 215 • Fat 1.4 g • Carbohydrates 46 g • Protein 6 g • Cholesterol <1 mg • Dietary Fiber 6 g • Sodium 119 mg
EXCHANGES 3 other carbs
CARB CHOICES 3

Amazing facts: One bushel of corn can sweeten more than 400 cans of soda. One bushel also produces 32 pounds of cornstarch and 1.6 pounds of corn oil.

Corn Tamale Casserole

Prep—Freeze—Bake

◆ Serves: 8

8 cups water
3 cups cornmeal
16-oz. can tomato sauce
6 cups frozen whole kernel corn,
    thawed and drained

1 cup chopped onion
¾ cup chopped green chiles
2 (4-oz.) cans chopped ripe olives,
    drained

Pour water into Dutch oven and bring to a boil over high heat. Add cornmeal and cook, stirring occasionally, until mixture becomes consistency of mush. Spray large nonstick skillet with cooking spray; pour tomato sauce into skillet. Add corn, onion, chiles and olives; cook, stirring frequently, until onion is softened and transparent. Spray 9 × 13-inch baking dish with cooking spray. Layer half the cornmeal mixture on bottom of dish; top with vegetable mixture and then remaining cornmeal mix. Cover with freezer-safe wrap and freeze. To bake: Preheat oven to 350°F. Bake casserole directly from freezer 2 hours, until cooked through. If baking without freezing, bake 45 to 60 minutes.

Shopping List:

PRODUCE
1 large onion

PACKAGED/CANNED
1-lb. pkg. cornmeal
2 (4-oz.) cans chopped
    green chiles

16-oz. can tomato
    sauce
2 (4-oz.) cans chopped
    ripe olives

FROZEN
3 (16-oz.) pkgs. frozen
    corn kernels

NUTRITION PER SERVING Calories 329 • Fat 2.4 g • Carbohydrates 73 g •
Protein 9 g • Cholesterol 0 mg • Dietary Fiber 7 g • Sodium 567 mg
EXCHANGES 3 vegetable • 3½ starch
CARB CHOICES 5

Tomato sauce provides a mega-dose of lycopene, a potential cancer fighter.

Crustless Vegetable Quiche

Prep — Bake — Chill

• Serves: 6

2 tbsp. vegetable broth
1 cup chopped onion
10-oz. pkg. frozen chopped broccoli
2 tbsp. water
¼ cup all-purpose flour
1 cup egg substitute

6 large egg whites
3 cups skim milk
¾ cup grated nonfat Parmesan cheese
¼ tsp. pepper
3 tablespoons Bacos (optional)

Preheat oven to 350°F. Spray 9 × 13-inch baking dish with cooking spray. Spray large nonstick skillet with cooking spray. Pour vegetable broth into skillet and heat over medium-high heat. Add onion and cook, stirring frequently, until golden brown. Add broccoli and 2 tablespoons water. Cover and cook, stirring occasionally, until tender, 4 to 5 minutes. Sprinkle flour over broccoli and stir until coated. Cook 3 to 4 minutes, stirring constantly. Spoon broccoli mixture into prepared baking dish. Combine egg substitute, egg whites, skim milk, Parmesan cheese and pepper in medium bowl; whisk mixture until frothy and blended. Pour mixture over broccoli; sprinkle with Bacos, if using. Bake 35 to 40 minutes, until knife inserted in center comes out clean. Serve immediately or cool to room temperature; cover and refrigerate up to 2 days. To reheat: Cover with foil and bake in 350°F oven 25 to 30 minutes, until heated through.

VIRTUOUS VEGETARIAN MEALS

Shopping List:

PRODUCE	PACKAGED/CANNED	FROZEN
1 large onion	Vegetable broth	10-oz. pkg. frozen
	1 jar Bacos (Betty	chopped broccoli
DAIRY	Crocker, optional)	
24 oz. skim milk		OTHER
3 oz. grated nonfat	SPICES	Flour
Parmesan cheese	Pepper	
8 oz. egg substitute		
6 large eggs		

NUTRITION PER SERVING Calories 161 • Fat 1 g • Carbohydrates 21 g • Protein 18 g • Cholesterol 2 mg • Dietary Fiber 2 g • Sodium 362 mg
EXCHANGES 2 very lean meat • ½ milk • 2 vegetable
CARB CHOICES 1

According to a research project conducted by the Honolulu Heart Program, the risk for stroke was two times greater in men who didn't drink milk compared to men who consumed 16 ounces or more each day.

Grandiose Grain Burgers

Prep—Cook—Freeze • Serves: 6

3 cups cooked lentils
1 tbsp. onion powder
2 large egg whites
¼ cup egg substitute
1½ tsp. garlic powder
½ tsp. ground cumin

1 tsp. dried sage
⅛ tsp. Tabasco sauce
1 cup cooked brown rice
¾ cup shredded carrots
½ cup cracker meal

Combine lentils, onion powder, egg whites, egg substitute, garlic powder, cumin, sage and Tabasco sauce in food processor or blender (you may need to divide this into two batches); process until smooth. Transfer mixture to medium bowl; add remaining ingredients and mix well. If mixture needs to be thickened, add 1 to 2 tablespoons additional cracker meal. Shape mixture into patties. Spray large nonstick skillet with cooking spray and heat over medium-high heat. Add patties and cook until browned, 6 to 7 minutes per side. Serve immediately or cool, wrap and freeze. Reheat grain burgers in microwave or oven (wrapped in foil). Serve on whole-grain rolls garnished with lettuce, tomatoes and sliced onions.

Shopping List:

PRODUCE	PACKAGED	
1 to 2 carrots or packaged shredded carrots	Lentils Brown rice Cracker meal	Garlic powder Ground cumin Sage
DAIRY	SPICES	
4 oz. egg substitute 2 large eggs	Tabasco sauce Onion powder	

NUTRITION PER SERVING Calories 207 • Fat 1.1 g • Carbohydrates 37 g • Protein 13 g • Cholesterol 0 mg • Dietary Fiber 6 g • Sodium 102 mg
EXCHANGES 1 very lean meat • 2 starch • 1 vegetable
CARB CHOICES 2

Along with a variety of soy products, lentils are an excellent source of flavonoids, antioxidants that may reduce the formation of artery-clogging plaque, reducing the risk of heart attack.

Mushrooms 'n' Barley

Prep—Cook—Chill   ◆ Serves: 6

3 cups + 1 tbsp. nonfat vegetable broth
1 cup chopped mushrooms
1 cup chopped onion
1½ cups pearled barley

Spray large nonstick skillet with cooking spray; add 1 tablespoon broth and heat over medium-high heat. Add mushrooms and onion to skillet; cook, stirring frequently, until vegetables are softened. Pour in remaining broth and bring to a boil over high heat. Stir in barley. Reduce heat to low, cover and simmer 40 to 45 minutes, until liquid is absorbed. If not serving immediately, spoon mixture into shallow baking dish, cover with plastic wrap and refrigerate. When ready to serve, reheat in microwave oven on High 5 to 7 minutes, until heated through.

Shopping List:

PRODUCE	PACKAGED/CANNED
½ lb. mushrooms	Pearled barley
1 large onion	3 (14½-oz.) cans
	vegetable broth

NUTRITION PER SERVING Calories 192 • Fat .7 g • Carbohydrates 42 g • Protein 6 g • Cholesterol 0 mg • Dietary Fiber 8 g • Sodium 438 mg
EXCHANGES 2 starch • 2 vegetable
CARB CHOICES 3

An excellent source of cholesterol-lowering fiber, one serving of pearled barley provides 11 percent of the RDA for iron as well as fair amounts of folate and niacin.

Peas 'n' Pasta Salad

Prep—Chill

8 oz. vermicelli, cooked and drained
½ cup mashed reduced-fat feta
  cheese
½ cup nonfat Italian salad dressing
2 tbsp. nonfat mayonnaise

1 cup chopped green onions
1 tbsp. Dijon mustard
¾ cup frozen baby peas, thawed
¼ cup chopped pimiento
¼ cup chopped ripe olives

Combine all ingredients in medium bowl and toss until mixed. Cover and refrigerate up to 3 days. Refrigerate at least 24 hours before serving for best flavor results.

Shopping List:

PRODUCE	PACKAGED	Dijon mustard
1 bunch green onions	8-oz. pkg. vermicelli	Pimientos
		4-oz. can chopped ripe
DAIRY		olives
4-oz. pkg. reduced-fat	**CONDIMENTS**	
feta cheese	4 oz. nonfat Italian salad	**FROZEN**
	dressing	10-oz. pkg. frozen baby
	Nonfat mayonnaise	peas

NUTRITION PER SERVING Calories 218 • Fat 3.7 g • Carbohydrates 38 g • Protein 8 g • Cholesterol 8 mg • Dietary Fiber 1 g • Sodium 432 mg
EXCHANGES 2 starch • 1 vegetable • 1 fat
CARB CHOICES 2

What's the difference between green and black olives? Maturity!

VIRTUOUS VEGETARIAN MEALS

Quinoa Pilaf

Prep — Cook — Chill   ◆ Serves: 6

3 cups vegetable broth
1½ cups uncooked quinoa
3 tbsp. chopped green onions
2 tsp. Mrs. Dash seasoning
1½ cups frozen mixed vegetables,
   thawed and drained

1 tsp. Butter Buds
Pepper to taste
2 tbsp. sliced almonds, lightly toasted

Pour vegetable broth into large saucepan; bring to a boil over high heat. Add quinoa, green onions and Mrs. Dash seasoning; cover and cook over medium-low heat 15 to 18 minutes, until all the water has been absorbed. Add vegetables, Butter Buds and pepper. Spray square baking dish with cooking spray; transfer quinoa mixture to baking dish. Top with almonds if serving immediately or refrigerate and reheat in microwave on High, adding almonds when ready to serve.

Shopping List:

PRODUCE	Quinoa	FROZEN
1 small bunch green	Sliced almonds	10-oz. pkg. frozen
onions		mixed vegetables
	SPICES	
PACKAGED CANNED	Mrs. Dash seasoning	
3 (14½-oz.) cans	Butter Buds	
vegetable broth	Pepper	

NUTRITION PER SERVING Calories 197 • Fat 3.8 g • Carbohydrates 35 g • Protein 7 g • Cholesterol 0 mg • Dietary Fiber 3 g • Sodium 450 mg
EXCHANGES 2 starch • 1 vegetable • ½ fat
CARB CHOICES 2

Quinoa supplies all the amino acids of a complete protein.

Ratatouille Pasta Sauce

Prep — Cook — Refrigerate or Freeze   ◆ Serves: 6

2 tbsp. vegetable broth
1 large bell pepper, thinly sliced
1 cup chopped onion
1 cup chopped celery
2 medium zucchini, sliced
1 tsp. garlic powder

2 (16-oz.) cans Italian-style tomatoes
6-oz. can tomato paste
1 tbsp. sugar
1 tbsp. lemon juice
1½ tbsp. Italian seasoning

VIRTUOUS VEGETARIAN MEALS

Spray large nonstick skillet with cooking spray; add vegetable broth and heat over medium-high heat. Add bell pepper, onion and celery to skillet; cook, stirring frequently, until vegetables are tender, about 5 minutes. Add zucchini, garlic powder, tomatoes, tomato paste, sugar, lemon juice and Italian seasoning. Bring to a boil over medium-high heat; reduce heat to low and simmer 10 to 15 minutes. Sauce can be refrigerated or frozen and served over favorite pasta or baked potatoes.

Shopping List:

PRODUCE	PACKAGED/CANNED	SPICES
1 large bell pepper (any color)	2 (16-oz.) cans Italian-style tomatoes	Italian seasoning
1 large onion	6-oz. can tomato paste	Garlic powder
1 small bunch celery	Vegetable broth	
2 zucchini	Sugar	
Lemon juice		

NUTRITION PER SERVING Calories 87 • Fat .7 g • Carbohydrates 20 g • Protein 4 g • Cholesterol 0 mg • Dietary Fiber 4 g • Sodium 696 mg
EXCHANGES 4 vegetable
CARB CHOICES 1

Timesaving tip: Keep frozen pepper strips on hand; simply grab the amount needed and cook from frozen or thawed state (1 large bell pepper = ¾ to 1 cup sliced peppers).

Refried Beans

♦ Serves: 4

16-oz. can pinto beans, rinsed and
   drained
¼ cup chunky-style salsa
1½ tsp. onion powder

¼ tsp. garlic powder
¼ tsp. chili powder
¼ tsp. ground cumin

Spray 2-quart saucepan with cooking spray. Add all the ingredients; bring to a boil over medium-high heat, stirring frequently. Reduce heat to low; simmer 10 to 12 minutes, stirring occasionally. Cool to room temperature. Process bean mixture in food processor or blender until smooth. Cover and refrigerate beans for up to 1 week. Serve with low-fat flour tortillas, taco shells or low-fat chips.

VIRTUOUS VEGETARIAN MEALS

Shopping List:

CANNED	SPICES
16-oz. can pinto beans	Onion powder
4-oz. jar chunky-style	Garlic powder
salsa	Chilli powder
	Ground cumin

NUTRITION PER SERVING Calories 96 • Fat .4 g • Carbohydrates 18 g • Protein 5 g • Cholesterol 0 mg • Dietary Fiber 0 g • Sodium 552 mg
EXCHANGES 1 starch
CARB CHOICES 1

Canned beans provide most of the same benefits as dried ones; just ½ cup cooked pinto beans provide one-third the daily value for fiber for women.

Rice and Black Bean Burritos

Prep—Cook—Refrigerate or Freeze   • Serves: 6

3½ cups canned black beans,
  drained
¾ cup salsa
⅓ cup chopped tomatoes
¼ cup chopped green chiles

1½ cups cooked rice
6 low-fat flour tortillas
1½ cups shredded nonfat cheddar
  cheese

Spray large nonstick skillet with cooking spray. Add beans, salsa, tomatoes and chiles to skillet; cook over medium-low heat, stirring frequently, until heated through. Add rice and mix well. Divide filling among tortillas; top with cheese. Roll tortillas up burrito style and place seam-side down on plate. Cover with plastic wrap and freeze until firm. Store burritos in individual plastic freezer bags. To reheat: Place in microwave-safe dish and heat on High 1 to 2 minutes per burrito. Serve with additional salsa, nonfat sour cream and chopped green onions.

Shopping List:

PRODUCE	PACKAGED/CANNED	BREAD
1 small tomato	4-oz. can chopped green chiles	19-oz. pkg. low-fat flour tortillas
DAIRY	6 oz. salsa	
6 oz. shredded nonfat cheddar cheese	2 (15-oz.) cans black beans	
	Rice	

NUTRITION PER SERVING Calories 338 • Fat 2.4 g • Carbohydrates 58 g • Protein 20 g • Cholesterol 0 mg • Dietary Fiber 5 g • Sodium 1,034 mg
EXCHANGES 1 very lean meat • 3½ starch • 1 vegetable
CARB CHOICES 4

Calcium-rich cheddar cheese promotes healthy heart, brain, muscle and nervous system function.

VIRTUOUS VEGETARIAN MEALS

80

Southwest Brown Rice and Green Chiles

Prep—Chill—Bake or Prep—Bake—Chill   • Serves: 6

1 tbsp. vegetable broth	1 cup nonfat ricotta cheese
¾ cup chopped onion	6 oz. chopped green chiles
4 cups cooked brown rice	¼ cup minced fresh cilantro
1 cup nonfat shredded cheddar cheese	½ tsp. ground cumin
	Pepper to taste

Preheat oven to 350°F. Spray 1½-quart baking dish with cooking spray. Spray large skillet with cooking spray; add vegetable broth and heat over medium heat. Add chopped onion; cook, stirring frequently, until softened and lightly browned. Remove from heat; combine onion, rice and remaining ingredients in casserole and mix well. Cover and refrigerate until ready to heat and serve or bake 35 minutes, until bubbly and lightly browned on top.

VIRTUOUS VEGETARIAN MEALS

Shopping List:

PRODUCE	8 oz. shredded, nonfat	Brown rice
1 medium onion	cheddar cheese	Vegetable broth
1 bunch fresh cilantro		
	PACKAGED/CANNED	SPICES
DAIRY	2 (4-oz.) cans chopped	Ground cumin
8 oz. nonfat ricotta	green chiles	Pepper
cheese		

NUTRITION PER SERVING Calories 222 • Fat 1.1 g • Carbohydrates 38 g • Protein 15 g • Cholesterol 7 mg • Dietary Fiber 1 g • Sodium 602 mg
EXCHANGES 2 starch • 2 vegetable • 1 very lean meat
CARB CHOICES 3

A good source of magnesium, brown rice can contribute to maintaining proper blood pressure. Brown rice is a good source of niacin, thiamin and vitamin B_6, vitamins essential for energy metabolism and production of red blood cells.

Southwest Couscous

Prep—Cook—Chill   ◆ Serves: 6

2 cups boiling water
1 cup uncooked couscous
15-oz. can black beans, rinsed and
  drained

1 cup chunky-style salsa
3½ tbsp. fresh cilantro, finely
  chopped
Pepper to taste

Bring 2 cups water to a boil in medium saucepan; add couscous, reduce
heat to low, cover and simmer 12 to 15 minutes, until water is completely
absorbed. Fluff couscous with a fork. Add beans, salsa, cilantro and pepper
to saucepan; cook over medium-low heat until completely heated through,
10 to 12 minutes. Serve at once or refrigerate and serve within 2 to 3 days.
Reheat in microwave or serve at room temperature. If serving chilled, add
additional salsa if desired.

Shopping List:

PRODUCE	PACKAGED/CANNED	SPICES
Cilantro	15-oz. can black beans	Pepper
	8 oz. chunky-style salsa	
	Couscous	

NUTRITION PER SERVING Calories 195 • Fat .4 g • Carbohydrates 38 g •
Protein 9 g • Cholesterol 0 mg • Dietary Fiber 7 g • Sodium 504 mg
EXCHANGES 2 starch • 2 vegetable
CARB CHOICES 3

*Couscous is a low-fat, low-sodium wheat product that contains a fair
amount of folate, a B vitamin important for the growth and regeneration of
red blood cells and for the formation of hemoglobin.*

Spinach-Cheese Calzones

Prep—Freeze—Bake or Prep—Bake—Freeze   • Serves: 6

1 lb. frozen bread dough, thawed and divided into 6 equal pieces
3 to 4 cups frozen chopped spinach, thawed and drained
1 cup nonfat ricotta cheese

1 tsp. garlic powder
⅓ cup egg substitute
2 tbsp. grated nonfat Parmesan cheese
1½ cups nonfat pasta sauce

Roll dough pieces on floured surface until about ¼ inch thick. Combine spinach, ricotta cheese, garlic powder, egg substitute and Parmesan cheese in a medium bowl; mix until blended. Divide filling among bread pieces; fold dough over top and crimp down with a fork. Preheat oven to 400°F. Line baking sheet with foil and spray with cooking spray. Arrange calzones on baking sheet; spray lightly with cooking spray. Calzones can be frozen at this point and baked after completely thawed or bake in preheated oven 15 to 20 minutes, until golden brown. Pour pasta sauce into microwave-safe bowl; cover and heat 1 to 2 minutes until warm. Serve with cooked calzones. Cooked calzones can be frozen, thawed and reheated; wrap individually with freezer wrap and store in plastic freezer bags to maintain freshness.

Shopping List:

DAIRY	PACKAGED	FROZEN
8 oz. nonfat ricotta cheese	16-oz. jar nonfat pasta sauce	1-lb. pkg. frozen bread dough
Grated nonfat Parmesan cheese		20-oz. pkg. frozen chopped spinach
Egg substitute	SPICES	
	Garlic powder	

NUTRITION PER SERVING Calories 316 • Fat 2.2 g • Carbohydrates 56 g • Protein 18 g • Cholesterol 6 mg • Dietary Fiber 4 g • Sodium 902 mg
EXCHANGES 1 lean meat • 4½ vegetable • 2 starch
CARB CHOICES 4

The best wrapping materials for freezing include freezer paper, plastic freezer wrap or bags and/or heavy-duty aluminum foil. These materials are moisture- and vapor-resistant, keeping foods safe from freezer burn.

Spinach Enchiladas

Prep—Freeze—Bake or Prep—Bake—Freeze ♦ Serves: 6

8 cups chopped fresh spinach
1½ cups shredded nonfat cheddar cheese
6 low-fat flour tortillas
3 cups low-fat enchilada sauce

Preheat oven to 400°F. Spray 9 × 13-inch baking dish with cooking spray. Steam or microwave spinach just until wilted, 2 to 4 minutes; drain well. Divide spinach and ¾ cup cheese among tortillas; roll tortillas. Pour 1 cup enchilada sauce on bottom of baking dish; arrange enchiladas on top. Top with remaining enchilada sauce and cheese. Bake 10 to 15 minutes, until hot and lightly browned. Enchiladas can be frozen before or after baking. If freezing before baking, wrap enchiladas separately (without sauce or cheese) in freezer wrap and store in plastic freezer bag. To bake uncooked enchiladas (from frozen state): Spread sauce on bottom of dish, top with enchiladas, remaining sauce and cheese. Bake 20 to 25 minutes in 400°F oven.

Shopping List:

PRODUCE	CANNED
2 lbs. fresh spinach leaves	28-oz. can low-fat enchilada sauce

DAIRY	BREAD
6 oz. shredded nonfat cheddar cheese	19-oz. pkg. low-fat flour tortillas

NUTRITION PER SERVING Calories 251 • Fat 1 g • Carbohydrates 42 g • Protein 16 g • Cholesterol 0 mg • Dietary Fiber 7 g • Sodium 1,419 mg
EXCHANGES 2 starch • 1 other carb • 2 very lean meat
CARB CHOICES 2

Spinach is rich in folic acid, a nutrient responsible for producing key chemicals for the brain and nervous system.

Spinach-Feta Stuffed Potatoes

Prep—Chill—Bake   • Serves: 4

4 large baking potatoes
2 (10-oz.) pkgs. frozen chopped
   spinach, thawed and drained
¼ cup grated nonfat Parmesan cheese

¼ cup nonfat cottage cheese
2 oz. reduced-fat feta cheese,
   crumbled
½ tsp. garlic powder

Preheat oven to 450°F. Pierce potatoes with a fork. Bake 45 to 60 minutes, until cooked through. (Potatoes can be microwaved on High 8 to 9 minutes per potato.) Cool 5 minutes. Cut potatoes in half; carefully scoop out pulp, leaving ¼-inch border. Combine potato pulp, spinach, Parmesan cheese, cottage cheese, feta cheese and garlic powder in medium bowl; mash with fork or mix with electric mixer until creamy and smooth. Spoon mixture back into potato shells. Line baking sheet with foil and spray with cooking spray. Arrange potatoes in single layer on baking sheet; cover and refrigerate until ready to serve. Let potatoes stand at room temperature 15 to 20 minutes before baking. Preheat oven to 425°F. Bake potatoes 10 to 15 minutes, until heated through.

VIRTUOUS VEGETARIAN MEALS

Shopping List:

PRODUCE	Nonfat cottage cheese	FROZEN
4 large baking potatoes	2 oz. reduced-fat feta cheese	2 (10-oz.) pkgs. frozen chopped spinach
DAIRY		
Grated nonfat Parmesan cheese	SPICES Garlic powder	

NUTRITION PER SERVING Calories 295 • Fat 2 g • Carbohydrates 61 g • Protein 13 g • Cholesterol 6 mg • Dietary Fiber 9 g • Sodium 269 mg
EXCHANGES 3 starch • 1 vegetable • ½ other carb
CARB CHOICES 4

Spinach, an excellent source of folate, has been associated with reducing depression.

Spinach Quiche

Prep—Bake—Freeze ◆ Serves: 6

1½ cups cooked brown rice
¾ cup egg substitute
1 tsp. low-sodium soy sauce
16-oz. pkg. frozen chopped spinach,
　thawed and drained

4 large egg whites
1½ cups nonfat half-and-half
1 cup shredded nonfat Swiss cheese
⅛ tsp. pepper

Preheat oven to 350°F. Spray 9- or 10-inch pie plate with cooking spray. Combine cooked rice, ¼ cup egg substitute and soy sauce in medium bowl and mix well. Spread mixture onto bottom of pie plate. Bake 10 to 12 minutes. Combine spinach, remaining egg substitute, egg whites, half-and-half and pepper in bowl and mix well. Spoon mixture over rice layer; top with cheese. Bake 40 to 45 minutes, until set. If not serving immediately, cool to room temperature. Quiche can be wrapped and frozen whole or sliced into individual servings, wrapped and frozen. Reheat in microwave or 350°F oven.

Shopping List:

DAIRY	PACKAGED	SPICES
12 oz. nonfat half-and-half	Brown rice	Pepper
4 oz. egg substitute	**CONDIMENTS**	**FROZEN**
4 large eggs	Low-sodium soy sauce	16-oz. pkg. frozen
¼ lb. nonfat Swiss cheese		chopped spinach

NUTRITION PER SERVING Calories 145 • Fat .7 g • Carbohydrates 19 g • Protein 13 g • Cholesterol 1 mg • Dietary Fiber 2 g • Sodium 343 mg
EXCHANGES 1 very lean meat • 1 starch • 1 vegetable
CARB CHOICES 1

Spinach contains two compounds, lutein and zeaxanthin, which have been shown to prevent age-related macular degeneration and vision loss.

Stuffed Peppers

Prep—Refrigerate or Freeze—Bake   ◆ Serves: 6

6 large green bell peppers
3 cups cooked lentils, drained
Garlic powder to taste
Onion powder to taste
Pepper to taste
2 tbsp. tomato paste

1 cup canned chopped tomatoes,
   drained
3 cups diced mushrooms
1 cup cooked brown rice
½ cup grated nonfat Parmesan cheese
   (optional)

Cut tops off bell peppers; remove core and seeds. Combine remaining ingredients except Parmesan cheese in medium bowl and mix well. Peppers can be refrigerated or frozen at this point. When ready to serve: If frozen, thaw peppers in refrigerator overnight. Preheat oven to 350°F. Spray 9 × 13-inch baking dish with cooking spray. Arrange peppers in single layer and bake 30 to 35 minutes, until cooked through (if not adding Parmesan cheese, cook an additional 5 to 10 minutes). Sprinkle with Parmesan cheese, if using, and bake 5 to 10 minutes, until browned on top.

Shopping List:

PRODUCE	3-oz. can tomato paste	SPICES
6 large green bell	Brown rice	Garlic powder
peppers	Lentils	Onion powder
½ lb. mushrooms	Grated nonfat	Pepper
	Parmesan cheese	
PACKAGED/CANNED	(optional)	
14-oz. can chopped		
tomatoes		

NUTRITION PER SERVING Calories 213 • Fat 1 g • Carbohydrates 39 g • Protein 14 g • Cholesterol 0 mg • Dietary Fiber 7 g • Sodium 134 mg
EXCHANGES 2 starch • 2 vegetable
CARB CHOICES 3

According to food experts, stirring rice while it simmers mashes the grains and makes the rice gummy and sticky.

Stuffed Portabellos

Prep—Chill—Bake ♦ Serves: 6

6 large portabello mushrooms
⅓ cup + 1 tbsp. vegetable broth
¾ tsp. garlic powder
¾ cup chopped onion
1½ tsp. minced garlic
1½ cups chopped tomatoes
2 tsp. Italian seasoning

½ cup seasoned bread crumbs
3 tbsp. grated nonfat Parmesan
   cheese
¾ cup shredded nonfat mozzarella
   cheese
¼ cup shredded reduced-fat
   mozzarella cheese

VIRTUOUS VEGETARIAN MEALS

Preheat oven to 425°F. Spray shallow baking dish with cooking spray. Remove stems from mushroom caps; chop and set aside. Place mushroom caps, smooth side down, in baking dish; pour ⅓ cup vegetable broth over mushrooms. Sprinkle with garlic powder; cover dish with foil and bake 13 to 15 minutes, until tender. Spray nonstick skillet with cooking spray; add 1 tablespoon vegetable broth and heat over medium-high heat. Add onion and garlic to skillet; cook, stirring occasionally, until onion is transparent and softened. Add mushroom stems, tomatoes and Italian seasoning; cook, stirring frequently, until vegetables are tender, 5 to 6 minutes. Remove from heat; stir in bread crumbs and Parmesan cheese and mix well. Divide mixture among mushroom caps. Combine cheeses in plastic bag; shake until mixed. Sprinkle cheese over mushroom caps. If not serving immediately, cover with plastic wrap or foil and refrigerate until ready to serve. Preheat broiler on high heat; remove wrap and broil mushrooms until cheese is melted and lightly browned.

Shopping List:

PRODUCE	Shredded nonfat	Seasoned bread
6 large portabello	mozzarella cheese	crumbs
mushrooms	Shredded reduced-fat	
1 onion	mozzarella cheese	SPICES
Minced garlic		Garlic powder
	PACKAGED/CANNED	Italian seasoning
DAIRY	Vegetable broth	
Grated nonfat	14½-oz. can chopped	
Parmesan cheese	tomatoes	

NUTRITION PER SERVING Calories 102 • Fat 1 g • Carbohydrates 13 g • Protein 10 g • Cholesterol 1 mg • Dietary Fiber 2 g • Sodium 340 mg
EXCHANGES 1 very lean meat • 3 vegetable
CARB CHOICES 0

Wow! There are about 38,000 species of mushrooms!

Tofu-Noodle Casserole

Prep — Chill — Bake   ♦ Serves: 6

1 tbsp. vegetable broth
1½ cups chopped celery
1 cup sliced mushrooms
2 cups skim milk
¼ cup all-purpose flour
12 oz. yolk-free egg noodles, cooked
  and drained

8 oz. baked extra-firm tofu, diced
3 tbsp. chopped green onions
Pepper to taste
3 tbsp. wheat germ

Preheat oven to 350°F. Spray 9 × 13-inch baking dish with cooking spray. Spray large saucepan with cooking spray; add vegetable broth and heat over medium-high heat. Add celery and cook until softened, 3 to 4 minutes; add mushrooms and cook just until mushrooms begin to soften and wilt. Slowly pour 1½ cups skim milk into saucepan and cook over medium-low heat. Combine remaining milk and flour in small bowl; mix until flour is dissolved and mixture is blended smooth. Slowly add to saucepan; cook, stirring constantly, until sauce thickens. Remove from heat. Combine drained noodles, sauce, baked tofu and green onions in large bowl; mix well. Season with pepper to taste. Spoon mixture into baking dish; sprinkle with wheat germ. Casserole can be covered and refrigerated at this point if desired or bake 30 to 35 minutes, until lightly browned and bubbly. Cool 5 to 8 minutes at room temperature before serving. If casserole is refrigerated allow it to stand at room temperature 20 to 30 minutes before baking.

Shopping List:

PRODUCE	DAIRY	All-purpose flour
1 bunch celery	1 pint skim milk	Wheat germ
1 small bunch green		
onions	PACKAGE/CANNED	SPICES
½ lb. mushrooms	12-oz. pkg. yolk-free	Pepper
8 oz. baked extra-firm	noodles	
tofu	Vegetable broth	

NUTRITION PER SERVING Calories 336 • Fat 4.4 g • Carbohydrates 55 g • Protein 20 g • Cholesterol 1 mg • Dietary Fiber 5 g • Sodium 105 mg
EXCHANGES 2 starch • ½ milk • 1 vegetable • 1 other carb • 1 fat
CARB CHOICES 4

You can make baked tofu by cutting fresh tofu into slices, pressing out the moisture between paper towels and baking at 350°F for 5 minutes per side.

FROM SEA TO SHINING SEA

Safe Food-Handling and Storage

Buying and storing raw fish or seafood safely:
- Don't purchase cooked seafood (i.e., shrimp, crab, lobster, smoked fish) if displayed in the same case as raw fish.
- Don't buy frozen seafood if the packages are open, torn or crushed on the edges. Select packages that are below the frost line in the store's freezer; check for frost or ice crystals, which may indicate that the fish has been stored for a long time or thawed and refrozen.
- Store fish or seafood in the coldest part of the refrigerator. All fresh fish/seafood should be kept at 32°F; fish kept at 40°F will lose quality faster.
- Keep fish or seafood cold until it is prepared.
- Discard live shellfish (i.e., lobster, crab, oysters, clams, mussels) if they die during storage or their shells crack or break.
- Store fish, seafood, meat and poultry on the bottom shelf of the refrigerator to prevent juices from dripping on other foods.
- Use fresh or defrosted fish or seafood in 1 to 2 days.
- The higher the fat content of the fish, the less time it will maintain its quality in the freezer: oily fish, 3 months; leaner fish, 6 months.
- Leftover cooked seafood can be refrigerated up to 2 days.

Preparing fish:
- Prepare fish for cooking by washing it with cold running water and patting it dry with paper towels.
- Always marinate fish or seafood in the refrigerator, not on the countertop.

Thawing seafood safely:
- In the refrigerator, 1 pound will thaw in 24 hours.
- One-pound packages will thaw in cold water in 1 hour (change water every 30 minutes to keep cold).
- Microwave 1-pound packages for 5 to 6 minutes on defrost setting.
- Thaw frozen fish in milk to draw out the frozen taste. Discard milk before cooking fish.

Cooking fish or seafood safely:
- Good cooking rule: Allow 10 minutes per inch (5 minutes per ½ inch) when baking, broiling, grilling, frying, poaching or steaming fish.

- Cook fish to an internal temperature of 140 to 145°F. FDA's Food Code recommends cooking most seafood to an internal temperature of 145°F for 15 seconds.
- If you don't have a meat thermometer, test for other signs that fish or seafood is properly cooked:
  - Cook fish until it becomes opaque and flakes easily. Slip the point of a sharp knife into the flesh of the fish and pull aside. The edges should be opaque, the center slightly translucent and the fish should flake easily. Allow the fish to stand 3 to 4 minutes to finish cooking.
  - Shrimp and lobster turn red/pink when finished cooking.
  - Scallops turn milky white or opaque and firm.
  - Clams, mussels and oysters should be brought to a boil until the shells open, 5 to 10 minutes; continue boiling 3 to 5 minutes longer to ensure proper cooking.
- If using a microwave to prepare fish or seafood, rotate the dish several times to ensure even cooking. Follow recommended standing times before testing for cooked temperature.

Refrigerating and freezing leftovers:
- Refrigerate or freeze cooked fish in shallow containers no deeper than 2 inches.
- Use refrigerated leftovers in 2 to 3 days.

For further safety tips regarding fish or seafood, call 1-888-SAFEFOOD.

To Freeze or Not to Freeze

- Frozen fish should be stored at −20°F. If vacuum-sealed with a FoodSaver®, fish can be frozen up to 2 years.
- Commercially frozen fish can be safely frozen for up to 6 months.
- Whole fish should be cleaned and scaled *before* freezing.

From Stovetop/Oven to Refrigerator or Freezer and Back Again

- Casseroles: Thaw or partially thaw in refrigerator and reheat in oven. If partially thawed, allow up to 50 percent more heating time.

Shortcuts with the Same Results (in Less Time)

- Baking whole fish: Wrap fish in aluminum foil and bake or barbecue. When fish is done cooking, you can easily remove it from the pan without the fish falling apart. Slip a spatula under the fish, slide it onto a clean platter and slide the foil out from underneath.
- Purchase a variety of bottled marinades at the supermarket (i.e., lemon-pepper, citrus-grill, honey-Dijon, teriyaki) to use for meals in less than 30 minutes.

Substituting One for the Other

Many of the recipes included in this section can be prepared with a variety of fish. For easy substitutions with similar results, follow these guidelines.

TYPE OF FISH	WHITE, LIGHT, DARKER OR DARK MEAT	FLAVOR	TEXTURE	BEST COOKING METHODS
Cod, Dover sole, Haddock,	white	light, delicate	flaky, tender	bake, microwave, poach,
Halibut, Flounder				poach, sauté, steam
Catfish, English Sole, Rock sole,	white	moderate	flaky, tender	bake, broil, deep-fry, microwave, poach, sauté, steam
Alaskan pollock, Giant sea bass, Grouper, Mahi-mahi, Orange roughy, Pacific Ocean perch, Rainbow trout, Red snapper, Striped bass	light	moderate	moderately firm	bake, broil, deep-fry, grill, microwave, poach
Salmon, Monkfish, Perch, Pink salmon, Pollock	darker	moderate	moderately firm	bake, broil, grill, microwave, poach, sauté steam
Mackerel, Tuna, Shark	dark	moderate	firm	broil, grill, microwave, poach, sauté, steam, stew

Always Room for Improvement

- Seasonings and spices: anise, basil, chives, coriander, dill, fennel, marjoram, parsley, rosemary, sage, tarragon.
- Keep the breading on fish when cooking by adding a little sugar to the breading mixture.
- To keep fish from sticking to the pan, place fish on top of a layer of chopped celery and onions and bake as directed.

Everything Old Is New Again!

- Add leftover cooked fish or seafood to soups, salads, casseroles or stir-fries.
- Combine cooked fish or seafood with cooked rice or pasta and homemade or store-bought sauce.

Baked Halibut with Blue Cheese

Prep—Chill—Bake   • Serves: 6

2½ cups nonfat blue cheese salad dressing
2-lbs. halibut fillets
1 large red onion, thinly sliced
2 tbsp. crumbled blue cheese

Spray 9 × 13-inch baking dish with cooking spray. Pour 1 cup salad dressing on bottom of pan. Top with halibut fillets and remaining dressing;
place onion slices on top and sprinkle with blue cheese. Cover and refrigerate several hours or overnight. Bake in preheated 350°F oven 15 to 20
minutes, until fish flakes easily with a fork.

Shopping List:

PRODUCE	FISH
1 large red onion	2-lbs. halibut fillets
DAIRY	CONDIMENTS
1 oz. blue cheese	20-oz. bottle nonfat
	blue cheese
	salad dressing

NUTRITION PER SERVING Calories 292 • Fat 4 g • Carbohydrates 26 g •
Protein 32 g • Cholesterol 50 mg • Dietary Fiber <1 g • Sodium 1,022 mg
EXCHANGES 1½ other carb • 4 very lean meat • 1 fat
CARB CHOICES 2

*Fish is a good source of cobalamin (vitamin B_{12}), a vitamin essential for the
production of dopamine (energy) and serotonin (well-being).*

FROM SEA TO
SHINING SEA

Baked Seafood Sandwich

Prep—Chill •Serves: 6

6-oz. can water-packed tuna, drained
well
6-oz. can crabmeat, drained well
½ cup chopped celery
¾ cup shredded nonfat cheddar
cheese

½ cup chopped red onion
¼ cup sliced canned water chestnuts
2 to 3 tbsp. nonfat mayonnaise
6 sourdough French rolls

Combine tuna, crabmeat, celery, cheese, red onion, water chestnuts and mayonnaise in medium bowl; mix well. Spread tuna mixture on bottoms of rolls; replace tops. Wrap sandwiches in foil and refrigerate up to 2 days. When ready to serve: Preheat oven to 350°F. Bake 12 to 15 minutes, until cheese is melted and sandwich is heated through.

Shopping List:

PRODUCE	CANNED	CONDIMENTS
1 small red onion	6-oz. can tuna packed	Nonfat mayonnaise
1 small bunch celery	in water	
	6-oz. can crabmeat	BREAD
DAIRY	6-oz. can sliced water	6 sourdough French
3 oz. shredded nonfat	chestnuts	bread rolls
cheddar cheese		

NUTRITION PER SERVING Calories 275 • Fat 4.9 g • Carbohydrates 34 g • Protein 22 g • Cholesterol 33 mg • Dietary Fiber <1 g • Sodium 710 mg
EXCHANGES 2 starch • 2 very lean meat • 1 fat
CARB CHOICES 2

Fish is one of the best sources of protein, vitamin B_{12} and potassium. It's also an excellent way to include heart-friendly omega-3 fatty acids in your diet.

Barbecued Grouper

Prep—Chill—Bake   ◆ Serves: 4

1-lb. grouper fillets
½ tsp. lemon pepper
⅓ cup barbecue sauce
1 tsp. lemon juice
⅛ tsp. cayenne pepper

Spray shallow baking dish with cooking spray. Arrange fish fillets in single layer in dish; sprinkle with lemon pepper. Combine remaining ingredients in small bowl; mix well. Spoon sauce over fish; cover and refrigerate several hours or overnight. Preheat oven to 400°F. Bake uncovered, 15 to 20 minutes, until fish flakes easily with a fork.

Shopping List:

FISH	SPICES
1-lb. grouper fillets	Lemon pepper
	Cayenne pepper
CONDIMENTS	
Barbecue sauce	
Lemon juice	

NUTRITION PER SERVING Calories 120 • Fat 1.5 g • Carbohydrates 3 g • Protein 22 g • Cholesterol 41 mg • Dietary Fiber <1 g • Sodium 229 mg
EXCHANGES 3 very lean meat
CARB CHOICES 0

Like this recipe with grouper? Try it with striped bass, mahi-mahi or catfish.

Breaded Trout with Almonds

Prep—Chill—Bake   • Serves: 4

1 tbsp. lemon juice	1½-lbs. rainbow trout fillets
Lemon pepper to taste	½ cup seasoned bread crumbs
¼ cup egg substitute	2 tbsp. sliced almonds

Spray shallow baking dish with cooking spray. Combine lemon juice, lemon pepper and egg substitute in small bowl. Dip fillets in lemon mixture and roll in bread crumbs to coat. Arrange in single layer in baking dish and sprinkle with sliced almonds. Cover and refrigerate up to several hours. Preheat oven to 400°F. Bake fish fillets 10 minutes, until fish is opaque and flakes easily with a fork.

Shopping List:

DAIRY	PACKAGED	SPICES
4 oz. egg substitute	Seasoned bread crumbs	Lemon pepper
FISH	Sliced almonds	
1½-lbs. rainbow trout fillets	Lemon juice	

NUTRITION PER SERVING Calories 277 • Fat 8 g • Carbohydrates 10 g • Protein 39 g • Cholesterol 96 mg • Dietary Fiber 1 g • Sodium 158 mg
EXCHANGES 5 very lean meat • ½ starch • 1 fat
CARB CHOICES 1

Almonds are loaded with minerals, including magnesium, phosphorus and zinc; they contain more magnesium than oatmeal or spinach.

Bread 'n' Bake Grouper Fillets

Prep—Chill—Bake

2-lbs. grouper fillets
12-oz. bottle (1½ cups) Lawry's Lemon Pepper Marinade
1½ cups seasoned bread crumbs

Cut several ⅛-inch-deep slashes in top of fillets; place in shallow baking dish. Pour marinade over fillets and turn until well coated. Cover and refrigerate at least 1 hour. Preheat oven to 350°F. Line broiler pan or cookie sheet with foil and spray with cooking spray. Arrange fillets in single layer on cookie sheet; sprinkle with bread crumbs and spray lightly with cooking spray. Bake 15 to 20 minutes, until fish flakes easily with a fork.

Shopping List:

FISH	PACKAGED
2-lbs. grouper fillets	12-oz. bottle Lawry's Lemon Pepper Marinade
	Seasoned bread crumbs

NUTRITION PER SERVING Calories 236 • Fat 2.7 g • Carbohydrates 18 g • Protein 33 g • Cholesterol 55 mg • Dietary Fiber 1 g • Sodium 2,030 mg
EXCHANGES ½ starch • ½ other carb • 4 very lean meat • ½ fat
CARB CHOICES 1

The custom of serving a slice of lemon with fish dates back to the Middle Ages. People believed it could help dissolve any fish bones that were accidentally swallowed.

FROM SEA TO SHINING SEA

Cajun-Style Orange Roughy

Prep—Chill—Broil

1½ tsp. Cajun seasoning
1½ tbsp. paprika
Pepper to taste
1½-lbs. orange roughy fillets

Line broiler pan with foil and spray with cooking spray. Combine Cajun seasoning, paprika and pepper in small plastic bag; shake until seasonings are blended. Arrange fillets on foil; sprinkle with seasoning mixture and spray lightly with cooking spray. Cover with plastic wrap and refrigerate up to 8 hours. Preheat broiler on high heat; cook fish on top rack 5 to 6 minutes, until fish flakes easily with a fork and is lightly browned.

Shopping List:

FISH	SPICES
1½-lbs. orange roughy fillets	Cajun seasoning
	Paprika
	Pepper

FROM SEA TO SHINING SEA

NUTRITION PER SERVING Calories 86 • Fat 1 g • Carbohydrates 1 g • Protein 17 g • Cholesterol 23 mg • Dietary Fiber 0 g • Sodium 131 mg
EXCHANGES 2½ very lean meat
CARB CHOICES 0

Did you know that the fat content of fish and shellfish vary according to seasons, the food the fish eat, the age of the fish, and whether or not they are reproducing or spawning? Fat levels tend to be higher in older and healthier fish during warmer months and nonreproductive or spawning seasons.

Cornmeal Crunch Orange Roughy

Prep — Bake — Refrigerate or Freeze   • Serves: 6

½ cup all-purpose flour
½ tsp. lemon pepper
¼ cup egg substitute
2 tbsp. skim milk
½ cup bread crumbs

½ cup cornmeal
1 tbsp. grated lemon peel
1 tsp. dried basil
1½-lbs. orange roughy fillets, cut into
    6 pieces

Preheat oven to 450°F. Spray shallow baking dish with cooking spray. Combine flour and lemon pepper in large plastic bag; shake well. Combine egg substitute and skim milk in small bowl; beat until mixed. Combine bread crumbs, cornmeal, lemon peel and basil on paper plate. Place moist fish in plastic bag and shake to coat with flour mixture. Dip in egg mixture and roll in crumb mixture until well coated and arrange in baking dish. Spray fish lightly with cooking spray and bake 10 to 12 minutes, until lightly browned and fish flakes easily when tested with a fork. Serve immediately or cool and refrigerate 1 to 2 days. Fish can be individually wrapped and frozen; reheat in microwave or thaw and heat in oven until crisp.

FROM SEA TO SHINING SEA

Shopping List:

PRODUCE	FISH	SPICES
Lemon peel	1½-lbs. orange roughy fillets	Lemon pepper
		Dried basil
DAIRY		
Skim milk	**PACKAGED**	
Egg substitute	Bread crumbs	
	Cornmeal	
	All-purpose flour	

NUTRITION PER SERVING Calories 193 • Fat 1.7 g • Carbohydrates 23 g • Protein 21 g • Cholesterol 23 mg • Dietary Fiber 2 g • Sodium 153 mg
EXCHANGES 1½ starch • 2 very lean meat
CARB CHOICES 2

According to a study published in the American Journal of Clinical Nutrition, *people who consumed two or more servings of fish per week had between 50 and 60 percent lower rates of stomach, colon and pancreatic cancers.*

Crab Pasta Salad

Prep—Chill   • Serves: 6

1 cup nonfat sour cream
1 cup nonfat mayonnaise
2½ tsp. dried dill
½ tsp. garlic powder

12-oz. pkg. shell pasta, cooked and
  drained
1¼ to 1½ cups flaked crabmeat

Combine sour cream, mayonnaise, dill and garlic powder in large bowl; mix well. Add pasta and crabmeat and toss until coated. Cover and refrigerate several hours or overnight. Serve on lettuce leaves with whole-wheat crackers or stuffed in a pita.

Shopping List:

DAIRY	CONDIMENTS
8 oz. nonfat sour cream	8 oz. nonfat mayonnaise
PACKAGED/CANNED	**SPICES**
12-oz. pkg. shell pasta	Dried dill
2 (6-oz.) cans crabmeat	Garlic powder

NUTRITION PER SERVING Calories 316 • Fat 2.3 g • Carbohydrates 50 g • Protein 20 g • Cholesterol 57 mg • Dietary Fiber 0 g • Sodium 560 mg
EXCHANGES 2 starch • 1 other carb • 2 very lean meat
CARB CHOICES 3

Fresh dill contains the stomach-soothing chemicals carvocral and limonene and may help ease indigestion.

Dilly of a Salmon Pita

Prep—Chill or Freeze

• Serves: 6

½ cup nonfat cream cheese, softened
¼ cup nonfat mayonnaise
2 tsp. dried dill
½ tsp. onion powder
¼ tsp. garlic powder

2 tbsp. lemon juice
¼ tsp. pepper
14-oz. can salmon, drained
6 whole pita breads, cut in half

Combine cream cheese, mayonnaise, dill, onion powder, garlic powder, lemon juice and pepper in food processor or mix with electric mixer until smooth. Stir in salmon and mix well. Divide mixture among pita pockets; wrap with freezer wrap and heavy-duty foil and store in plastic freezer bags (or refrigerate up to 2 days). Thaw in refrigerator overnight.

Shopping List:

DAIRY	CONDIMENTS	Garlic powder
4 oz. nonfat cream cheese	Nonfat mayonnaise	Pepper
	Lemon juice	
		BREAD
CANNED	SPICES	6 pita breads
14-oz. can salmon	Dried dill	
	Onion powder	

NUTRITION PER SERVING Calories 223 • Fat 4.6 g • Carbohydrates 24 g • Protein 20 g • Cholesterol 36 mg • Dietary Fiber <1 g • Sodium 787 mg
EXCHANGES 1 starch • ½ other carb • 2 lean meat
CARB CHOICES 2

Salmon is high in protein, which is essential for repairing cells. This catch of the day also contains essential fatty acids called omega-3 acids. Salmon delivers a substance called DMAE, an antioxidant membrane stabilizer, which appears to increase muscle tone for firmer-looking skin (serving size 4–6 oz.).

Flashy Flounder

Prep—Chill—Bake

1 lb. flounder
2 tbsp. nonfat mayonnaise
2 tbsp. nonfat sour cream
¼ tsp. ground cumin
¼ tsp. cayenne pepper

¼ tsp. onion powder
¼ tsp. garlic powder
½ cup cornflake crumbs
2 tbsp. wheat germ

Spray shallow baking dish with cooking spray; place fish in dish. Combine mayonnaise, sour cream, cumin, cayenne pepper, onion powder and garlic powder in small bowl; mix until smooth. Spread all the mayonnaise mixture over top of fish. Combine cornflake crumbs and wheat germ in small plastic bag; shake until mixed. Sprinkle crumb mixture over fish, coating completely. Cover and refrigerate several hours or until ready to serve. Preheat oven to 425°F. Bake uncovered, 18 to 20 minutes, until fish flakes easily with a fork.

Shopping List:

DAIRY	PACKAGED	SPICES
Nonfat sour cream	Cornflake crumbs	Ground cumin
	Wheat germ	Cayenne pepper
FISH		Onion powder
1 lb. flounder	**CONDIMENTS**	Garlic powder
	Nonfat mayonnaise	

NUTRITION PER SERVING Calories 143 • Fat 1 g • Carbohydrates 14 g • Protein 19 g • Cholesterol 1 mg • Dietary Fiber 0 g • Sodium 245 mg
EXCHANGES 2½ lean meat • ½ other carb
CARB CHOICES 1

Flounder, cod, Dover sole and haddock are white fish with a light, delicate flavor and flaky, tender texture.

Fruit 'n' Nut Tuna Sandwiches

Prep—Chill

12-oz. can water-packed tuna,
drained well
1 cup chopped pear
¼ cup diced jicama
⅓ cup chopped walnuts

1 tbsp. sweet pickle relish
⅓ cup nonfat mayonnaise, or as
needed
6 pita breads, cut in half
6 romaine lettuce leaves

Combine tuna, pear, jicama, walnuts and pickle relish in medium bowl; stir in mayonnaise (adding more as needed for desired consistency). Cover and refrigerate up to 24 hours. When ready to serve, line pita pockets with romaine lettuce leaves; fill with tuna mixture or prepare the night before, wrap securely and take for a quick lunch the next day.

Shopping List:

PRODUCE	CANNED/PACKAGED	CONDIMENTS
1 pear	12-oz. can water-packed	Nonfat mayonnaise
Romaine lettuce	tuna	Sweet pickle relish
2 oz. jicama	Chopped walnuts	
		BREAD
		6 pita breads

NUTRITION PER SERVING Calories 254 • Fat 4.9 g • Carbohydrates 29 g • Protein 23 g • Cholesterol 10 mg • Dietary Fiber 2 g • Sodium 532 mg
EXCHANGES ½ fruit • 1 starch • ½ other carb • 2 very lean meat • 1 fat
CARB CHOICES 2

Pears are actually a member of the rose family. They not only ripen better off the tree but also ripen from the inside out.

Halibut Italiano

Prep—Chill—Bake • Serves: 4

2 tsp. vegetable broth
4 tsp. minced garlic
16-oz. can Italian-style stewed
   tomatoes
1½ tsp. Italian seasoning

½ lb. mushrooms, quartered
1 tbsp. lemon juice
½ tsp. pepper
1-lb. halibut fillets

Spray small saucepan with cooking spray; add vegetable broth and heat over medium-high heat. Add garlic and cook 1 to 2 minutes; add tomatoes, Italian seasoning, mushrooms, lemon juice and pepper. Cook, stirring occasionally, 10 to 15 minutes; remove from heat. While sauce is cooling, spray shallow baking dish with cooking spray; arrange halibut in single layer in dish. Pour sauce over fish; cover and refrigerate several hours, if desired. Preheat oven to 400°F. Remove cover and bake 12 to 15 minutes, until fish flakes easily with a fork.

Shopping List:

PRODUCE	PACKAGED/CANNED	SPICES
½ lb. mushrooms	Vegetable broth	Italian seasoning
1 lemon or lemon juice	16-oz. can Italian-style	Pepper
Minced garlic	stewed tomatoes	
FISH		
1-lb. halibut fillets		

NUTRITION PER SERVING Calories 158 • Fat 2.9 g • Carbohydrates 7 g • Protein 26 g • Cholesterol 36 mg • Dietary Fiber 1 g • Sodium 518 mg
EXCHANGES ½ fat • 3 very lean meat • 1 vegetable
CARB CHOICES 0

Tomato seeds may contain a powerful clot-fighting compound, helping to reduce the risk of heart disease and stroke.

FROM SEA TO SHINING SEA

Honey Dijon Salmon

Prep—Chill—Broil ◆ Serves: 4

1⅓-lbs. salmon fillet, cut into 4 pieces
1½ tsp. garlic powder
1 tbsp. Dijon mustard

1 tbsp. honey
1 tbsp. grated lemon peel
¼ tsp. ground pepper

Line broiler pan with foil and spray with cooking spray. Arrange salmon in single layer in pan; sprinkle salmon on both sides with garlic powder. Combine mustard, honey, lemon peel and pepper in small cup; mix until completely blended. Spread mixture over salmon; cover with plastic wrap and refrigerate 30 to 60 minutes. Heat broiler on high heat; cook salmon 5 to 6 minutes per side, until fish flakes easily with a fork.

Shopping List:

PRODUCE	CONDIMENTS	SPICES
Lemon	Honey	Garlic powder
	Dijon mustard	Pepper
FISH		
1⅓-lbs. salmon fillet		

NUTRITION PER SERVING Calories 170 • Fat 5.4 g • Carbohydrates 8 g • Protein 23 g • Cholesterol 27 mg • Dietary Fiber 0 g • Sodium 126 mg
EXCHANGES ½ other carb • 3 lean meat
CARB CHOICES 1

A 3-ounce serving of heart-healthy salmon supplies more than 200 percent of your need for vitamin B₁₂, a vitamin that helps maintain proper amounts of homocysteine in the blood.

Honey-Orange Snapper

Prep—Chill—Broil   • Serves: 6

¾ cup honey
2 cups orange juice
¾ cup lime juice

2-lbs. red snapper fillets
¾ tsp. Mrs. Dash seasoning
1 tbsp paprika

Combine honey, orange juice and lime juice in blender; process until smooth. Cut several slashes about ¼-inch-deep on top of fish. Pour honey mixture into bottom of shallow baking dish; place fish in baking dish and roll in marinade until coated on all sides. Cover and refrigerate 1 hour. Preheat broiler on high heat. Line broiler pan with foil and spray with cooking spray. Remove fish from baking dish, reserving marinade, and arrange in single layer on broiler pan; sprinkle with Mrs. Dash seasoning and paprika. Broil fish fillets 5 to 6 minutes; turn over and broil 5 minutes longer, until fish flakes easily with a fork. While fish is broiling, pour marinade into saucepan or microwave-safe dish and heat to boiling. Serve over fish.

Shopping List:

FISH	SPICES	BEVERAGES
2-lbs. red snapper fillets	Mrs. Dash seasoning	16 oz. orange juice
	Paprika	6 oz. lime juice
CONDIMENTS		
6 oz. honey		

NUTRITION PER SERVING Calories 330 • Fat 2.3 g • Carbohydrates 46 g • Protein 32 g • Cholesterol 56 mg • Dietary Fiber 1 g • Sodium 100 mg
EXCHANGES 2 fruit • 1 other carb • 4½ very lean meat
CARB CHOICES 3

Oranges are such a good source of potassium that the Food and Drug Administration has approved marketing orange juice with the following label: "Diets containing foods that are good sources of potassium and low in sodium may reduce the risk of high blood pressure and stroke." One 8-ounce serving of orange juice provides 450 mg of potassium, about 11 percent of the daily value.

Lazy Man's Lemon Sole

Prep—Chill—Bake   • Serves: 4

1-lb. sole fillet
½ cup fresh lemon juice
2 tbsp. grated nonfat Parmesan cheese
¾ tsp. lemon pepper
Lemon slices, for garnish (optional)

Spray shallow baking dish with cooking spray. Place sole in baking dish; pour lemon juice over top, cover with plastic wrap and refrigerate at least 1 hour. Line broiler pan or baking sheet with foil and spray with cooking spray. Remove fish from baking dish and place on baking sheet; sprinkle with Parmesan cheese and lemon pepper. Broil 4 to 5 minutes, until fish flakes easily with a fork. Garnish with lemon slices, if desired.

Shopping List:

PRODUCE	FISH
1 or 2 lemons	1-lb. sole fillet

DAIRY	SPICES
Grated nonfat Parmesan cheese	Lemon pepper

NUTRITION PER SERVING Calories 107 • Fat 1.1 g • Carbohydrates 4 g • Protein 20 g • Cholesterol 53 mg • Dietary Fiber 0 g • Sodium 105 mg
EXCHANGES 3 very lean meat
CARB CHOICES 0

Lemons do far more than pucker your lips. They are loaded with disease-fighting flavonoids, potassium, folic acid and vitamin C.

Pineapple Tuna Wraps

Prep—Chill

3-oz. pkg. nonfat cream cheese,
  softened
3 tbsp. nonfat mayonnaise
3 (6-oz.) cans water-packed tuna,
  drained
1 cup crushed pineapple in juice,
  drained well

1½ tsp. dried parsley
1 tbsp. slivered almonds
Pepper to taste
6 low-fat flour tortillas

Combine cream cheese and mayonnaise in medium bowl; beat with electric mixer until blended creamy and smooth. Add tuna, pineapple, parsley and almonds; mix well. Season with pepper. Divide mixture among tortillas; roll and wrap with plastic wrap. Store in refrigerator up to 2 days.

FROM SEA TO SHINING SEA

Shopping List:

DAIRY	CONDIMENTS	BREAD
3-oz. pkg. nonfat cream cheese	Nonfat mayonnaise	19-oz. pkg. low-fat tortillas
	SPICES	
CANNED	Dried parsley	OTHER
3 (6-oz.) cans tuna packed in water	Pepper	Slivered almonds
8-oz. can crushed pineapple in juice		

NUTRITION PER SERVING Calories 250 • Fat 3 g • Carbohydrates 26 g • Protein 29 g • Cholesterol 15 mg • Dietary Fiber 1 g • Sodium 407 mg
EXCHANGES 1 starch • ½ fruit • 3 very lean meat • ½ other carb
CARB CHOICES 2

Omega-3 fatty acids in tuna work as an anti-inflammatory agent, making it an excellent choice for post-workout food. Merely 2 ounces of tuna provides 13 grams protein, almost all the 16 grams needed to build 1 pound of muscle.

Salmon Bake with Dill

Prep—Bake—Chill   ◆ Serves: 6

2-lbs. salmon fillet	1 large cucumber, diced
Garlic powder to taste	2 tsp. skim milk
½ cup plain nonfat yogurt	1 tsp. sugar
½ cup nonfat sour cream	½ tsp. dry mustard
1 tbsp. fresh dill	¼ tsp. pepper

Preheat oven to 350°F. Using shallow pan with rack, pour cold water into pan about 1 inch deep. Spray large sheet of aluminum foil with cooking spray; arrange salmon on foil and place on rack. Sprinkle salmon generously with garlic powder. Cover salmon with foil; bake 25 to 30 minutes, until fish flakes easily with a fork. While salmon is cooking, combine remaining ingredients in food processor or blender. Cover and refrigerate. Salmon can be served hot or cold with dill sauce.

Shopping List:

PRODUCE	DAIRY	PACKAGED
1 large cucumber	4 oz. plain nonfat yogurt	Sugar
Fresh dill	4 oz. nonfat sour cream	
	Skim milk	SPICES
		Garlic powder
	FISH	Dry mustard
	2-lbs. salmon fillet	Pepper

NUTRITION PER SERVING Calories 176 • Fat 5.2 g • Carbohydrates 6 g • Protein 26 g • Cholesterol 27 mg • Dietary Fiber 1 g • Sodium 75 mg
EXCHANGES 1 vegetable • 3 lean meat
CARB CHOICES 0

Flaky fish finishes first! Whether fish is baked, broiled, poached, microwaved or grilled, the best test for doneness is to make sure it flakes easily when pierced with a fork.

Salmon Casserole

Prep—Chill—Bake or Prep—Bake—Chill Serves: 6

½ cup egg substitute
2 tbsp. skim milk
6½-oz. can salmon, drained
1 cup nonfat cottage cheese
10-oz. pkg. frozen chopped broccoli,
  thawed and drained

¾ tsp. onion powder
1 large tomato, thinly sliced
½ cup shredded nonfat mozzarella
  cheese
1 tbsp. grated nonfat Parmesan
  cheese

Combine egg substitute, skim milk, salmon, cottage cheese, broccoli and
onion powder in a medium bowl and mix until ingredients are blended.
Spray 9-inch pie plate with cooking spray; spoon mixture into pie plate.
Cover and refrigerate up to several hours. Just before serving: Preheat oven
to 350°F. Bake casserole 25 to 30 minutes. Top with tomato and cheeses.
Bake an additional 10 to 15 minutes, until lightly browned. Remove from
oven and let stand 5 minutes before serving. Casserole can also be baked,
refrigerated and reheated if desired.

FROM SEA TO
SHINING SEA

Shopping List:

PRODUCE	Grated nonfat	SPICES
1 large tomato	Parmesan cheese	Onion powder
	Skim milk	
DAIRY	4 oz. egg substitute	FROZEN
8-oz. nonfat cottage		10-oz. pkg. frozen
cheese		chopped broccoli
Shredded nonfat	CANNED	
mozzarella cheese	6½-oz. can salmon	

NUTRITION PER SERVING Calories 147 • Fat 3 g • Carbohydrates 8 g •
Protein 21 g • Cholesterol 27 mg • Dietary Fiber 3 g • Sodium 479 mg
EXCHANGES 3 very lean meat • 1 vegetable
CARB CHOICES 0

*Salmon contains coenzyme Q_{10}, an enzyme that may strengthen weak
heart muscles.*

Seafood-Rice Casserole

Prep—Chill—Bake   • Serves: 6

¼ cup vegetable broth	2 tbsp. lemon juice
⅓ cup minced onion	1½ cups canned crabmeat
¼ cup all-purpose flour	1 lb. cooked small shrimp
½ cup skim milk	3 cups cooked rice
1½ cups nonfat half-and-half	¾ cup shredded nonfat cheddar
½ tsp. pepper	cheese
1 tbsp. chopped red bell pepper	2 tbsp. grated nonfat Parmesan
1 cup sliced water chestnuts	cheese

Spray 2½-quart casserole with cooking spray. Spray medium saucepan with cooking spray; add vegetable broth and heat over medium-high heat. Add onion and cook, stirring frequently, until softened. Gradually add flour, stirring until blended. Add skim milk and half-and-half; stirring constantly, cook mixture over medium heat until thick and bubbly. Remove from heat; stir in pepper, bell pepper, water chestnuts, lemon juice, crabmeat, shrimp, cooked rice and cheddar cheese. Spoon mixture into casserole dish. Casserole can be covered and refrigerated at this point up to overnight. When ready to serve: Preheat oven to 350°F. Bake 25 minutes, until bubbly and browned. Sprinkle with Parmesan cheese; bake an additional 5 minutes, until browned on top.

Shopping List:

PRODUCE	12 oz. half-and-half	SPICES
1 small onion	4 oz. skim milk	Pepper
1 red bell pepper		
Lemon juice	**PACKAGED/CANNED**	**OTHER**
	3 (6-oz.) cans crabmeat	1 lb. cooked small
DAIRY	8-oz. can sliced water	shrimp
3 oz. shredded nonfat	chestnuts	
cheddar cheese	Vegetable broth	
Grated nonfat	Rice	
Parmesan cheese	All-purpose flour	

NUTRITION PER SERVING Calories 323 • Fat 1.8 g • Carbohydrates 50 g • Protein 23 g • Cholesterol 89 mg • Dietary Fiber 1 g • Sodium 427 mg
EXCHANGES ½ milk • 1½ starch • 1 vegetable • 1 other carb • 2 very lean meat
CARB CHOICES 3

Americans increase their intake of rice each year by about 1 pound. According to the latest statistics, rice consumption is about 25 pounds per person per year.

Spanish Snapper Olé

Prep—Chill—Bake   • Serves: 6

1½-lbs. red snapper fillets, cut into 6   1 green bell pepper, sliced into rings
   pieces   1 large tomato, thinly sliced
¼ tsp. garlic powder   1 red onion, thinly sliced
¼ tsp. onion powder   ¾ cup Garlic Lemon Marinade
¼ tsp. pepper   Lemon slices, for garnish (optional)
¼ tsp. paprika

Spray shallow baking dish with cooking spray. Arrange fish in baking dish; sprinkle with garlic powder, onion powder, pepper and paprika. Arrange bell pepper, tomato and onion slices on top of fish; pour marinade over top. Cover with plastic wrap and refrigerate several hours. Preheat oven to 375°F. Remove cover and bake 10 to 12 minutes, until fish flakes easily with a fork. Garnish with lemon slices, if desired.

FROM SEA TO SHINING SEA

Shopping List:

PRODUCE	FISH	Survival Co.) or
1 green bell pepper	1½-lbs. red snapper	similar product
1 large tomato	fillets	
1 red onion		SPICES
1 lemon (optional)	PACKAGED	Garlic powder
	14-oz. bottle Garlic	Onion powder
	Lemon	Paprika
	Marinade (Garlic	Pepper

NUTRITION PER SERVING Calories 144 • Fat 1.7 g • Carbohydrates 8 g • Protein 24 g • Cholesterol 42 mg • Dietary Fiber 1 g • Sodium 156 mg
EXCHANGES 2 vegetable • 3 very lean meat
CARB CHOICES 1

Fish is the most well-known source of omega-3 acids, EPA (epicosapentaenoic acid) and DHA (docosahexaenoic acid). For optimal health benefits, include 650 mg of omega-3s in your diet daily.

10-Minute Teriyaki Fish

Prep—Chill—Broil   • Serves: 4

1 lb. flounder, cod or haddock
¼ cup low-sodium teriyaki sauce
1 tbsp. honey
½ tsp. ground ginger
½ tsp. garlic powder
Paprika to taste

Line broiler pan with foil and spray with cooking spray. Arrange fish on broiler pan and pat dry with paper towels. Combine remaining ingredients in small bowl and mix until blended. Pour sauce over fish. Cover and refrigerate until ready to serve or up to overnight. Just before serving: Remove fish from refrigerator and let stand at room temperature 10 to 15 minutes. Preheat broiler on high heat. Sprinkle fish with paprika and broil 4 to 5 minutes per side, until lightly browned and fish flakes easily with a fork.

Shopping List:

FISH	CONDIMENTS	SPICES
1 lb. flounder, cod or haddock	4 oz. low-sodium teriyaki sauce	Ground ginger Garlic powder
	Honey	Paprika

NUTRITION PER SERVING Calories 127 • Fat .8 g • Carbohydrates 8 g • Protein 21 g • Cholesterol 49 mg • Dietary Fiber 0 g • Sodium 382 mg
EXCHANGES 3 very lean meat • ½ fruit
CARB CHOICES 1

Thaw frozen fish in milk. The milk draws out the frozen taste and provides a fresh-caught flavor.

MEATS AND MORE

Safe Food-Handling and Storage

- Thaw frozen ground meats in the refrigerator, never at room temperature.
- Store raw meat, poultry and fish or seafood on the bottom shelf of the refrigerator to prevent juices from dripping on other foods.
- When thawing meat in the refrigerator, allow 1 day for every 5 pounds.
- Meat that is thawed or partially cooked in the microwave must be transferred to another heat source (barbecue, oven, broiler) immediately to complete the cooking process.
- Ground meat and poultry can be refrigerated 1 to 2 days; freeze meat/poultry not used within that time period.
- *Always* marinate meat/poultry in a covered dish in the refrigerator.
- *Never* serve marinade that has been used on raw meat, poultry or fish/seafood without properly boiling for 4 to 5 minutes (stovetop or microwave).
- *Never* put cooked meat on the same platter used for raw meat (unless it has been thoroughly washed and dried).
- Cook roasts and steaks to at least 145°F (rare); ground beef to at least 160°F; and whole poultry to 180°F for doneness.
- Poultry is safely cooked when juices run clear and meat is no longer pink.
- Grilling, broiling or skillet-cooking: Cook evenly by turning meat or poultry at least once while cooking.
- Oven baking: Do not set oven temperatures lower than 325°F.
- Microwave: Cover meat or poultry while cooking. Turn patties, rotate casserole dish or stir ground meat several times while cooking. Allow microwaved meat or poultry to stand at room temperature 5 minutes to complete the cooking process.
- Never stuff poultry that will be cooked in a microwave.
- Prepare stuffing and place in poultry cavity or in pockets of thick sliced meat or poultry just before roasting.
- Discard any leftover batter or breading after it has come in contact with raw food.
- Do not leave raw or cooked food out of the refrigerator for more than 2 hours.

- Leftover cooked poultry or beef and meat casseroles can be refrigerated up to 3 to 4 days.
- Leftover cooked meat or poultry patties or nuggets can be refrigerated for 1 to 2 days.
- Cool leftovers in the refrigerator, not on the stovetop.
- Divide large portions into smaller ones before refrigerating; foods cool faster that way.

For further safety tips regarding meat/poultry call the FSIS Meat and Poultry Hotline: 1-800-535-4555 or 202-720-3333 (Washington, D.C., area)

To Freeze or Not to Freeze

- Most raw ground meats can be safely frozen for 3 to 4 months. If vacuum-sealed with a FoodSaver®, ground meat can be frozen up to 1 year.
- Chops, steaks, roasts, whole chickens or turkeys can be safely frozen for up to 1 year.
- Poultry parts can be frozen for up to 6 months.
- Meat or poultry that will be used within one week of purchase can be safely frozen in the store-packaged foam, plastic-wrapped tray. If it will be frozen longer than a week, rewrap or overwrap to prevent freezer burn. If vacuum-sealed with a FoodSaver®, meat can be frozen 2 to 3 years without freezer burn.
- Meat and poultry defrosted in the refrigerator may be refrozen before or after cooking. If other thawing methods are used, meat or poultry must be cooked before refreezing.
- Meat that has been partially thawed but still has ice crystals on it can be refrozen.
- Casseroles: Thaw or partially thaw in refrigerator and reheat in oven. If partially thawed, allow up to 50 percent more heating time.
- Do *not* freeze:
  - Stuffed poultry
  - Battered or bread-crumb-topped foods
  - Luncheon meats

From Stovetop/Oven to Refrigerator or Freezer and Back Again

- Allow 24 hours to thaw casseroles in refrigerator. Do not thaw at room temperature.
- Poultry that has thawed but is still cold can be cooked, refrozen, thawed and reheated.
- To reheat leftovers: Cover and heat to 165°F until hot and steaming throughout.

- Reheating a whole turkey is *not* recommended. Slice breast meat and reheat with other turkey pieces to 165°F until hot and steaming.

Shortcuts with the Same Results (in Less Time)
- Heat a can of low-fat condensed cream soup (cream of celery, chicken or mushroom) and serve over cooked meat or poultry.
- Purchase a variety of bottled marinades at the supermarket (i.e., lemon-pepper, citrus-grill, honey-Dijon, teriyaki) to use for meals in less than 30 minutes.
- Purchase packaged cooked and cubed chicken breast fillets, tenders, or cubes (available in the meat or produce section of your supermarket).
- Holiday shortcut: According to the USDA, it is safe to cook an unstuffed frozen turkey. Allow 50 percent longer cooking time than what is recommended for a thawed turkey.
- Add vegetables (onions, carrots, celery, potatoes) directly to pan while baking meat or poultry for great flavor.
- For easier slicing: Freeze fresh meat or poultry 30 minutes before slicing, chopping or cutting into cubes.
- Cut clean-up time: Marinate meat or poultry in a plastic bag; flip the bag several times for even coating. You can also marinate meat in a FoodSaver® square canister. Vacuum-packing opens the pores of the meat and will marinate it in 20 minutes or less.
- Mix meatloaf ingredients with a potato masher or combine ingredients in a plastic bag and mash contents until they are completely mixed.
- Brown ground beef and store 1-to 2-cup servings in plastic freezer bags.
- For faster cooking, prepare meat loaf in small, rounded loaves or muffin pans.
- Repackage meat/poultry in meal-size portions for easier and quicker defrosting.

Always Room for Improvement
- Seasonings and spices:
  - Beef: basil, bay leaves, coriander, cumin, dill, marjoram, mint, sage, tarragon, thyme
  - Chicken: basil, coriander, cumin, dill, mint, rosemary, tarragon
  - Pork: anise, basil, chervil, coriander, cumin, dill, fennel, mint, marjoram, rosemary, sage, tarragon, thyme
  - Turkey: rosemary, sage, thyme

Everything Old Is New Again!

- Meat sauce: Use as topping for pasta, pizza and baked potatoes.
- Leftover meat or poultry: Add to stir-fry dishes, casseroles, soups, salads or wraps.
- Mix leftover meat or poultry with other leftovers (grains, pasta, potatoes), and heat in microwave or oven.

Laura's Lean Beef is available in the fresh meat case at most grocery stores. For a location near you, contact Laura's Lean Beef at: 2285 Executive Drive, Lexington, KY 40505, 800-ITS-LEAN or www.lauraslean-beef.com.

Baked-in-Buns Sloppy Joes

Prep—Freeze—Bake   • Serves: 8

2 lbs. Laura's lean ground beef (see   2 (16-oz.) cans Manwich® Sloppy Joe
  p. 124)   sauce
¾ cup chopped green bell pepper   8 low-calorie hamburger buns, cut in
1½ tbsp. onion powder   half
1½ tsp. garlic powder

Spray large nonstick skillet with cooking spray; add ground beef, bell pepper, onion powder and garlic powder and cook, stirring, over medium heat until beef is cooked through. Add sauce; cook, stirring frequently, until meat mixture is heated through. Scoop out centers of tops and bottoms of hamburger buns. Divide sloppy joe mixture among bun bottoms; replace tops. Wrap individual sandwiches in heavy-duty foil. Preheat oven to 350°F. Bake sandwiches 15 to 20 minutes. Sandwiches can be wrapped and stored in freezer bags before baking; bake directly from freezer at 350°F for 30 to 40 minutes.

Shopping List:

PRODUCE	CANNED	BREAD
1 small green bell pepper	2 (16-oz.) cans Manwich Sloppy Joe sauce	8 low-calorie hamburger buns
BEEF	**SPICES**	
2 lbs. Laura's lean ground beef	Onion powder Garlic powder	

NUTRITION PER SERVING Calories 324 • Fat 6.6 g • Carbohydrates 34 g • Protein 27 g • Cholesterol 61 mg • Dietary Fiber 3 g • Sodium 1,003 mg
EXCHANGES 2 starch • 1 vegetable • 3 very lean meat • 1 fat
CARB CHOICES 2

Complete your Baked-in-Buns Sloppy Joe meal with frozen corn on the cob (microwaved in minutes) and chunky-style applesauce.

MEATS AND MORE

Barbecue Meat Loaf Muffins

Prep—Bake—Freeze   • Serves: 6

1½ lbs. Laura's lean ground beef (see
   p. 124)
¾ cup + 2 tbsp. cracker meal
2 tbsp. wheat bran
1½ tsp. Mrs. Dash seasoning
5-oz. can evaporated skim milk

¼ cup egg substitute
¾ cup chopped green bell pepper
¾ tsp. garlic powder
½ tsp. onion powder
1 tsp. chili powder
¾ cup barbecue sauce

Preheat oven to 375°F. Spray 6 large or 12 regular muffin cups with cooking spray. Combine all ingredients except barbecue sauce in medium bowl and mix well. Shape beef mixture to fit muffin cups and press down lightly. Brush top of "muffins" with barbecue sauce and bake 25 to 30 minutes, until meat is cooked through. Cool to room temperature; wrap and store in plastic freezer bags for up to 6 weeks. To reheat: Thaw in microwave on low heat or refrigerator overnight. Bake in 350°F oven 15 to 20 minutes, until heated through. Serve with additional warmed barbecue sauce.

Shopping List:

PRODUCE
1 small green pepper

DAIRY
4 oz. egg substitute

PACKAGED/CANNED
5-oz. can evaporated
   skim milk

Cracker meal
Wheat bran

BEEF
1½ lbs. Laura's lean
   ground beef

CONDIMENTS
6 oz. barbecue sauce

SPICES
Mrs. Dash seasoning
Onion powder
Garlic powder
Chili powder

NUTRITION PER SERVING Calories 369 • Fat 6 g • Carbohydrates 34 g •
Protein 41 g • Cholesterol 71 mg • Dietary Fiber 1 g • Sodium 572 mg
EXCHANGES 1 starch • 1 other carb • 5 very lean meat • 1 fat
CARB CHOICES 2

Although the origins of chili powder have been traced to ancient Aztecs who combined chile peppers and oregano, the present blend of dried chiles, garlic powder, red peppers, oregano and cumin is said to be the creation of early Texans.

MEATS AND MORE

Chicken, Corn and Chile Burritos

Prep—Chill—Bake   • Serves: 6

1 lb. low-fat cooked, cubed chicken
   breast cuts, diced
¼ cup chopped onion
1½ cups salsa, divided
¾ cup creamed corn

¾ cup whole corn kernels
2 tbsp. chopped green chiles
1½ cups shredded nonfat cheddar
   cheese
6 low-fat flour tortillas

Spray 10-inch baking dish with cooking spray. Combine chicken, onion, ¾ cup salsa, creamed corn, corn kernels, chiles and ½ cup cheese in medium bowl; mix well. Spoon mixture down center of tortillas; fold both sides over and place, seam side down, in baking dish. Pour remaining salsa over top; sprinkle with remaining cheese. Cover and refrigerate until ready to bake and serve. Preheat oven to 350°F. Remove cover and bake burritos 15 to 20 minutes, until bubbly hot and lightly browned.

Shopping List:

PRODUCE	MEAT	4-oz. can chopped
1 small onion	3 (6-oz.) pkgs. cooked	green chiles
	chicken breast cuts	12 oz. salsa
DAIRY		6 low-fat flour tortillas
6 oz. shredded nonfat	PACKAGED/CANNED	
cheddar cheese	8-oz. can creamed corn	
	8-oz. can whole corn	
	kernels	

MEATS AND MORE

NUTRITION PER SERVING Calories 329 • Fat 3 g • Carbohydrates 39 g • Protein 33 g • Cholesterol 53 mg • Dietary Fiber 3 g • Sodium 1,733 mg EXCHANGES 3½ very lean meat • 2 starch • 2 vegetable CARB CHOICES 3

According to Mayan legend, tortillas were invented approximately
10,000 B.C.

Chick 'n' Artichoke Casserole

Prep—Chill—Bake   • Serves: 6

1 cup all-purpose flour
2 tsp. Mrs. Dash seasoning
¼ tsp. pepper
1½ lb. low-fat chicken tenders, cut in half
2 cups + 3 tbsp. nonfat chicken broth
1 cup white wine
2 tbsp. tomato paste

½ tsp. garlic powder
2 (10-oz.) pkgs. frozen artichoke hearts, cooked and drained
¼ cup chopped green onions
1 cup sliced mushrooms
Cooked rice, pasta or couscous (not included in nutritional information)

Combine flour, Mrs. Dash seasoning and pepper in a plastic bag; add chicken tenders and toss until coated. Spray large nonstick skillet with cooking spray; add 1 to 3 tablespoons chicken broth (as needed) and heat over medium-high heat. Add chicken strips and cook 8 to 10 minutes, until lightly browned. Spray 9 × 13-inch baking dish with cooking spray. Place chicken strips in baking dish. Combine remaining broth, wine, tomato paste and garlic powder in bowl; mix well. Pour mixture over chicken, cover and refrigerate up to 24 hours. When ready to bake and serve: Bring casserole to room temperature. Preheat oven to 350°F. Bake, covered, 25 to 30 minutes; add artichoke hearts, green onions and mushrooms. Cover casserole and bake 10 to 15 minutes, until heated through. Serve over cooked rice, pasta or couscous.

Shopping List:

PRODUCE	PACKAGED/CANNED	SPICES
½ lb. mushrooms	2 (14½-oz.) cans nonfat chicken broth	Mrs. Dash seasoning
1 small bunch green onions	8 oz. white wine	Garlic powder
	Tomato paste	Pepper
BEEF	Flour	
1½ lb. low-fat chicken tenders	Rice, pasta or couscous	**FROZEN**
		2 (10-oz.) pkgs. frozen artichoke hearts

NUTRITION PER SERVING Calories 332 • Fat 5 g • Carbohydrates 28 g • Protein 37 g • Cholesterol 85 mg • Dietary Fiber 1 g • Sodium 501 mg
EXCHANGES 4½ very lean meat • 3 vegetable • ½ other carb • 1 fat
CARB CHOICES 2

Boost immunity with heart! Artichoke hearts are a good source of folate, vitamin C and iron.

MEATS AND MORE

Chili 'n' Noodles

Prep—Cook—Refrigerate or Freeze   • Serves: 6

1 cup Morningstar Farms Crumbles
1 cup boiling water
2 (16-oz.) cans diced tomatoes
⅓ cup tomato paste
1 cup chopped onion
¾ cup chopped red bell pepper
1 tbsp. chopped canned jalapeños
2 tbsp. chili powder
1½ tsp. cumin powder

2 tsp. garlic powder
1 tsp. dried oregano
¼ tsp. ground allspice
15-oz. can red kidney beans, drained
15-oz. can canned black beans, drained
8 oz. spaghetti, cooked and drained
⅜ cup grated nonfat Parmesan cheese (optional)

Combine all ingredients except beans, spaghetti and Parmesan cheese in large saucepan or Dutch oven; bring to a boil over medium heat. Reduce heat to low, cover and simmer 1 hour. Add kidney and black beans; cook, stirring occasionally, 40 to 45 minutes. Chili can be refrigerated or frozen at this point. When ready to serve: Heat in saucepan or microwave. Serve over cooked spaghetti and top with Parmesan cheese, if desired.

Shopping List:

PRODUCE
1 large red bell pepper
1 large onion

PACKAGED/CANNED
2 (16-oz.) cans diced tomatoes
6-oz. can tomato paste
4-oz. can chopped jalapeños

15-oz. can red kidney beans
15-oz. can black beans
8 oz. spaghetti
Grated nonfat Parmesan cheese (optional)

SPICES
Chili powder
Cumin powder

Garlic powder
Dried oregano
Ground allspice

FROZEN
16-oz. pkg. Morningstar Farms Crumbles (textured soy protein)

NUTRITION PER SERVING Calories 372 • Fat 2.2 g • Carbohydrates 70 g • Protein 22 g • Cholesterol 0 mg • Dietary Fiber 10 g • Sodium 928 mg
EXCHANGES 4 starch
CARB CHOICES 5

Soy crumbles, also known as textured soy protein or textured vegetarian protein, are low in fat and high in soy protein and can lower the risk of several types of cancer.

Chinese Chicken Bake

Prep—Chill—Bake   • Serves: 6

1½-lbs. boneless, skinless chicken   ½ tsp. ground ginger
   breasts   ¼ tsp. garlic powder
⅗ cup low-sodium soy sauce   ¼ tsp. pepper
1 tsp. dry mustard

Spray shallow baking dish with cooking spray; arrange chicken breasts in
single layer in dish. Combine soy sauce, mustard, ginger, garlic powder and
pepper in small bowl; mix until blended. Pour sauce over chicken; cover
and refrigerate overnight. Preheat oven to 350°F. Bake 15 minutes; remove
chicken and brush generously with marinade in pan. Bake an additional
10 to 15 minutes, until chicken is cooked through and lightly browned.

Shopping List:

MEAT	SPICES
1½-lbs. boneless,	Dry mustard
skinless chicken	Ground ginger
breasts	Garlic powder
	Pepper
CONDIMENTS	
Low-sodium soy sauce	

NUTRITION PER SERVING Calories 117 • Fat .9 g • Carbohydrates 3 g •
Protein 24 g • Cholesterol 53 mg • Dietary Fiber 0 g • Sodium 796 mg
EXCHANGES 2 lean meat • ½ vegetable
CARB CHOICES 0

No dry mustard in the house? No problem—substitute 1 tablespoon
prepared mustard for 1 teaspoon dry mustard.

Fiesta Tacos

Prep—Cook—Refrigerate or Freeze   • Serves: 6

1 tbsp. chili powder
1½ tsp. paprika
2¼ tsp. cumin
1½ tsp. onion powder
1¼ tsp. garlic powder
Dash cayenne pepper
1 cup Morningstar Farms Crumbles
1 cup boiling water
¾ cup canned nonfat refried beans

2 tbsp. chopped canned green chiles
12 baked taco shells
1 cup shredded nonfat cheddar
   cheese
½ cup shredded lettuce
½ cup chopped tomato
¾ cup salsa (more as needed)
¼ cup nonfat sour cream

Combine chili powder, paprika, cumin, onion powder, garlic powder and cayenne pepper in plastic bag; shake until completely mixed. Place crumbles in medium saucepan; pour boiling water over top. Sprinkle with seasoning mix and mix well. Add refried beans and green chiles. Bring to a boil over medium-high heat. Immediately reduce heat to low and simmer, stirring frequently, 10 to 15 minutes. Taco filling can be refrigerated or frozen at this point. When ready to serve: Heat taco shells 2 to 3 minutes in 350°F oven (1 minute in toaster oven). Heat taco filling in saucepan or microwave until heated through. Spoon taco mixture into shells and garnish with cheese, lettuce, tomatoes, salsa and sour cream as desired.

MEATS AND MORE

Shopping List:

PRODUCE	PACKAGED/CANNED	Cumin
4 oz. shredded lettuce or 1 head lettuce	16-oz. can nonfat refried beans	Onion powder
1 medium tomato	4-oz. can chopped green chiles	Garlic powder
		Cayenne pepper
DAIRY	6 to 8 oz. salsa	**FROZEN**
4 oz. shredded nonfat cheddar cheese	12 baked taco shells	½ lb. Morningstar Farms Crumbles
Nonfat sour cream	**SPICES**	(textured soy protein)
	Chili powder	
	Paprika	

NUTRITION PER SERVING Calories 217 • Fat 5 g • Carbohydrates 29 g • Protein 14 g • Cholesterol 0 mg • Dietary Fiber 4 g • Sodium 652 mg
EXCHANGES 1 very lean meat • 1½ starch • 1 vegetable • 1 fat
CARB CHOICES 2

Soy protein is loaded with saponins, which may block cholesterol absorption. As little as 25 grams soy protein each day may lower cholesterol levels by 10 percent.

Hot Diggity Dogs and Beans

Prep—Chill—Bake ♦ Serves: 6

32-oz. can (4 cups) nonfat baked beans
6 nonfat hot dogs, cut into chunks
¾ cup barbecue sauce
¾ cup packed brown sugar
1 small onion, grated

Spray 2-quart casserole with cooking spray. Combine all ingredients in casserole; cover and refrigerate until ready to heat and serve or bake in 350°F oven for 45 to 60 minutes.

Shopping List:

PRODUCE	PACKAGED/CANNED	CONDIMENTS
1 small onion	32-oz. can nonfat baked beans	6 oz. barbecue sauce
MEAT	Brown sugar	
1 lb. nonfat hot dogs		

NUTRITION PER SERVING Calories 327 • Fat .6 g • Carbohydrates 68 g • Protein 15 g • Cholesterol 15 mg • Dietary Fiber 6 g • Sodium 1,243 mg
EXCHANGES 1 very lean meat • 2 starch • 2½ other carbs
CARB CHOICES 0

Baked beans, rich in folic acid, can lower triglyceride levels, reducing the risk of heart disease.

Layered Taco Salad

1 lb. Laura's lean ground beef (see p. 124)
¾ tsp. onion powder
½ tsp. garlic powder
2 cups Southwest-style salsa, divided
1¼-oz. envelope taco seasoning mix
¼ cup water
6 cups shredded lettuce

1½ cups diced tomato
½ cup shredded carrots
1 red onion, thinly sliced
1 green bell pepper, thinly sliced
4-oz. can chopped green chiles
1 cup shredded nonfat cheddar cheese
6 oz. baked tortilla chips

Spray medium nonstick skillet with cooking spray and heat over medium-high heat. Add beef, breaking into small pieces; sprinkle with onion powder and garlic powder. Cook, stirring frequently, until beef is browned; drain well. Add 1 cup salsa, taco seasoning and water; bring to a boil over high heat. Reduce heat to low and simmer, uncovered, 15 to 20 minutes. Remove beef mixture from heat and cool to room temperature. Beef mixture can be frozen or refrigerated at this point until ready to serve. In a large glass bowl, layer lettuce, tomato, carrots, onion, bell pepper and green chiles. Top with beef mixture and shredded cheese. Pour remaining salsa over salad; sprinkle with crumbled baked tortilla chips and serve.

Shopping List:

PRODUCE	DAIRY	4-oz. can chopped
2 (6-oz.) pkgs. shredded lettuce	4 oz. shredded nonfat cheddar cheese	green chiles
2 medium tomatoes		1¼-oz. pkg. taco seasoning mix
1 carrot	MEAT	6 oz. baked tortilla
1 medium red onion	1 lb. Laura's lean	chips (1 g fat per
1 medium green bell pepper	ground beef	serving)
	PACKAGED/CANNED	SPICES
	16-oz. jar Southwest-style salsa	Onion powder
		Garlic powder

NUTRITION PER SERVING Calories 313 • Fat 4.5 g • Carbohydrates 41 g • Protein 26 g • Cholesterol 41 mg • Dietary Fiber 3 g • Sodium 1,352 mg
EXCHANGES 3 vegetable • 1½ starch • 2 very lean meat • 1 fat
CARB CHOICES 3

Meat is one of the best ways to get your daily value of 6 milligrams B_{12} for prevention of fatigue, memory loss and other neurological problems.

MEATS AND MORE

133

Mad About Meat Loaf

Prep—Bake—Freeze   ◆ Serves: 8

2 lbs. Laura's lean ground beef (see   ¼ cup chopped onion
   p. 124)   ¼ cup chopped green bell pepper
¾ cup tomato sauce   1 tsp. Mrs. Dash seasoning
¾ cup seasoned bread crumbs   ½ tsp. garlic powder
½ cup egg substitute   ½ tsp. Italian seasoning

Preheat oven to 350°F. Spray loaf pan with cooking spray. Combine all
ingredients in large bowl and mix well. Press meat mixture into loaf pan
and bake 50 to 60 minutes, until cooked through and browned. If not
serving immediately, cool to room temperature. Wrap in heavy-duty foil
and store in plastic freezer bags. To serve: Place foil-wrapped frozen meat
loaf in 350°F oven 55 to 60 minutes or wrap in plastic wrap and thaw in
microwave. Wrap thawed meat loaf in foil and bake in 350°F 20 minutes
until heated through.

Shopping List:

PRODUCE	MEAT	SPICES
1 small green pepper	2 lbs. Laura's lean	Garlic powder
1 small onion	ground beef	Italian seasoning
		Mrs. Dash seasoning
DAIRY	**PACKAGED/CANNED**	
4 oz. egg substitute	6-oz. can tomato sauce	
	Seasoned bread	
	crumbs	

NUTRITION PER SERVING Calories 195 • Fat 5 g • Carbohydrates 10 g •
Protein 24 g • Cholesterol 61 mg • Dietary Fiber 1 g • Sodium 219 mg
EXCHANGES 3 very lean meat • 2 vegetable • 1 fat
CARB CHOICES 1

*Onions contain some 50 different phytochemicals. The best of the lot may be
the allyic sulfides, a group of cancer-fighting phytochemicals. These
substances bolster a cell's defense system so the cell can more readily detoxify
incoming carcinogens.*

MEATS AND MORE

Mandarin Orange Chicken

Prep — Chill — Bake

1½-lbs. boneless, skinless chicken
  breasts
1½ tsp. garlic powder, divided
½ cup low-sodium soy sauce
½ cup sherry

½ cup orange juice
¾ tsp. ground ginger
16-oz. can mandarin oranges in juice,
  drained and liquid reserved

Spray 9 × 13-inch shallow baking dish with cooking spray; arrange chicken breasts in single layer and sprinkle with ¾ teaspoon (or more if desired) garlic powder. Combine soy sauce, sherry, orange juice, ginger and ¾ teaspoon garlic powder in small bowl or plastic bag. Blend or shake until ingredients are mixed. Pour marinade over chicken; cover with plastic wrap and refrigerate at least 6 hours or overnight. When ready to serve: Preheat oven to 350°F. Drain marinade into small saucepan; add 1 to 2 tablespoons reserved juice from oranges and bring to a boil over high heat. Reduce heat to low and simmer 5 to 10 minutes. Bake chicken 15 to 20 minutes; pour cooked marinade over chicken. Add mandarin oranges; continue baking 15 to 20 minutes, until chicken is cooked through.

Shopping List:

MEAT	CONDIMENTS	BEVERAGES
1½-lbs. boneless skinless chicken breasts	Low-sodium soy sauce	4 oz. orange juice
	SPICES	OTHER
CANNED	Garlic powder	Sherry
16-oz. can mandarin oranges in juice	Ground ginger	

NUTRITION PER SERVING Calories 195 • Fat .6 g • Carbohydrates 16 g • Protein 28 g • Cholesterol 57 mg • Dietary Fiber 2 g • Sodium 993 mg
EXCHANGES 1 fruit • 4 very lean meat
CARB CHOICES 1

Most canned mandarin oranges are satsumas, small Japanese fruits that are almost seedless.

Perfect Peppercorn Sauce for Chicken, Turkey or Pork Tenders

Prep—Bake—Chill   • Serves: 6

¾ cup plain nonfat yogurt
⅓ cup nonfat sour cream
3 tbsp. grated nonfat Parmesan
   cheese

3 tbsp. nonfat mayonnaise
1½ tsp. black peppercorns, crushed
1½-lbs. low-fat chicken, turkey or
   pork tenders, cooked

Combine all ingredients except tenders and blend until smooth. Cover and refrigerate sauce up to 1 week. Serve over baked, grilled, broiled or sautéed tenders. Sauce can also be used as vegetable dip or baked potato topping.

Shopping List:

DAIRY	MEAT	SPICES
6 oz. plain nonfat yogurt	1½-lbs. low-fat chicken,	Whole black
4 oz. nonfat sour cream	turkey or pork tenders	peppercorns
Grated nonfat		
Parmesan cheese	CONDIMENTS	
	Nonfat mayonnaise	

NUTRITION PER SERVING Calories 146 • Fat .5 g • Carbohydrates 6 g • Protein 29 g • Cholesterol 57 mg • Dietary Fiber 0 g • Sodium 298 mg
EXCHANGES 3 very lean meat • ½ other carb
CARB CHOICES 0

While whole-milk yogurt supplies 34 percent of the daily need for calcium, nonfat yogurt is the real calcium booster, meeting 56 percent of the recommended amount of calcium.

Polynesian Chicken Tenders

Prep—Bake—Freeze   ◆ Serves: 6

½ cup all-purpose flour
1½ tsp. garlic powder, divided
1½-lbs. low-fat chicken tenders
½ cup egg substitute
3 tbsp. white wine vinegar
3 tbsp. brown sugar
1½ cups nonfat chicken broth

1½ cups pineapple chunks in juice,
   drained
1½ cups chopped green bell pepper
¾ cup chopped carrots
1½ tsp. curry powder
¾ tsp. ground ginger

Spray large nonstick skillet with cooking spray and heat over medium-high heat. Combine flour and ½ teaspoon garlic powder on paper plate and mix well. Dip chicken tenders in egg substitute and roll in flour mixture. Brown chicken pieces in skillet 5 to 8 minutes, until cooked through. Remove from skillet and drain well. Allow skillet to cool slightly and respray with cooking spray. Return skillet to heat and add vinegar, brown sugar, 1 teaspoon garlic powder, chicken broth, pineapple, bell pepper, carrots, curry powder and ginger; cook over medium heat, stirring constantly, until mixture becomes thick. Stir in cooked chicken. Serve over cooked rice or couscous. Chicken mixture can be cooked and cooled to room temperature; freeze in plastic freezer bags. To reheat: Microwave directly from freezer 1 to 3 minutes per serving.

MEATS AND MORE

Shopping List:

PRODUCE	MEAT	Brown sugar
2 large carrots	1½-lbs. low-fat chicken	Flour
2 medium green bell	tenders	
peppers		CONDIMENTS
	PACKAGED/CANNED	White wine vinegar
DAIRY	16-oz. can pineapple	
4 oz. egg substitute	chunks in juice	SPICES
	14½-oz. can nonfat	Curry powder
	chicken broth	Ground ginger
		Garlic powder

NUTRITION PER SERVING Calories 240 • Fat .8 g • Carbohydrates 31 g • Protein 29 g • Cholesterol 57 mg • Dietary Fiber 2 g • Sodium 444 mg
EXCHANGES 4 very lean meat • 1 fruit • ½ other carb • 1 vegetable
CARB CHOICES 2

Leftover cooked poultry dishes can be refrigerated and served for 3 to 4 days.

Rosemary Oven-Fried Chicken

Prep—Chill—Bake or Prep—Bake—Refrigerate or Freeze ◆ Serves: 6

⅔ cup seasoned bread crumbs
⅓ cup grated nonfat Parmesan cheese
¾ tsp. dried rosemary
¾ tsp. dried thyme
½ tsp. garlic powder
½ tsp. onion powder

Pepper to taste
1½-lbs. boneless, skinless chicken
   breasts
1¼ cups plain nonfat yogurt
Cooking spray

Line baking sheet with foil and spray with cooking spray. Combine bread crumbs, Parmesan cheese, rosemary, thyme, garlic powder, onion powder and pepper in plastic bag; shake until ingredients are well mixed. Dip chicken in yogurt; place in plastic bag and shake until well coated. Arrange chicken in single layer on baking sheet. Sprinkle with remaining crumbs and spray lightly with cooking spray. Chicken can be covered and refrigerated until ready to serve. Preheat oven to 400°F. Bake chicken 25 to 35 minutes, until golden brown and crisp. Chicken can be cooled, wrapped individually and frozen; thaw in refrigerator overnight or heat directly from freezer in microwave on High until heated through 1 to 2 minutes. For crisp chicken, broil 1 to 2 minutes after heating.

Shopping List:

DAIRY	MEAT	SPICES
10 oz. plain nonfat yogurt	1½-lbs. boneless, skinless chicken breasts	Dried rosemary
Nonfat Parmesan cheese		Dried thyme
		Garlic powder
	PACKAGED	Onion powder
	Seasoned bread crumbs	Pepper

NUTRITION PER SERVING Calories 187 • Fat 1.2 g • Carbohydrates 14 g • Protein 29 g • Cholesterol 72 mg • Dietary Fiber <1 g • Sodium 432 mg
EXCHANGES 1 other carb • 4 very lean meat
CARB CHOICES 1

Throughout history, rosemary has been used as everything from a meat preservative and love charm, to plague deterrent, tonic for indigestion and remedy for headaches and baldness. Even today, it is associated with reducing the risk of cancer and arteriosclerosis.

St. Paddy's Day Any Day Special

Prep—Freeze—Bake   • Serves: 6

4 cups shredded cabbage
2 cups uncooked rice
1½ cups chopped onions
1 lb. Laura's lean ground beef, (see
  p. 124)
1 tsp. Mrs. Dash seasoning

¾ tsp. pepper
3 tbsp. brown sugar
32-oz. can (4 cups) low-sodium
  tomato juice
2 cups water

Spray 9 × 13-inch baking dish with cooking spray. Layer cabbage, rice, onions and beef; repeat layers starting with cabbage. Sprinkle Mrs. Dash seasoning, pepper and brown sugar over layers in baking dish. Combine tomato juice and water and mix until blended; pour over top of casserole. Cover with freezer-safe wrap and freeze until ready to serve. To serve: Preheat oven to 325°F. Bake frozen casserole 2 hours, until completely heated through.

Shopping List:

PRODUCE	PACKAGED/CANNED	SPICES
2 medium onions	32-oz. can low-sodium	Mrs. Dash seasoning
1 lb. cabbage	tomato juice	Pepper
	14-oz. pkg. rice	
MEAT	Brown sugar	
1 lb. Laura's lean		
ground beef		

NUTRITION PER SERVING Calories 403 • Fat 3.7 g • Carbohydrates 70 g • Protein 21 g • Cholesterol 41 mg • Dietary Fiber 4 g • Sodium 34 mg
EXCHANGES 4 starch • 2 vegetable • 1 very lean meat
CARB CHOICES 5

Uncut cabbage will keep for several months if refrigerated, but for a timesaver, purchase packaged shredded cabbage in the produce section of your local supermarket.

Southwest-Style Meat Loaf

Prep—Bake—Refrigerate or Freeze   • Serves: 6

1½ lbs. Laura's lean ground beef
¾ cup (2½ oz.) low-fat tortilla chips, crushed
¼ cup egg substitute

15¼-oz. can (1¾ cups) corn kernels
1¼ cups chunky, Southwest-style salsa
¼ tsp. pepper

Preheat oven to 375°F. Line baking sheet or small baking pan with foil and spray with cooking spray. Combine ground beef, crushed tortilla chips, egg substitute, corn kernels, 1 cup salsa and pepper in medium bowl and mix just until ingredients are combined. Shape meat mixture into loaf and place on foil. Spread remaining salsa on top. Bake 1 hour, until completely cooked through. Serve immediately; refrigerate, reheat and serve later; or freeze, thaw and reheat.

Shopping List:

DAIRY	PACKAGE/CANNED	Low-fat tortilla chips
Egg substitute	15¼-oz. can whole corn kernels	(1 g fat per serving)
MEAT	12-oz. jar chunky,	SPICES
1½ lbs. Laura's lean ground beef	Southwest-style salsa	Pepper

NUTRITION PER SERVING Calories 264 • Fat 5.7 g • Carbohydrates 26 g • Protein 26 g • Cholesterol 61 mg • Dietary Fiber 1 g • Sodium 593 mg
EXCHANGES 3 very lean meat • 1 fat • 1 starch • 2 vegetable
CARB CHOICES 2

Make the trade! Switching to low-fat tortilla chips saves at least 50 calories and 6 or more grams of fat per ounce!

Spicy Overnight Chicken

Prep—Chill—Bake   ◆ Serves: 4

1-lb. boneless, skinless chicken
   breasts
6 to 8 tbsp. apple juice, divided
2 tbsp. mustard seed
1½ tsp. ground turmeric
1 tsp. ground coriander
½ tsp. ground cinnamon

1 tsp. ground cloves
½ tsp. crushed red pepper
2 tbsp. paprika
½ tsp. pepper
½ cup orange juice
¼ cup nonfat chicken broth

Spray shallow baking dish with cooking spray. Arrange chicken breasts in baking dish and brush with 2 to 4 tablespoons apple juice to moisten. Combine remaining ingredients in food processor or blender and process until completely blended. Pour over chicken. Cover and refrigerate for 24 hours. Bring chicken to room temperature. Preheat oven to 325°F. Bake chicken 20 to 25 minutes, until tender. Remove from oven and pour marinade into separate bowl. Preheat broiler on high heat. Broil chicken 5 to 6 minutes per side, basting several times with marinade.

Shopping List:

MEATS	SPICES	Paprika
1-lb. boneless, skinless	Mustard seed	Pepper
chicken breasts	Ground tumeric	
	Ground coriander	BEVERAGES
CANNED	Ground cinnamon	8 oz. apple juice
Nonfat chicken broth	Ground cloves	4 oz. orange juice
	Crushed red pepper	

NUTRITION PER SERVING Calories 167 • Fat 1.7 g • Carbohydrates 13 g • Protein 27 g • Cholesterol 57 mg • Dietary Fiber 0 g • Sodium 247 mg
EXCHANGES 1 fruit • 3½ very lean meat
CARB CHOICES 1

Chicken is rich in niacin, the B vitamin that helps all cells obtain the energy they need to stay healthy. One 3-ounce serving of chicken provides half the daily need for niacin.

Tarragon Chicken Bake

Prep—Chill—Bake or Prep—Bake—Refrigerate or Freeze • Serves: 6

10¾-oz. can low-fat condensed cream of celery soup, undiluted
1 cup nonfat half-and-half
2 tsp. dried tarragon
¼ tsp. pepper

3 cups low-fat chicken, cooked and cubed
8 oz. linguine, cooked and drained
⅓ cup grated nonfat Parmesan cheese

Preheat oven to 350°F. Spray 2-quart baking dish with cooking spray. Combine soup, half-and-half, tarragon, pepper and chicken in medium bowl; mix well. Stir in linguine; spoon mixture into baking dish. Sprinkle with Parmesan cheese. Bake 30 to 35 minutes, until bubbly and hot. Casserole can be refrigerated and baked later, or baked and refrigerated or frozen. To reheat: Thaw completely and reheat in microwave oven about 3 minutes per serving.

Shopping List:

DAIRY	MEAT	PACKAGED/CANNED
8 oz. nonfat half-and-half	1-lb. boneless, skinless chicken tenders or 3 (6-oz.) pkgs. cooked chicken breast cuts	10¾-oz. can low-fat condensed cream of celery soup
Grated nonfat Parmesan cheese		8 oz. linguine
		SPICES
		Dried tarragon
		Pepper

NUTRITION PER SERVING Calories 310 • Fat 3.3 g • Carbohydrates 40 g • Protein 24 g • Cholesterol 46 mg • Dietary Fiber <1 g • Sodium 847 mg
EXCHANGES 3 very lean meat • 1 starch • 1½ other carb
CARB CHOICES 3

Americans purchase an average of 100 cans of Campbell's soup every second of every day in the month of January!

Tequila Chicken Strips

Prep—Chill—Bake ◆ Serves: 6

1½-lbs. boneless, skinless chicken
   tenders
Mrs. Dash seasoning to taste
Garlic powder to taste
Pepper to taste

½ of a 6-oz. can frozen lime juice
   concentrate, thawed
1½ oz. tequila
1 tbsp. grated lime peel
1½ tsp. minced garlic

Spray shallow baking dish with cooking spray. Arrange chicken tenders in baking dish; season with Mrs. Dash seasoning, garlic powder and pepper to taste. Combine remaining ingredients in small bowl and mix until blended. Pour over chicken; cover and refrigerate overnight. Preheat oven to 350°F. Toss chicken with marinade to coat; spoon marinade over top. Bake 25 to 35 minutes, until chicken tenders are golden brown and cooked through.

Shopping List:

PRODUCE	SPICES	FROZEN
Lime zest	Mrs. Dash seasoning	6-oz. can frozen lime
	Garlic powder	juice concentrate
MEAT	Pepper	
1½-lbs. boneless,	Minced garlic	**OTHER**
skinless chicken		Tequila
tenders		

NUTRITION PER SERVING Calories 130 • Fat .5 g • Carbohydrates 2 g • Protein 25 g • Cholesterol 57 mg • Dietary Fiber 0 g • Sodium 192 mg
EXCHANGES 3½ very lean meat
CARB CHOICES 0

Slow down . . . don't eat too fast! It takes about 20 minutes for your brain to recognize that your stomach is full.

Turkey Enchiladas

Prep—Freeze—Bake • Serves: 6

1 tsp. onion powder
4-oz. can chopped green chiles,
 drained, divided
⅓ cup picante sauce
¼ cup nonfat sour cream
⅙ tsp. chili powder

3 cups chopped, cooked low-fat
 turkey breast meat
1½ cups shredded nonfat cheddar
 cheese, divided
6 low-fat flour tortillas
14-oz. can low-fat enchilada sauce

Combine onion powder, chiles, picante sauce, sour cream, chili powder, turkey and ¾ cup cheese in a medium bowl; mix well. Divide the mixture evenly among tortillas, placing down center of each tortilla. Roll tortillas and place, seam side down, on baking sheet. Cover with plastic wrap and freeze 30 to 40 minutes, until slightly frozen. Place tortillas in plastic freezer bags (package according to the number you need for each meal). To prepare after freezing: Preheat oven to 325°F. Spray baking dish with cooking spray. Pour ½ cup enchilada sauce on bottom of dish; arrange frozen enchiladas on top of sauce and cover with additional ½ to ¾ cups sauce. Bake enchiladas 45 minutes; top with ¾ cup cheese and bake 20 to 30 minutes, until enchiladas are heated through and cheese is melted.

Shopping List:

DAIRY	MEAT	4-oz. can chopped
6 oz. shredded nonfat	1 lb. boneless turkey	green chiles
cheddar cheese	breast or 1½ lb.	Picante sauce
4 oz. nonfat sour cream	cooked turkey meat	6 low-fat flour tortillas
	PACKAGED/CANNED	SPICES
	14-oz. can low-fat	Chili powder
	enchilada sauce	Onion powder

NUTRITION PER SERVING Calories 232 • Fat 3.9 g • Carbohydrates 27 g • Protein 24 g • Cholesterol 31 mg • Dietary Fiber 1 g • Sodium 956 mg
EXCHANGES 3 very lean meat • 1 starch • 2 vegetable
CARB CHOICES 2

To speed up the cooking process, thaw frozen enchiladas in the microwave; bake 30 minutes, top with cheese and bake 10 to 15 minutes longer until cheese is melted.

Veggie 'n' Beef Burgers

Prep—Chill—Grill or Broil or
Prep—Cook—Refrigerate or Freeze

• Serves: 4

1 lb. Laura's lean ground beef (see
   p. 124)
10-oz. pkg. frozen chopped spinach,
   thawed and drained

2 tsp. Italian seasoning
½ tsp. garlic powder
½ tsp. onion powder
Pepper to taste

Combine all ingredients in a medium bowl and mix well. Shape into four large patties. Arrange on plate; cover and refrigerate until ready to cook or up to 24 hours. Preheat grill, broiler or skillet and cook to desired doneness. Burgers can also be cooked, refrigerated or frozen and reheated if desired.

Shopping List:

MEAT	SPICES	FROZEN
1 lb. Laura's lean ground beef	Italian seasoning Garlic powder Onion powder Pepper	10-oz. pkg. frozen chopped spinach

NUTRITION PER SERVING Calories 166 • Fat 4.8 g • Carbohydrates 5 g • Protein 24 g • Cholesterol 61 mg • Dietary Fiber 2 g • Sodium 62 mg
EXCHANGES 3 very lean meat • 1 vegetable • 1 fat
CARB CHOICES 0

Spinach, rich in antioxidants lutein and zeaxanthin, not only fends off age-related macular degeneration, but may also protect against cataracts.

MEATS AND MORE

Very Versatile Meat Sauce

Prep—Cook—Refrigerate or Freeze   • Serves: 6

1½ lbs. Laura's lean ground beef (see p. 124)
1¼ cups chopped onions
¾ tsp. minced garlic
¾ cup chopped celery
28-oz. canned diced tomato, undrained
¼ cup tomato paste
¼ tsp. dried parsley

2 tsp. Italian seasoning
½ tsp. dried basil
¼ tsp. pepper
⅛ tsp. crushed red pepper
¾ tsp. sugar
16-oz. can tomato sauce
1½ cups sliced mushrooms
6 cups cooked pasta

Spray Dutch oven with cooking spray and heat over medium-high heat. Add ground beef, onions, garlic and celery and cook, stirring frequently, until vegetables are tender and meat is no longer pink. Stir in remaining ingredients except mushrooms and pasta; bring to a boil over high heat. Reduce heat to low and simmer, uncovered, 45 minutes. Add mushrooms and cook 15 to 20 minutes, until softened. Sauce can be refrigerated or frozen. When ready to serve: Thaw sauce in refrigerator or microwave; reheat on stovetop or in microwave oven. Serve over favorite cooked pasta or baked potatoes.

MEATS AND MORE

Shopping List:

PRODUCE	PACKAGED/CANNED	SPICES
2 medium onions	12 oz. pasta of choice	Minced garlic
1 small bunch celery	Sugar	Dried parsley
¼ to ⅓ lb. sliced mushrooms	28-oz. can diced tomatoes	Italian seasoning
	6-oz. can tomato paste	Dried basil
MEAT	16-oz. can tomato sauce	Pepper
1½ lbs. Laura's lean ground beef		Crushed red pepper

NUTRITION PER SERVING Calories 305 • Fat 5.7 g • Carbohydrates 35 g • Protein 28 g • Cholesterol 61 mg • Dietary Fiber 4 g • Sodium 786 mg
EXCHANGE 1½ starch • 2 vegetable • 3 very lean meat • 1 fat
CARB CHOICES 2

For vegetarians or those who don't eat red meat: Substitute 1½ pounds textured soy protein crumbles or extra-lean ground turkey for ground beef.

SOUPS AND STEWS FOR
ALL SEASONS

❖

Did you know that the difference between soups and stews is the cooking method, not the particular combination of ingredients?

Safe Food-Handling and Storage
- Place soup directly in refrigerator to chill; do not leave on stovetop. Pour into shallow container so it will cool more quickly. Cover after cooling to retain moisture.
- Divide soups or stews into several containers before freezing. This allows soups/stews to chill evenly and defrost in less time.
- Leftover soups and stews can be refrigerated 3 to 4 days.

To Freeze or Not to Freeze
- Most soups or stews can be frozen without changing the nutritional quality, texture or flavor of the foods, but certain ingredients are better if they are added just before serving.
  - Cooked potatoes become mushy and watery after freezing; for best results, add cooked potatoes while reheating.
  - Soups thickened with cornstarch or flour may separate when they are reheated; for best results, add thickening ingredients while reheating.
  - Some fish and/or shellfish may become tough when reheated; thaw soup or stew in refrigerator overnight and reheat at very low temperature, stirring frequently, until heated through.
- Instead of freezing completed soups, freeze components (broth, cooked meat, chicken, fish, rice) and combine when reheating.
- Individual-size servings of soup can be frozen in foil-lined bowls, removed from the bowls and vacuum-sealed in bags. The bags can go directly into boiling water to thaw and heat.

From Stovetop to Refrigerator or Freezer and Back Again

From stovetop to fridge:
- Chill soups and stews as soon as possible—do not leave sitting out at room temperature for more than 2 hours.
- Pour soups/stews into shallow containers without lids and refrigerate. Cover containers tightly once foods are chilled.

- Don't use large containers for cooling. This does not allow for equal chilling—some of the hot vapors can increase the refrigerator temperature above the maximum safe temperature of 40°F.
- Use plastic or glass containers with tight-fitting lids.
- Most cooked soups or stews can be safely refrigerated for up to 3 days.
- Soups or stews containing fish or shellfish should not be refrigerated more than 1 day.

From stovetop to freezer:
- Use containers specifically designed for freezer use.
- Freezing will cause the soup or stew to expand. Leave about 1½ inches of space between the soup and the lid.
- Always label and date containers with name of recipe and date frozen or use-by date.
- Most soups and stews can be safely frozen for up to 3 months. Vacuum-packed soups can be frozen up to 2 years.
- For best results, add raw noodles to soups either after thawing (cook during reheating process) or to cooled soup before freezing (noodles will soften and finish cooking when soup is reheated).

Best methods for thawing:
- Thaw in refrigerator overnight or in microwave on defrost setting.
- For best results, thoroughly thaw soups/stews before reheating them. They will reheat more evenly and you won't be left with "cold spots."

Reheating:
- For best results, thoroughly thaw soups/stews before reheating. They will reheat more evenly, and you won't be left with "cold spots."
- Soups made with milk, eggs, cheese or cream can be safely frozen, but they may curdle when reheated. Cook over very low heat, stirring frequently, or thaw in microwave and reheat on stovetop.
- Broth-based soups can be reheated over medium heat, stirring occasionally, until thoroughly heated.
- Bring sauces, soups and gravy to a boil when reheating.

Shortcuts with the Same Results (in Less Time)
- Canned broth (chicken, beef or vegetable)
- Precut fresh or canned vegetables (especially ones that always need to be sliced or chopped)
- Frozen vegetables: Place frozen vegetables in a colander. Pour boiling water over the top and add vegetables to your favorite soups, stews, skillet meals or casseroles.
- Precooked packaged potatoes (whole, shredded, cubed)

- Cut flour tortillas into strips and add to boiling soup a few at a time as a quick and low-fat substitute for dumplings.

Always Room for Improvement

- Remove fat from soups by adding a lettuce leaf to the pot; remove before serving.
- Skim grease or fat from soup by dragging a piece of bread across the surface.
- If soup is too thin:
  - Microwave a baked potato until soft; peel, mash, add to soup and cook until heated through.
  - Puree a portion of the soup; stir it back into the pot and cook until heated through.
- If soup is too salty, add a raw potato. The potato will absorb the extra salt.
- Extra seasonings and spices:
  - Chives, cumin, dill, fennel, marjoram, mint, tarragon, thyme

Everything Old Is New Again!

- Leftover chili: Combine chili with fresh-cut or canned vegetables (i.e., corn, bell peppers, onions). Prepare low-fat or fat-free cornbread mix (try Krusteaz brand); drop batter by tablespoons over top of chili. Bake 25 to 30 minutes at 350°F, until lightly browned and heated through. Top with shredded cheese, if desired.
- Save leftover meat, poultry, vegetables, noodles, rice and potatoes and add to canned broth for a quick-and-easy soup.

Beef 'n' Barley Stew

Prep—Refrigerate or Freeze   • Serves: 8

½ cup quick-cooking barley
2 lbs. Laura's lean ground beef (see p. 124)
2 tsp. garlic powder
1½ cups diced celery
1½ cups diced carrots

16-oz. can diced tomatoes, drained
2½ cups chopped onions
2 (14-oz.) cans nonfat beef broth
½ cup Worcestershire sauce
2 tsp. sugar
½ tsp. pepper

Cook barley according to package directions and set aside. Spray large soup pot with cooking spray. Add ground beef and garlic powder to pot; cook, stirring frequently, until beef is browned. Add celery, carrots, tomatoes and onions; cook over low heat 10 to 12 minutes, until vegetables are softened. Add broth, Worcestershire sauce, sugar and pepper. Bring to a boil; add cooked barley. Reduce heat to low and cook 25 to 30 minutes, until heated through. Refrigerate or freeze; thaw, heat and serve.

Shopping List:

PRODUCE	PACKAGED/CANNED	CONDIMENTS
1 small bunch celery	2 (14½-oz.) cans nonfat	Worcestershire sauce
2 large carrots	beef broth	
1 lb. onions	16-oz. can diced	SPICES
	tomatoes	Garlic powder
MEAT	Sugar	Pepper
2 lbs. Laura's lean	Quick-cooking barley	
ground beef		

NUTRITION PER SERVING Calories 245 • Fat 5 g • Carbohydrates 22 g • Protein 25 g • Cholesterol 61 mg • Dietary Fiber 4 g • Sodium 638 mg
EXCHANGES 3 very lean meat • 3 vegetable • ½ starch
CARB CHOICES 1

Fun fact: Long before batons, ancient Greek marathon racers carried celery and awarded the prized vegetable to winners at sporting events.

Beet Borscht

Prep—Chill   • Serves: 4

32-oz. jar Manischewitz borscht with beets
15-oz. can shredded beets, drained
1 small potato, quartered
¼ cup nonfat sour cream

Combine all ingredients except sour cream in large saucepan; bring to a boil over high heat. Reduce heat to low and simmer 45 to 60 minutes. Remove from heat and cool 15 to 20 minutes; remove 1 cup shredded beets from soup and set aside. Pour remaining mixture into blender or food processor and process until smooth. Pour into bowl; add reserved beets. Cover and refrigerate up to 1 week. Garnish with sour cream before serving.

Shopping List:

PRODUCE	PACKAGED/CANNED
1 small potato	32-oz. jar Manischewitz borscht with beets
DAIRY	15-oz. can shredded
Nonfat sour cream	beets

NUTRITION PER SERVING Calories 145 • Fat .1 g • Carbohydrates 33 g • Protein 3 g • Cholesterol 0 mg • Dietary Fiber 5 g • Sodium 808 mg
EXCHANGES 3 vegetable • 1 starch
CARB CHOICES 2

Beets, high in folate, are low in calories, with only 44 calories per ³⁄₄ cup serving.

Brunswick Stew

2 lbs. Laura's lean ground beef (see
  p. 124)
2 tbsp. onion powder
1 bay leaf
2 (14½-oz.) cans (3½ cups) crushed
  tomatoes

14½-oz. can (1¾ cup) low-fat
  creamed corn
14½-oz. can (1¾ cup) whole-kernel
  corn
1 cup barbecue sauce
Tabasco sauce to taste

Spray large Dutch oven with cooking spray. Add ground beef and onion powder; cook, stirring frequently, until beef is browned. Add remaining ingredients and cook over low heat for 1 hour; stir frequently to prevent sticking. Cool to room temperature; remove bay leaf. Cover and refrigerate until ready to serve or freeze. Thaw completely and reheat on stovetop or in microwave oven.

Shopping List:

MEAT	14½-oz. can low-fat	SPICES
2 lbs. Laura's lean	creamed corn	Onion powder
ground beef	14½-oz. can whole-	Bay leaf
	kernel corn	
CANNED		
2 (14½-oz.) cans	CONDIMENTS	
crushed tomatoes	8 oz. barbecue sauce	
	Tabasco sauce	

NUTRITION PER SERVING Calories 266 • Fat 5.8 g • Carbohydrates 29 g •
Protein 25 g • Cholesterol 61 mg • Dietary Fiber 4 g • Sodium 541 mg
EXCHANGES 3 very lean meat • 1 starch • 1 vegetable • ½ other carb •
1 fat
CARB CHOICES 2

Fun fact: One ear of corn averages 800 kernels in 16 rows. One pound of corn has approximately 1,300 kernels, and 100 bushels produces approximately 7,280,000 kernels.

Chicken and Rice Soup

Prep—Cook—Refrigerate or Freeze   ♦ Serves: 8

10½ cups nonfat chicken broth	2 cups uncooked rice
¼ tsp. dried rosemary	4 cups cubed, cooked, low-fat chicken
¼ tsp. pepper	28-oz. can diced tomatoes with
4 cups frozen mixed vegetables	roasted garlic, undrained

In a large soup pot or Dutch oven, combine chicken broth, rosemary and pepper; bring to a boil over high heat. Add mixed vegetables and rice; cover and simmer over low heat 12 to 15 minutes, until rice is tender. Stir in chicken and tomatoes; cook over medium-high heat 5 to 10 minutes, until completely heated through.

Shopping List:

MEAT	PACKAGED/CANNED	SPICES
1½ lb. boneless, skinless chicken breasts	28-oz. can diced tomatoes with roasted garlic	Dried rosemary Pepper
	6 (14½-oz.) cans nonfat chicken broth	**FROZEN**
	14-oz. pkg. instant rice	2 (16-oz.) pkgs. frozen mixed vegetables

NUTRITION PER SERVING Calories 209 • Fat 3.5g • Carbohydrates 21 g • Protein 23 g • Cholesterol 53 mg • Dietary Fiber 5 g • Sodium 1,636 mg
EXCHANGES 2 vegetables • 1 starch • 2 very lean meat
CARB CHOICES 1

Beyond garlic breath, the benefits of garlic are great. The complex mixture of chemicals that make up garlic display antiviral, antibacterial, anticancer, anti–blood clotting, decongestive, cholesterol-reducing and immunity-boosting properties.

Chicken and Stars Soup

Prep—Cook—Refrigerate or Freeze   • Serves: 6

8½ cups nonfat chicken broth, divided
1½ cups chopped onions
1½ cups chopped celery
2¼ cups chopped carrots

1 cup pasta stars (pastina)
4 cups cubed cooked chicken
¼ tsp. pepper
2 tbsp. dried parsley

Pour 1 tablespoon chicken broth into large soup pot or Dutch oven and heat over medium-high heat. Add onions and celery; cook, stirring frequently, 4 to 5 minutes, until lightly browned. Add remaining chicken broth, carrots and pasta (only if serving immediately or storing in refrigerator). Bring to a boil over medium-high heat, reduce heat to medium and cook 15 to 20 minutes, until vegetables and rice are tender. Add cooked chicken, pepper and parsley and heat through. To freeze, omit pasta. Heat soup over low heat until thawed. Bring to a boil over high heat; add cooked pasta to soup and sprinkle with pepper and parsley.

Shopping List:

PRODUCE	PACKAGED/CANNED	SPICES
1 large bunch celery	5 (14½-oz.) cans nonfat	Dried parsley
2 large onions	chicken broth	Pepper
6 carrots	6 oz. pasta stars	
	(pastina)	

NUTRITION PER SERVING Calories 231 • Fat 3.5 g • Carbohydrates 23 g • Protein 23 g • Cholesterol 72 mg • Dietary Fiber 3 g • Sodium 1,487 mg
EXCHANGES 1 starch • 2 vegetable • 3 meat
CARB CHOICES 2

Pasta is rich in B vitamins, easy to digest and low in fat and sodium.

Chicken Tortilla Soup

Prep—Cook—Refrigerate or Freeze

8 cups + 2 tbsp. nonfat chicken
broth, divided
1 cup chopped onion
2 tsp. minced garlic
¼ cup chopped green chiles
2 cups cubed, cooked low-fat chicken

1 cup frozen corn kernels
½ cup frozen bell pepper strips
¼ cup chopped fresh cilantro
1 tbsp. lime juice
2 tsp. cumin
Baked tortilla chips

Spray large soup pot with cooking spray; add 2 tablespoons chicken broth and heat over medium-high heat. Add onion, garlic and chiles to pot; cook, stirring frequently, 3 to 5 minutes, until softened. Add remaining broth, chicken, corn, bell pepper, cilantro, lime juice and cumin; bring to a boil over high heat. Reduce heat to low and simmer 10 to 15 minutes. Soup can be refrigerated or frozen; reheat on stovetop or in microwave oven. Just before serving, garnish with baked tortilla strips.

Shopping List:

PRODUCE	PACKAGED/CANNED	SPICES
1 bunch cilantro	4-oz. can chopped	Ground cumin
1 large onion	green chiles	
Minced garlic	5 (14½-oz.) cans nonfat	FROZEN
	chicken broth	10-oz. pkg. frozen
MEAT	Lime juice	pepper strips
¾ lb. boneless, skinless	Baked tortilla chips	10-oz. pkg. frozen corn
chicken breast or 2		kernels
(6-oz.) pkgs. cooked		
chicken cuts		

NUTRITION PER SERVING Calories 90 • Fat 2 g • Carbohydrates 7 g •
Protein 11 g • Cholesterol 26 mg • Dietary Fiber 1 g • Sodium 1,013 mg
EXCHANGES ½ starch • 1 very lean meat
CARB CHOICES 0

*To reduce water-retention and help control blood pressure, select
low-sodium broth or make your own chicken stock with a variety of spices
and seasonings.*

SOUPS AND STEWS
FOR ALL SEASONS

Chicken Vegetable Soup

Prep—Cook—Refrigerate or Freeze   • Serves: 6

3 cups cubed, cooked low-fat chicken
1 tsp. onion powder
¼ tsp. garlic powder
28-oz. can diced tomatoes with
  roasted garlic, undrained
1 cup chopped celery
1 cup diced carrots

1 cup potato cubes
1 cup nonfat chicken broth
½ cup water, if needed
4 cups frozen mixed vegetables (of
  choice)
¾ tsp. Mrs. Dash seasoning
½ tsp. pepper

Combine chicken, onion powder, garlic powder, tomatoes, celery, carrots, potatoes, chicken broth and water in Dutch oven or large soup pot. Bring to a boil over high heat. Reduce heat to low and simmer 15 to 20 minutes, until vegetables are tender. Add frozen vegetables, Mrs. Dash seasoning and pepper. Cook 10 to 15 minutes until heated through. Serve immediately or freeze. Reheat on stovetop or in microwave until hot.

Shopping List:

PRODUCE
1 small bunch celery
1 large carrot
16-oz. pkg. cubed
  potatoes (refrigerated)

MEAT
1-lb. boneless skinless
  chicken breasts or

tenders or 3 (6-oz.)
pkgs. cooked chicken
breast cuts

CANNED
28-oz. can diced
tomatoes with
roasted garlic
14½-oz. can nonfat
chicken broth

SPICES
Mrs. Dash seasoning
Onion powder
Garlic powder
Pepper

FROZEN
2 (16-oz.) pkgs. frozen
  vegetables of choice

NUTRITION PER SERVING Calories 246 • Fat 3.6 g • Carbohydrates 28 g • Protein 26 g • Cholesterol 57 mg • Dietary Fiber 9 g • Sodium 972 mg
EXCHANGES 1 starch • 3 vegetable • 2 very lean meat
CARB CHOICES 2

Potatoes, rich in vitamin C, rate as one of the superfoods for healthy skin.

SOUPS AND STEWS FOR ALL SEASONS

Chili with Winter Squash and Beans

Prep—Cook—Refrigerate or Freeze   • Serves: 6

¾ lb. extra-lean ground turkey
1 cup diced onion
¾ tsp. garlic powder
¾ tsp. Mrs. Dash seasoning
2 (28-oz.) cans diced tomatoes with
  green chiles
1¼-oz. pkg. chili seasoning mix

2 (14½-oz.) cans nonfat beef broth
15-oz. can black beans, drained
2 medium zucchinis, diced
2 medium yellow squash, diced
2 cups diced green bell peppers
1 cup diced celery
¾ cup diced carrot

Spray Dutch oven with cooking spray and heat over medium-high heat. Add ground turkey and onion; sprinkle with garlic powder and Mrs. Dash seasoning. Cook, stirring frequently, 5 to 8 minutes, until turkey and onion are browned. Add remaining ingredients; bring to a boil over high heat. Reduce heat to low and simmer 25 to 30 minutes, until vegetables are tender. Chili can be served immediately, refrigerated 3 to 4 days or frozen and reheated in the microwave.

Shopping List:

PRODUCE	MEAT	tomatoes with green
1 medium onion	¾ lb. extra-lean ground	chiles
2 medium zucchini	turkey	
2 medium yellow		SPICES
squash	CANNED	1¼-oz. pkg. chili
1 small bunch celery	15-oz. can black beans	seasoning mix
1 large carrot	2 (14½-oz.) cans nonfat	Garlic powder
2 large green bell	beef broth	Mrs. Dash seasoning
peppers	2 (28-oz.) cans diced	

NUTRITION PER SERVING Calories 236 • Fat 1.6 g • Carbohydrates 35 g • Protein 21 g • Cholesterol 23 g • Dietary Fiber 6 g • Sodium 1,432 mg
EXCHANGES 4 vegetable • 1 starch • 1½ lean meat
CARB CHOICES 2

Just ¾ cup of black beans provides 25 percent of a woman's RDA for magnesium, an essential mineral that functions in more than 300 enzymes.

Chunky Gazpacho

Prep — Chill • Serves: 6

2 cups chopped bell pepper, divided
1¼ cups chopped green onions,
   divided
2 large cucumbers, peeled and
   chopped, divided
2 (16-oz.) cans stewed tomatoes
1¼ cups vegetable broth
1 to 2 tbsp. red wine vinegar

½ to 1 tsp. garlic powder
1 tsp. ground celery seeds
⅓ cup bread crumbs
1 tsp. sugar
2 to 3 drops Tabasco sauce
Pepper to taste
1½ cups nonfat croutons

Set aside 1 cup bell pepper, ½ cup green onions and 1 cup cucumber; store in plastic bag. Combine remaining ingredients except croutons in blender and blend until smooth. Pour gazpacho into bowl; cover and refrigerate until ready to serve. When ready to serve, add reserved vegetables and top with croutons.

Shopping List:

PRODUCE	14 ½-oz. can vegetable	CONDIMENTS
2 large bell peppers	broth	Tabasco sauce
½ to ¾ lb. green onions	Bread crumbs	Red wine vinegar
2 large cucumbers	5-oz. pkg. nonfat	
	croutons	SPICES
PACKAGED/CANNED	Sugar	Garlic powder
2 (16-oz.) cans stewed		Ground celery seeds
tomatoes		Pepper

NUTRITION PER SERVING Calories 117 • Fat .7 g • Carbohydrates 28 g •
Protein 4 g • Cholesterol 0 mg • Dietary Fiber 3 g • Sodium 541 mg
EXCHANGES ½ starch • 4 vegetable
CARB CHOICES 2

Tomatoes are one of the best sources of lycopene, a potent antioxidant that has been shown to prevent certain types of cancer.

SOUPS AND STEWS
FOR ALL SEASONS

Cockaleekie Soup

Prep—Cook—Refrigerate or Freeze   • Serves: 8

7 (14½-oz.) cans nonfat chicken
   broth
1 cup uncooked rice
3 large leeks, white parts only, sliced

6 cups low-fat cooked chicken cuts
Pepper to taste
4 cups frozen mixed vegetables

Pour chicken broth into large soup pot; bring to a boil over high heat. Add rice and leeks to broth. Cook over medium heat 20 to 25 minutes until rice and leeks are tender. Add cooked chicken to soup; season as desired. Cool to room temperature and store in refrigerator or freezer-safe containers. To reheat: Thaw soup and heat in saucepan on stovetop or in microwave oven until heated through. Add frozen mixed vegetables, reduce heat to medium and cook 10 to 12 minutes until heated through.

Shopping List:

PRODUCE	skinless chicken	SPICES
3 large leeks	breasts or tenders	Pepper
MEAT	PACKAGED/CANNED	FROZEN
5 (6-oz.) pkgs. cooked	7 (14½-oz.) cans nonfat	2 (16-oz.) pkgs. frozen
chicken breast cuts	chicken broth	mixed vegetables of
or 2-lb. boneless	5.7-oz. pkg. white rice	choice

NUTRITION PER SERVING Calories 93 • Fat .5 g • Carbohydrates 20 g • Protein 3 g • Cholesterol <1 mg • Dietary Fiber 4 g • Sodium 1,293 mg
EXCHANGES ½ starch • 2 vegetable
CARB CHOICES 1

As a member of the genus Allium, *leeks may help protect against stomach cancer.*

Crab Bisque

Prep—Cook—Refrigerate   • Serves: 4

2 tbsp. vegetable broth
2 cups chopped red bell peppers
1 cup chopped green onions
1 cup chopped celery
⅔ cup shredded carrot
½ cup chopped red onion
¼ tsp. cayenne pepper
2 tsp. dried tarragon, divided

28-oz. can diced tomatoes
3 cups clam juice
1 cup dry white wine
12-oz. can crabmeat
½ cup sherry
1 cup evaporated skim milk
Pepper to taste

Heat vegetable broth in large pot over medium heat. Add bell pepper, green onion, celery, carrot and red onion; cook 10 to 12 minutes, until vegetables are softened. Sprinkle cayenne pepper and 1 teaspoon tarragon over vegetables. Add tomatoes, clam juice, wine and 1 teaspoon tarragon; bring to a boil over high heat. Reduce heat to low and simmer 30 to 45 minutes. Add crabmeat; cook 5 to 8 minutes, until heated through. Add sherry, evaporated skim milk and pepper. Cook, stirring frequently, until soup thickens and is heated through. Soup can be refrigerated up to 3 days. Reheat on stovetop or in microwave.

Shopping List:

PRODUCE	PACKAGED/CANNED	8 oz. dry white wine
2 to 3 red bell peppers	28-oz. can diced	4 oz. sherry
½ to ¾ lb. bunch green	tomatoes	
onions	12-oz. can crabmeat	SPICES
1 small bunch celery	8-oz. can evaporated	Dried tarragon
1 small red onion	skim milk	Cayenne pepper
1 to 2 carrots	Vegetable broth	Pepper
	24 oz. clam juice	

NUTRITION PER SERVING Calories 293 • Fat 2.3 g • Carbohydrates 27 g • Protein 25 g • Cholesterol 48 mg • Dietary Fiber 4 g • Sodium 1,737 mg
EXCHANGES 3 very lean meat • 4 vegetable • ½ other carb
CARB CHOICES 2

Why do onions bring tears to your eyes? Onions release a gas called propanethiol-S that, when mixed with water in the eye, forms a weak acid that irritates the eye. As a result, tear ducts flood the eyes to get rid of the acid.

Cucumber Bisque

Prep—Chill

2 large cucumbers, peeled, seeded
   and grated
1 cup nonfat half-and-half
1 cup nonfat plain yogurt
1 cup nonfat sour cream
2 tbsp. lime juice

2 tsp. grated lime peel
¾ tsp. onion powder
2 to 3 drops Tabasco sauce
Pepper to taste
½ cup chopped green onion

Combine cucumbers, half-and-half, yogurt, sour cream, lime juice, lime peel and onion powder in a large bowl; mix until all ingredients are blended. Cover and refrigerate overnight. Just before serving, season soup with Tabasco sauce and pepper; garnish with green onions.

Shopping List:

PRODUCE	DAIRY	CONDIMENTS
2 large cucumbers	8 oz. nonfat half-and-	Tabasco sauce
1 small bunch green	half	
onions	8-oz. carton nonfat	SPICES
1 lime	plain yogurt	Onion power
	8 oz. nonfat sour cream	Pepper

NUTRITION PER SERVING Calories 135 • Fat <1 g • Carbohydrates 22 g • Protein 8 g • Cholesterol 1 mg • Dietary Fiber 2 g • Sodium 87 mg
EXCHANGES 3 vegetable • ½ other carb
CARB CHOICES 1

We should be a strong nation! Dairy products, a good source of calcium, account for 29 percent of all food consumed in the United States.

SOUPS AND STEWS
FOR ALL SEASONS

Fish Chowder

• Serves: 6

2 tbsp. vegetable broth
1 cup chopped onion
1½ cups chopped carrots
1 cup chopped celery
2 cups cubed, peeled potatoes
2½ cups water

½ tsp. crushed bay leaf
½ tsp. dried thyme
½ tsp. dried dill
1½ lb. halibut fillet, cut into chunks
1½ cups nonfat half-and-half
Pepper to taste

Spray large soup pot or Dutch oven with cooking spray. Pour vegetable broth into pot and heat over medium-high heat. Add onion and cook until softened, about 5 minutes. Add carrots, celery, potatoes, water, bay leaf, thyme and dill. Cover pot and cook over medium-low heat 15 to 20 minutes, until vegetables are tender. Add fish; simmer until fish is cooked through, 8 to 10 minutes. Gradually stir in half-and-half; cook over medium heat, stirring frequently, but do not boil. Season with pepper. If not serving immediately, cool to room temperature, cover and refrigerate up to 3 days.

Shopping List:

PRODUCE	DAIRY	CANNED
1 large onion	12 oz. nonfat half-and-	Vegetable broth
2 potatoes	half	
2 carrots		SPICES
1 small bunch celery	FISH	Bay leaf
	1½-lb. halibut fillet	Dried thyme
		Dried dill
		Pepper

NUTRITION PER SERVING Calories 221 • Fat 2.9 g • Carbohydrates 20 g • Protein 27 g • Cholesterol 37 mg • Dietary Fiber 3 g • Sodium 117 mg
EXCHANGES 3 very lean meat • 1 starch • 1 vegetable
CARB CHOICES 1

Halibut, the largest flatfish that can weigh as much as 300 pounds is an excellent source of protein. A four-ounce serving has approximately 110 calories, 23 grams of protein, less than 1 gram of saturated fat and 35 mg of cholesterol.

Fish Stew

• Serves: 6

1 tbsp. + 1 cup vegetable broth
  divided
1 cup sliced onion
¾ cup sliced celery
¾ cup diced bell pepper
¾ cup sliced carrot
½ tsp. garlic powder
1 cup canned chopped tomatoes

2 cups peeled, cubed potatoes
1 cup water
1 cup low-sodium tomato juice
1 tbsp. lemon juice
1 tsp. Italian seasoning
Pepper to taste
1 lb. halibut, cut into 1-inch cubes
1 lb. cod, cut into 1-inch cubes

Spray large soup pot or Dutch oven with cooking spray. Pour 1 tablespoon vegetable broth into pot and heat over medium-high heat. Add onion, celery, bell pepper and carrot; sprinkle with garlic powder and cook over medium-high heat, stirring frequently, until vegetables are softened. Add tomatoes, potatoes, remaining broth, water, tomato juice, lemon juice, Italian seasoning and pepper. Reduce heat to low, cover and simmer until potatoes are tender, 10 to 15 minutes. Add fish to pot; cook, uncovered, over medium-low heat until fish flakes easily with a fork, 10 to 12 minutes. Cover and refrigerate up to 3 days. Soup can be reheated in microwave or on stovetop.

Shopping List:

PRODUCE	FISH	8-oz. can chopped
1 large onion	1 lb. halibut	tomatoes
16-oz. pkg. cubed	1 lb. cod	
potatoes (refrigerated)		SPICES
1 to 2 large carrots	CANNED	Italian seasoning
1 large bell pepper	14½-oz. vegetable	Garlic powder
1 small bunch celery	broth	Pepper
Lemon juice	8 oz. low-sodium	
	tomato juice	

NUTRITION PER SERVING Calories 225 • Fat 2.6 g • Carbohydrates 19 g • Protein 32 g • Cholesterol 57 mg • Dietary Fiber 2 g • Sodium 601 mg
EXCHANGES 1 starch • 1 vegetable • 3 very lean meat
CARB CHOICES 1

Halibut, also known as the king of flatfish, is an excellent source of vitamin
B_{12}, *which helps produce myelin, the protective coating that surrounds delicate nerve tissue.*

SOUPS AND STEWS
FOR ALL SEASONS

Jambalaya

Prep—Cook—Refrigerate or Freeze   • Serves: 6

2 (14½-oz.) cans nonfat chicken
  broth, divided
1½ tsp. minced garlic
¾ cup chopped onion
1½ cups sliced celery
16-oz. can diced tomatoes with
  roasted garlic
2 cups cooked low-fat chicken breast
  cuts

3 tbsp. Worcestershire sauce
¼ tsp. pepper
¼ tsp. dried parsley
¼ tsp. dried tarragon
¼ tsp. dried chives
¼ tsp. dried chervil
2 to 3 drops Tabasco sauce
3 cups cooked white rice

Spray large soup pot or Dutch oven with cooking spray. Pour ¼ cup chicken broth into pot and heat over medium-high heat. Add garlic, onion and celery to pot; cook, stirring frequently, until vegetables are tender. Add remaining broth and tomatoes; bring to a boil over high heat. Reduce heat to low, cover and simmer 30 to 35 minutes. Add chicken, Worcestershire sauce, pepper, parsley, tarragon, chives, chervil and Tabasco sauce; cook over medium-low heat until heated through, 10 to 15 minutes. Serve jambalaya over cooked rice. Jambalaya can be frozen and reheated; cook rice just before serving or add leftover cooked rice to stew while reheating.

Shopping List:

PRODUCE	PACKAGED/CANNED	CONDIMENTS
1 medium onion	16-oz. can diced	Tabasco sauce
1 small bunch celery	tomatoes with	Worcestershire sauce
Minced garlic	roasted garlic	
	2 (14½-oz.). cans	SPICES
MEAT	chicken broth	Dried parsley
2 (6-oz.) pkgs. cooked	Rice	Dried tarragon
chicken breast cuts		Dried chives
		Dried chervil
		Pepper

NUTRITION PER SERVING Calories 170 • Fat 1.4 g • Carbohydrates 34 g •
Protein 6 g • Cholesterol 1 mg • Dietary Fiber 5 g • Sodium 204 mg
EXCHANGES 1½ starch • 2 vegetable
CARB CHOICES 2

One bottle of Tabasco sauce should last a long, long time. A 2-ounce bottle contains at least 720 drops of sauce.

Matzo Balls for Quick-Fix Soup

Prep—Cook—Refrigerate or Freeze   ♦ Serves: 6

4 large egg whites
¼ cup egg substitute
¾ cup matzo meal
1 tbsp. dried minced onion

¾ tsp. Mrs. Dash seasoning
1½ tsp. dried parsley
Pepper to taste

Pour egg whites into medium bowl; beat with electric mixer or whisk until stiff. Gradually add egg substitute and mix lightly. Combine matzo meal, onion, Mrs. Dash seasoning, parsley and pepper in plastic bag; shake until ingredients are blended. Add crumb mixture to egg mixture, stirring until ingredients are blended. Form mixture into 1-inch balls and place in 10 cups boiling water. Reduce heat to low, cover and simmer until matzo balls are soft and fluffy, 20 to 30 minutes. Using slotted spoon, carefully remove matzo balls from water; drain well. Line baking sheet with foil; arrange matzo balls in single layer on baking sheet, cover with plastic wrap and freeze 10 to 15 minutes. Remove from freezer; store matzo balls in plastic freezer bags until ready to serve. Add frozen matzo balls to boiling chicken broth and cook over medium heat until thawed and heated through. If desired, add frozen mixed vegetables to soup; bring to a boil and cook just until vegetables are tender. For a full meal, add cooked chicken.

Shopping List:

DAIRY	SPICES
4 large eggs	Dried minced onion
Egg substitute	Mrs. Dash seasoning
	Dried parsley
PACKAGED	Pepper
Matzo meal	

NUTRITION PER SERVING Calories 83 • Fat .2 g • Carbohydrates 15 g • Protein 5 g • Cholesterol 0 mg • Dietary Fiber <1 g • Sodium 51 mg
EXCHANGES 1 starch
CARB CHOICES 1

Check labels on egg substitutes before purchase; some are higher in calories and fat but do not provide better flavor or more nutritional value.

Mushroom Barley Soup

Prep—Chill ◆ Serves: 6

3 tbsp. dried porcini or shiitake
  mushrooms
1½ cups hot water
3 (14½-oz.) cans nonfat beef broth
3 carrots, cut into 1-inch slices
1½ cups chopped celery
¾ cup chopped onion

¼ tsp. garlic powder
2 cups fresh shiitake mushrooms,
  trimmed and sliced
6 cups sliced white mushrooms
½ cup pearled barley
Salt and pepper to taste

Place dried mushrooms in bowl; pour 1½ cups hot water over mushrooms and let stand until softened, 15 to 20 minutes. Remove mushrooms with slotted spoon. Spray Dutch oven with cooking spray; add 2 tablespoons broth and heat over medium-high heat. Add carrots, celery, onion and garlic powder; cook, stirring occasionally, until softened, 8 to 10 minutes. Add mushrooms, remaining broth and barley; season with salt and pepper to taste. Bring to a boil over high heat; reduce heat to medium-low and simmer until barley is tender, 35 to 40 minutes. Store soup in refrigerator up to 1 week; reheat on stovetop or in microwave when ready to serve.

Shopping List:

PRODUCE	3 oz. dried porcini or	SPICES
3 carrots	shiitake mushrooms	Garlic powder
1 bunch celery		Salt
1 medium onion	PACKAGED/CANNED	Pepper
1 lb. white mushrooms	3 (14½-oz.) cans nonfat	
⅓ lb. shiitake	beef broth	
mushrooms	Pearled barley	

NUTRITION PER SERVING Calories 154 • Fat 1 g • Carbohydrates 34 g • Protein 6 g • Cholesterol <1 mg • Dietary Fiber 6 g • Sodium 845 mg
EXCHANGES 3 vegetable • 1 starch
CARB CHOICES 2

The Mushroom Council of California recommends cooking shiitake mushrooms before eating them because they contain an enzyme that may cause an upset stomach.

Not Grandma's Noodle Soup

Prep—Cook—Refrigerate or Freeze • Serves: 6

8¼ cups nonfat chicken broth
3 cups sliced mushrooms
1 cup sliced green onions
¼ tsp. dried tarragon
¼ tsp. dried chervil
1 tsp. dried parsley

¼ tsp. pepper
2½ cups uncooked yolk-free noodles
2 cups cubed, cooked low-fat chicken
10-oz. pkg. frozen chopped spinach,
    thawed and drained

Combine chicken broth, mushrooms, green onions, tarragon, chervil, parsley and pepper in soup pot; bring to a boil over high heat. Add noodles; bring to a boil over high heat. Reduce heat to medium and cook until noodles are tender, 7 to 9 minutes. Stir in chicken and spinach; cook over medium heat until heated through, 5 to 10 minutes. Freeze leftover soup in covered containers; thaw and reheat on stovetop or in microwave.

Shopping List:

PRODUCE	PACKAGED/CANNED	Dried parsley
1 lb. fresh mushrooms	5 (14½-oz.) cans nonfat	Pepper
1 bunch large green	chicken broth	
onions	5 oz. yolk-free noodles	FROZEN
		10-oz. pkg. frozen
MEAT	SPICES	chopped spinach
2 (6-oz.) pkgs. cooked	Dried tarragon	
chicken breast cuts	Dried chervil	

NUTRITION PER SERVING Calories 184 • Fat 2.6 g • Carbohydrates 21 g • Protein 19 g • Cholesterol 35 mg • Dietary Fiber 2 g • Sodium 941 mg
EXCHANGES 1 vegetable • 1 starch • 2 very lean meat
CARB CHOICES 1

A mushroom is more than merely a fungus! A good source of fiber, complex carbohydrates, folate and vitamin C, mushrooms contribute to the fight against heart disease.

Portabello Mushroom Soup

Prep—Cook—Refrigerate or Freeze ◆ Serves: 4

3 (14½ oz.) cans vegetable broth
3 medium onions, quartered
3 cloves garlic, peeled
1 lb. portabello mushrooms, cut into
large chunks

Salt and pepper to taste
2 tbsp. sherry
¼ cup evaporated skim milk
2 cups sliced button mushrooms
1 cup cooked barley or orzo pasta

Preheat oven to 400°F. Line baking sheet with foil and spray with cooking spray. Coat baking sheet with 1 teaspoon broth. Arrange onions and garlic cloves on baking sheet; top with portabello mushrooms and drizzle with 1 teaspoon broth. Season with salt and pepper. Roast vegetable mixture 20 to 25 minutes, until browned. Remove baking sheet from oven and drizzle mushrooms with sherry. Combine vegetables and 5 cups broth in large bowl. Puree soup in food processor or blender (do this in several batches); pour into soup pot. Add evaporated skim milk and button mushrooms. Cook over medium heat, stirring constantly, until heated through. Soup can be frozen at this point. Add cooked barley or orzo before reheating. Soup can be reheated on stovetop or in microwave oven.

Shopping List:

PRODUCE	PACKAGED/CANNED	Quick-cooking barley or
1 lb. portabello	3 (14½-oz.) cans	orzo pasta
mushrooms	vegetable or beef	Sherry
⅓ to ½ lb. mushrooms	broth	
3 medium onions	5-oz. can evaporated	SPICES
1 head garlic	skim milk	Salt
		Pepper

NUTRITION PER SERVING Calories 149 • Fat .7 g • Carbohydrates 31 g • Protein 8 g • Cholesterol <1 mg • Dietary Fiber 9 g • Sodium 1,116 mg
EXCHANGES ½ starch • 4 vegetable
CARB CHOICES 2

After reviewing 19 studies, scientists at the University of North Carolina at Chapel Hill concluded that people who ate six cloves of garlic a week are 30 percent less likely to develop colon cancer and half as likely to get stomach cancer as those who rarely eat garlic.

Potato-Leek Soup

1 lb. potatoes, peeled and cubed
1 lb. leeks, trimmed and finely
  chopped
4½ cups water

2½ cups skim milk
¾ tsp. Mrs. Dash seasoning
Salt and pepper to taste
1 cup nonfat sour cream

Combine all ingredients except sour cream in soup pot; bring to a boil over high heat. Reduce heat to low and cook, covered, until potatoes are soft, 1 hour. Remove ½ to ¾ cup potato cubes from soup and set aside. Pour remaining soup into blender or food processor and process until smooth and creamy. Return to soup pot; add potato cubes and cook over low heat until heated through. Serve with sour cream. Soup can be served hot or cold.

Shopping List:

PRODUCE	DAIRY	SPICES
1 lb. potatoes	8 oz. nonfat sour cream	Mrs. Dash seasoning
1 lb. leeks	20 oz. skim milk	Salt
		Pepper

NUTRITION PER SERVING Calories 179 • Fat .5 g • Carbohydrates 35 g •
Protein 9 g • Cholesterol 2 mg • Dietary Fiber 3 g • Sodium 98 mg
EXCHANGES 1½ starch • 2 vegetable
CARB CHOICES 2

Potatoes are the most popular vegetable among Americans, with head lettuce and onions following in second and third place.

SOUPS AND STEWS
FOR ALL SEASONS

Pumpkin-Cider Soup

• Serves: 6

2 tbsp. nonfat chicken broth
1 cup chopped onion
15-oz. can pumpkin
1 cup water
2 cups apple cider
¼ cup packed brown sugar
¼ tsp. cinnamon

⅛ tsp. nutmeg
1 large apple, peeled and chopped
¼ tsp. pepper
6 tbsp. nonfat sour cream (optional)
Chopped chives, for garnish
   (optional)

Spray large soup pot or Dutch oven with cooking spray. Add broth and heat over medium-high heat; add onion and cook until softened and transparent. Add remaining ingredients except sour cream and chives, if using; cook over medium-high heat, stirring constantly, and bring to a boil. Reduce heat to low, cover and simmer 1 hour, stirring occasionally. Remove from heat and cool slightly. Blend soup in several batches in blender until smooth and creamy. Return to soup pot and heat 5 to 6 minutes over medium heat. Serve with nonfat sour cream and chopped chives, if desired.

Shopping List:

PRODUCE	DAIRY	Nonfat chicken broth
1 large onion	Nonfat sour cream	Brown sugar
1 large apple	(optional)	
Chives (optional)		SPICES
	PACKAGED/CANNED	Ground cinnamon
	15-oz. can pumpkin	Ground nutmeg
	16 oz. apple cider	Pepper

NUTRITION PER SERVING Calories 129 • Fat .4 g • Carbohydrates 24 g • Protein 2 g • Cholesterol 0 mg • Dietary Fiber 2 g • Sodium 33 mg
EXCHANGES 2 fruit
CARB CHOICES 2

The largest pumpkin ever grown and recorded weighed in at 1,061 pounds—
that would pack a lot of pies!

Southwest Chicken Stew

Prep—Cook—Refrigerate or Freeze

1 tbsp. nonfat chicken broth
1 cup chopped onion
1 tsp. minced garlic
1½ tsp. chili powder
½ tsp. ground cumin
⅛ tsp. cayenne pepper
15-oz. can red kidney beans, drained
15-oz. can black beans, drained

15-oz. can Mexican-style stewed
  tomatoes
11-oz. can corn kernels, drained
4-oz. can chopped green chiles
4½ cups cubed, cooked low-fat
  chicken
3 tbsp. chopped fresh cilantro
Pepper to taste

Spray large nonstick skillet with cooking spray. Add chicken broth and heat over medium-high heat. Add onion, garlic, chili powder, cumin and cayenne pepper to skillet and cook, stirring frequently, until onion is transparent and soft, 3 to 5 minutes. Add kidney beans, black beans, tomatoes with juice, corn and chiles. Bring to a boil over high heat. Reduce heat to medium and cook, stirring occasionally, until mixture becomes thick, 10 to 15 minutes. Add chicken, cilantro and pepper; heat through. Serve immediately or refrigerate up to 3 days. Stew can be frozen and reheated after thawing.

Shopping List:

PRODUCE	CANNED	4-oz. can chopped
1 large onion	15-oz. can red kidney	green chiles
Cilantro	beans	
Minced garlic	15-oz. can black beans	SPICES
	15-oz. can Mexican-	Chili powder
MEAT	style stewed	Ground cumin
4 (6-oz.) pkgs. cooked	tomatoes	Cayenne pepper
chicken breast cuts	11-oz. can corn kernels	Pepper

SOUPS AND STEWS FOR ALL SEASONS

NUTRITION PER SERVING Calories 320 • Fat 1.7 g • Carbohydrates 45 g • Protein 35 g • Cholesterol 49 mg • Dietary Fiber 4 g • Sodium 1,121 mg
EXCHANGES 4 very lean meat • 2 starch • 1 vegetable • 1 fat
CARB CHOICES 0

Beans are the ultimate healthy diet food, packing protein, fiber and at least six essential vitamins and minerals into a low-calorie, low-fat package.

Superfoods Vegetable Stew

Prep—Cook—Refrigerate   ✦ Serves: 8

3 tbsp. + 2 cups vegetable broth
2 sweet potatoes, cut into ½-inch
   cubes
1 large red onion, cut into thin
   wedges
¾ tsp. garlic powder
2 large red bell peppers, cut into
   ½-inch pieces
1 tsp. ground cumin
1 tsp. ground coriander

¾ tsp. Mrs. Dash seasoning
¼ tsp. pepper
2 (15½-oz.) cans chickpeas, drained
2 (14½-oz.) cans diced tomatoes
12-oz. pkg. fresh baby spinach
2 tbsp. cornstarch
2 tbsp. water
4 cups cooked rice or couscous
   (optional)

Spray Dutch oven with cooking spray; add 3 tablespoons vegetable broth to pan and heat over medium-high heat. Add sweet potatoes and onion to pan; sprinkle with garlic powder and cook, stirring frequently, until tender, 5 to 6 minutes. Add bell peppers, cumin, coriander, Mrs. Dash seasoning and pepper; cook, stirring frequently, until peppers are tender, 4 to 5 minutes. Stir in chickpeas, tomatoes, spinach and remaining vegetable broth. Bring to a boil over high heat; reduce heat to low, and simmer, uncovered, 12 to 15 minutes, until heated through. Combine cornstarch and water in a small cup; mix well. Gradually add cornstarch mixture to stew; bring to a boil over high heat. Cook over high heat, stirring constantly, until stew thickens, about 1 minute. Serve over cooked rice or couscous if desired. Do not freeze. Stew can be refrigerated and reheated up to 4 days.

Shopping List:

PRODUCE	PACKAGED/CANNED	Rice or couscous
2 large sweet potatoes	2 (14½-oz.) cans	(optional)
1 large red onion	vegetable broth	
2 large red bell peppers	2 (15½-oz.) cans	SPICES
12-oz. pkg. baby	chickpeas (garbanzo	Garlic powder
spinach	beans)	Ground cumin
	2 (14½-oz.) cans diced	Ground coriander
	tomatoes	Mrs. Dash seasoning
	Cornstarch	Pepper

NUTRITION PER SERVING Calories 194 • Fat 2.5 g • Carbohydrates 37 g • Protein 9 g • Cholesterol 0 mg • Dietary Fiber 9 g • Sodium 880 mg
EXCHANGES 4 vegetable • 1 starch
CARB CHOICES 2

*Researchers have found that cumin seed works as an
immune-system booster.*

Sweet Onion Soup

Prep—Cook—Refrigerate or Freeze   • Serves: 8

7 (14½-oz.) cans nonfat beef broth
12 whole Vidalia onions, sliced
1 tsp. garlic powder
Pepper to taste
½ cup grated nonfat Parmesan cheese

Spray large nonstick skillet with cooking spray and heat over high heat.
Add 1 tablespoon beef broth to skillet to coat. Add one-third to one-half
of onions (do not crowd); sprinkle with some of the garlic powder. Cook
over high heat, stirring frequently until onions are golden, 5 to 7 minutes.
Transfer onions to large bowl and repeat cooking with remaining onions,
adding broth as needed to keep onions moist. Remove 1 to 2 cups cooked
onions from bowl and set aside. Place remaining onions in large soup pot.
Add remaining beef broth to pot and bring to a boil over high heat. Reduce
heat to low, cover and simmer 1 to 1½ hours. Pour soup into large glass
or metal bowl. In small batches, transfer soup to blender or food processor,
filling container about half full. Puree soup and pour back into soup pot.
Add reserved onions, season with pepper and cook over medium heat until
heated through, 10 to 15 minutes. Soup can be frozen at this point. Reheat
on stovetop or in microwave and sprinkle with Parmesan cheese before
serving.

Shopping List:

PRODUCE	PACKAGED/CANNED	SPICES
12 Vidalia or other sweet onions	7 (14½-oz.) cans nonfat beef broth Grated nonfat Parmesan cheese	Garlic powder Pepper

NUTRITION PER SERVING Calories 117 • Fat .6 g • Carbohydrates 24 g •
Protein 6 g • Cholesterol 0 mg • Dietary Fiber 4 g • Sodium 1,360 mg
EXCHANGES 5 vegetable
CARB CHOICES 2

*Sweet onions, including Vidalia, Maui and Walla-Walla, must contain at
least 6 percent sugar to be called "sweet."*

Tomato Soup

2 cups low-sodium tomato juice	1 tsp. onion powder
2 cups nonfat chicken broth	½ tsp. pepper
2 tsp. dried parsley	½ tsp. crumbled bay leaves
1½ tsp. celery flakes	¼ tsp. dried basil

Combine all ingredients in a large saucepan and bring to a boil over high heat. Reduce heat to low, cover and simmer 30 minutes. Cool to room temperature; refrigerate or freeze. Great with simple sandwiches or wraps.

Shopping List:

CANNED	SPICES
16 oz. low-sodium	Celery flakes
tomato juice	Dried parsley
15½-oz. can nonfat	Bay leaves
chicken broth	Dried basil
	Onion powder
	Pepper

NUTRITION PER SERVING Calories 34 • Fat .1 g • Carbohydrates 7 g • Protein 4 g • Cholesterol 0 mg • Dietary Fiber 2 g • Sodium 836 mg EXCHANGES 2 vegetable CARB CHOICES ½

According to British mythology, bay leaves had the power to ward off disease, witchcraft and lightning.

Vegetable Beef Stew

Prep — Cook — Refrigerate or Freeze ◆ Serves: 6

1½ lbs. Laura's extra-lean ground
  beef (see p. 124)
1 tsp. garlic powder
1½ cups chopped onions
2 (29-oz.) cans chopped tomatoes,
  undrained
10-oz. pkg. frozen baby carrots

2 (10-oz.) pkgs. frozen mixed
  vegetables of choice
16-oz. pkg. precooked, diced potatoes
½ tsp. crushed bay leaf
¼ tsp. celery seeds
Pepper to taste

Spray Dutch oven with cooking spray. Place ground beef in pan, breaking into small pieces; sprinkle with garlic powder. Add onions; cook over medium-high heat, stirring frequently, until meat is browned and onions are soft. Add tomatoes with juice, carrots, mixed vegetables, potatoes, bay leaf and celery seeds to meat mixture; bring to a boil over high heat. Reduce heat to low, cover and simmer until vegetables are tender, 30 to 40 minutes; season with pepper to taste. Stew can be refrigerated up to 3 days; if freezing, omit potatoes and add during reheating.

Shopping List:

PRODUCE	PACKAGED/CANNED	mixed vegetable of
16-oz. pkg. precooked,	2 (29-oz.) cans diced	choice
diced potatoes	tomatoes	
2 small onions		SPICES
	FROZEN	Garlic powder
MEAT	10-oz. pkg. baby or	Celery seeds
1½ lbs. Laura's extra-	crinkle-cut carrots	Bay leaf
lean ground beef	2 (10-oz.) pkgs. frozen	Pepper

NUTRITION PER SERVING Calories 340 • Fat 5.6 g • Carbohydrates 43 g • Protein 29 g • Cholesterol 61 mg • Dietary Fiber 10 g • Sodium 621 mg
EXCHANGES 3 vegetable • 2 starch • 2 very lean meat • 1 fat
CARB CHOICES 3

Laura's Lean Beef is the first red meat to be certified by the American Heart Association.

Vegetable Broth with Tomatoes

Prep—Cook—Refrigerate or Freeze   ◆ Serves: 8

1 tbsp. + 8 cups vegetable broth,
   divided
4 cups chopped onions
1 cup chopped carrots
¾ cup chopped celery
1½ tsp. garlic powder

2 (28-oz.) cans diced tomatoes with
   roasted garlic, undrained
¼ tsp. pepper
2 tsp. dried parsley
Cooked pasta, canned beans or
   cooked chicken (optional)

Spray large stockpot or Dutch oven with cooking spray; pour in 1 table-spoon vegetable broth and heat over medium-high heat. Add onions, carrots and celery; cook, stirring frequently, until lightly browned and tender, 10 to 12 minutes. Add remaining broth, garlic powder, tomatoes with juice and pepper; bring to a boil over high heat. Reduce heat to low and simmer, uncovered, 30 to 45 minutes; stir in parsley. Soup can be refrigerated or frozen. Add cooked pasta, canned beans or cooked chicken when reheating if desired. Thaw in refrigerator or microwave on low heat; bring to a boil, add desired ingredients, cook 15 to 20 minutes and serve.

Shopping List:

PRODUCE	CANNED	SPICES
2 lbs. onions	4 (15 ½-oz.) cans	Dried parsley
1 to 2 carrots	vegetable broth	Garlic powder
1 small bunch celery	2 (28-oz.) cans diced	Pepper
	tomatoes with	
	roasted garlic	

NUTRITION PER SERVING Calories 78 • Fat .4 g • Carbohydrates 17 g • Protein 3 g • Cholesterol 0 mg • Dietary Fiber 3 g • Sodium 1,733 mg EXCHANGES 3 vegetable
CARB CHOICES 1

Thanks to seventeenth-century Europeans, we have orange, not purple, carrots. Beta-carotene–rich orange carrots were developed during World War II to improve night vision of aviators.

Veggie-Packed Lentil Stew

Prep—Cook—Refrigerate or Freeze ♦ Serves: 8

2 (28-oz.) cans Italian-style stewed
   tomatoes
2 cups low-sodium tomato juice
16-oz. can kidney beans, drained
15-oz. can garbanzo beans, drained
4 medium carrots, thinly sliced
1 cup chopped onion
2 cups chopped bell pepper

1 cup lentils
2 tbsp. chili powder
1 tsp. dried basil
1 tsp. Italian seasoning
1½ tsp. garlic powder
1 tsp. ground cumin
Chopped chives, for garnish
   (optional)

Spray Dutch oven with cooking spray. Add all ingredients except chives; bring to a boil over high heat. Reduce heat to low, cover and simmer until lentils and vegetables are tender, 40 to 45 minutes. Sprinkle with chopped chives before serving, if desired. Stew can be refrigerated or frozen; reheat on stovetop or in microwave oven.

Shopping List:

PRODUCE
4 carrots
1 large onion
2 large bell peppers
Chives (optional)

PACKAGED/CANNED
2 (28-oz.) cans Italian-
   style stewed
   tomatoes

16 oz. low-sodium
   tomato juice
16-oz. can kidney beans
15-oz. can garbanzo
   beans
Lentils

SPICES
Chili powder
Dried basil

Garlic powder
Ground cumin
Italian seasoning

NUTRITION PER SERVING Calories 272 • Fat 2.4 g • Carbohydrates 51 g • Protein 16 g • Cholesterol 0 mg • Dietary Fiber 10 g • Sodium 762 mg
EXCHANGES 2 starch • 4 vegetable
CARB CHOICES 3

Garbanzo beans, an excellent source of magnesium, also contain digestive enzymes that help prevent the formation of cancer cells.

SIMPLE SIDES

Safe Food-Handling and Storage
- Wash fruits and vegetables with cool tap water before use. Thick-skinned produce may be scrubbed with a brush. Do not use soap.

To Freeze or Not to Freeze
- For best results, blanch fresh vegetables before freezing.
- Frozen vegetables can be refrozen if they still have ice crystals, but for best quality, use as soon as possible.
- Plain vegetables (without sauce) can be refrozen if not left at room temperature longer than 1 to 2 hours.
- Prepare large batches of rice; cool to room temperature. Divide rice into desired servings and package in plastic freezer bags. Freeze bags flat to save room. Remove as needed and thaw at room temperature for stir-fries, soups, side dishes or casseroles.

From Stovetop to Refrigerator or Freezer and Back Again
- Frozen vegetables can be cooked and refrozen separately or prepared as ingredients in a casserole or other dish and refrozen.

Shortcuts with the Same Results (in Less Time)
- Serve iceberg or romaine lettuce wedges instead of torn salad greens.
- Wash and core lettuce before refrigerating so it's ready to serve when needed.
- Microwave potatoes (9 to 12 minutes per potato) rather than baking, or microwave 5 to 6 minutes and bake 15 to 20 at 450°F.
- Cut baking time for potatoes: Let baking potato stand in boiling water for 15 minutes; finish baking for 30 minutes at 425 to 450°F.
- Use instant varieties of grains (rice, barley).
- Forget-about-it rice: Boil water, add rice, stir and turn off heat. Cover pan and leave on stovetop several hours.

Always Room for Improvement
- Extend the life of sweet onions (Vidalia, Walla-Walla, etc.) by wrapping in newspaper and storing in a cool, dark place.
- Do not store onions and potatoes together. Onions emit a gas that makes potatoes spoil faster.

- Keep potatoes from budding by placing an apple in the bag.
- Make mashed potatoes fluffier: Add a pinch of baking soda along with the other ingredients.
- Wrap celery in aluminum foil before refrigerating, and it will stay fresh for several weeks.
- To ripen a tomato fast: Put the tomato in a perforated bag or covered bowl with an apple. The apple releases ethylene gas that speeds up the ripening process.
- Do not wash vegetables before storing them; they will spoil faster.
- Do not cover the pot when cooking green vegetables; they will retain their bright green color.
- Keep cauliflower white while boiling, steaming or microwaving by adding ½ teaspoon sugar to the water.
- Use cooking water from boiled potatoes in place of milk for lighter and fluffier mashed potatoes. Drain potatoes; gradually add liquid and mash or whip until desired consistency.
- Keep salad greens crisper by:
  - Washing, drying and storing in salad spinner in the refrigerator.
  - Washing and drying in salad spinner; rolling in paper towels; dampening towels with water; sealing in plastic bags and refrigerating. Storing salad greens this way will keep them fresh for 5 to 7 days.

Everything Old Is New Again!
- Cooked vegetables: Add to soups, stews or salads.
- Baked potatoes:
  - Reheat leftover baked potatoes: Dip them in water and bake 20 minutes in a 350°F oven.
  - Cut leftover potatoes into ½-inch pieces, sprinkle with seasonings and spray lightly with cooking spray. Bake at 425°F 35 to 45 minutes, until crisp.
  - Cut leftover potato skins into strips, season as desired and spray with cooking spray. Bake skins at 400°F for 10 minutes, until crisp. Add shredded cheese or bacon bits, if desired.
  - Make hash browns: Cut potato into cubes, add chopped onions and cook in hot skillet.
  - Prepare mashed potatoes with skim milk and low-fat margarine, nonfat yogurt or broth.
- Mashed potatoes:
  - Form into patties and bake or "fry" in hot skillet until lightly browned and crisp.
  - Use to thicken soups and sauces.

- Rice: Serve cold in salad, make rice pudding or add to soups, stews or casseroles.
- Save leftover parsley stems, celery leaves, asparagus, broccoli stalks and other vegetable trimmings. Store in plastic freezer bags and freeze. Use for soups, stews and sauces.

Baked Beans

Prep—Chill—Bake   ◆ Serves: 8

16-oz. can black beans, drained
16-oz. can kidney beans, drained
1 cup barbecue sauce
2 tbsp. brown sugar

Spray shallow baking dish with cooking spray. Combine all ingredients in casserole and mix well. Cover and refrigerate until ready to serve or up to 3 days; bake at 350°F for 1½ hours. Beans can also be baked, chilled and reheated in microwave.

Shopping List:

PACKAGED/CANNED	CONDIMENTS
16-oz. can black beans	8-oz. barbecue sauce
16-oz. can kidney beans	
Brown sugar	

NUTRITION PER SERVING Calories 148 • Fat 1 g • Carbohydrates 28 g • Protein 8 g • Cholesterol 0 mg • Dietary Fiber 5 g • Sodium 694 mg
EXCHANGES 1½ starch • ½ other carb
CARB CHOICES 2

According to Bottom Line/Health, *a high-fiber diet can lower cholesterol just as effectively as cholesterol-lowering statin drugs.*

SIMPLE SIDES

Cheese Ravioli

Prep—Cook—Freeze   • Serves: 8

1½ cups nonfat ricotta cheese
½ cup grated nonfat Parmesan cheese
2 tsp. Italian seasoning
½ cup egg substitute
¾ tsp. garlic powder
¼ tsp. pepper

¼ tsp. ground nutmeg
64 wonton wrappers
3 cups nonfat tomato pasta sauce
¾ cup nonfat sour cream
⅓ cup chopped fresh basil

Combine ricotta cheese and Parmesan cheese in medium bowl; mix well. Stir in Italian seasoning, egg substitute, garlic powder, pepper and nutmeg. Mix until ingredients are completely blended. Lay 32 wonton wrappers on flat surface. Spoon 1 to 1½ tablespoons cheese mixture onto center of each wrapper. Brush edge of wrapper lightly with water and top with remaining wrappers. Press edges to seal. Bring 3 quarts water to a boil over high heat; drop ravioli into boiling water and cook 4 to 5 minutes. Remove ravioli with slotted spoon and place in shallow dish sprayed with cooking spray.

Pour pasta sauce into medium saucepan; bring to a boil over medium-high heat. Reduce heat to low; gradually stir in sour cream, stirring constantly until mixture is blended. Add fresh basil and heat 2 to 3 minutes; do not boil. Pour sauce over cooked ravioli and serve. Ravioli can be prepared and frozen in plastic freezer bags for 3 to 4 weeks. Cook frozen ravioli in boiling water and top with sauce when ready to serve. For best results, do not freeze ravioli with sauce.

Shopping List:

PRODUCE	4 oz. egg substitute	SPICES
Fresh basil	6 oz. nonfat sour cream	Garlic powder
		Nutmeg
DAIRY		Pepper
12 oz. nonfat ricotta	PACKAGED	Italian seasoning
cheese	64 wonton wrappers	
Grated nonfat	24 oz. nonfat tomato	
Parmesan cheese	pasta sauce	

SIMPLE SIDES

NUTRITION PER SERVING Calories 263 • Fat 0 g • Carbohydrates 46 g • Protein 17 g • Cholesterol 8 mg • Dietary Fiber <1 g • Sodium 688 mg
EXCHANGES 1 very lean meat • 1½ starch • 1 other carb • 1 vegetable
CARB CHOICES 3

By simply substituting nonfat sour cream for regular, you'll save 187 calories and 24 grams fat per ½ cup serving.

Chicken Fried Rice

Prep — Cook — Refrigerate or Freeze   ◆ Serves: 6

2 tbsp. nonfat chicken broth
3 cups cooked brown rice
1½ cups cubed, cooked low-fat
    chicken

3 tbsp. low-sodium soy sauce
2 tsp. curry powder
¾ cup chopped green onions
¾ cup egg substitute

Spray large nonstick skillet or wok with cooking spray. Add chicken broth and heat over medium-high heat. Add cooked rice, chicken, soy sauce, curry powder and green onions to skillet and cook, stirring frequently, until ingredients are heated through. Pour egg substitute over rice mixture and cook, stirring frequently, until cooked through. Serve immediately or store fried rice in plastic freezer bags; reheat in microwave oven 1 to 2 minutes per serving when ready to serve.

Shopping List:

PRODUCE	MEAT	CONDIMENTS
1 bunch small green onions	6-oz. pkg. cooked chicken breast cuts	Low-sodium soy sauce
DAIRY	**PACKAGED/CANNED**	**SPICES**
6 oz. egg substitute	Nonfat chicken broth Brown rice	Curry powder

NUTRITION PER SERVING Calories 180 • Fat 2.4 g • Carbohydrates 24 g • Protein 15 g • Cholesterol 26 mg • Dietary Fiber <1 g • Sodium 226 mg
EXCHANGES 1½ starch • 2 very lean meat
CARB CHOICES 2

Grand savings: You save 152 calories, 11.2 grams of fat, and 101 milligrams cholesterol per serving compared to "regular" fried rice!

SIMPLE SIDES

Chile-Corn Muffins

Prep—Bake—Freeze   ◆ Serves: 12

1 cup all-purpose flour
¾ cup cornmeal
1 tsp. baking soda
½ tsp. baking powder
½ cup plain nonfat yogurt
½ cup skim milk
1½ tsp. lemon juice

½ cup egg substitute
2 tbsp. honey
1 cup shredded nonfat cheddar
  cheese
2 tbsp. chopped green chiles
¾ cup canned corn kernels, drained

Preheat oven to 350°F. Spray 12 muffin cups with cooking spray. Combine flour, cornmeal, baking soda and baking powder in large bowl; mix well. Combine yogurt, skim milk and lemon juice in medium bowl; mix until completely blended and let stand 5 to 8 minutes. Stir in egg substitute, honey, cheese, green chiles and corn; mix well. Add to flour mixture and mix until all ingredients are moistened. Fill muffin cups two-thirds full; bake 15 to 20 minutes, until toothpick inserted in center comes out clean. Cool to room temperature; muffins can be individually wrapped and stored in plastic freezer bag in freezer. Reheat directly from freezer in microwave on High 1 to 1½ minutes per muffin.

Shopping List:

DAIRY	PACKAGED/CANNED	BAKING
4 oz. nonfat plain yogurt	4-oz. can chopped	All-purpose flour
4 oz. skim milk	green chiles	Cornmeal
4 oz. shredded nonfat	6-oz. can whole corn	Baking soda
cheddar cheese	kernels	Baking powder
4 oz. egg substitute	Lemon juice	
	Honey	

NUTRITION PER SERVING Calories 113 • Fat .4 g • Carbohydrates 21 g • Protein 6 g • Cholesterol <1 mg • Dietary Fiber 2 g • Sodium 221 mg
EXCHANGES 1½ other carb
CARB CHOICES 1

Honey, nature's original sweetener, is a concentrated source of energy, one of the best sweeteners for battling fatigue, because the natural sugars are easily and readily absorbed by the body.

SIMPLE SIDES

Corn Cakes

4½ tbsp. all-purpose flour	2 tbsp. egg substitute
1½ cups cornmeal	¾ cup salsa
1½ tsp. baking powder	¾ cup canned corn kernels, drained
1 cup skim milk	3 tbsp. diced red bell pepper
2 large egg whites	

Combine all ingredients in large mixing bowl; mix until blended. Spray large nonstick skillet with cooking spray and heat over medium-high heat. Spoon batter by tablespoons into hot skillet and cook until bubbles appear on top; turn corn cakes over and cook until lightly browned. Wrap in freezer-safe wrap and store in plastic freezer bags. To reheat: Cook in microwave on High 30 to 45 seconds per cake and serve with additional salsa.

Shopping List:

PRODUCE	PACKAGED/CANNED
1 red bell pepper	8-oz. can corn kernels
	Salsa
DAIRY	All-purpose flour
8 oz. skim milk	Cornmeal
2 large eggs	Baking powder
Egg substitute	

NUTRITION PER SERVING Calories 170 • Fat 1.4 g • Carbohydrates 34 g • Protein 6 g • Cholesterol 1 mg • Dietary Fiber 5 g • Sodium 204 mg
EXCHANGES 1½ starch • 2 vegetable
CARB CHOICES 2

Although fiber values between white and yellow corn may differ slightly, all other nutrient values are equal.

SIMPLE SIDES

Creamy Coleslaw

Prep — Chill

3½ cups shredded cabbage
½ cup shredded apple
2 tbsp. cider vinegar

¼ cup apple juice
½ cup nonfat sour cream
Pepper to taste

Combine cabbage and apple in large bowl. Combine remaining ingredients in small bowl, blender or food processor and mix until blended. Toss cabbage mixture with dressing just before serving.

Shopping List:

PRODUCE	DAIRY	SPICES
1 small apple	4 oz. nonfat sour cream	Pepper
1 lb. cabbage		
	CONDIMENTS	BEVERAGES
	Cider vinegar	Apple juice

NUTRITION PER SERVING Calories 54 • Fat 0 g • Carbohydrates 11 g •
Protein 3 g • Cholesterol 0 mg • Dietary Fiber 2 g • Sodium 35 mg
EXCHANGES 1 vegetable • ½ fruit
CARB CHOICES 1

Did you know that an apple, onion and potato all have the same taste? The differences in flavor are caused by their smell. Pinch your nose, close your eyes, take a bite of each and see if you can tell the difference—they all taste sweet!

SIMPLE SIDES

Creole Mixed Salad Greens and Tomatoes

Prep—Chill

2 cups spinach leaves, stemmed and torn into bite-size pieces
2 cups watercress leaves, torn into bite-size pieces
2 cups chicory greens, torn into bite-size pieces

2 cups endive leaves, cut in half
¾ cup chopped red onion
½ cup chopped celery
2 cups cherry tomatoes, cut in half
1 cup nonfat French salad dressing

Combine greens, red onion, celery and tomatoes in large bowl and toss until mixed; cover with plastic wrap and refrigerate several hours. Just before serving, toss with French dressing.

Shopping List:

PRODUCE		CONDIMENTS
16-oz. pkg. fresh spinach leaves	1 head endive	Nonfat French salad
1 large bunch watercress leaves	1 red onion	dressing (select from
1 large bunch chicory	1 bunch celery	a variety of choices:
	1 pint cherry tomatoes	spicy, Catalina or other)

NUTRITION PER SERVING Calories 69 • Fat .4 g • Carbohydrates 15 g • Protein 2 g • Cholesterol 0 mg • Dietary Fiber 2 g • Sodium 272 mg
EXCHANGES 3 vegetable
CARB CHOICES 1

What exactly is Creole cooking? It's a combination of French and Spanish cuisines that takes on an entirely new and enticing flavor of its own.

192

Cucumbers 'n' Onions with Garlic Yogurt

Prep—Chill
✦ Serves: 6

3 large cucumbers, seeded and sliced
1 large red onion, thinly sliced
⅓ cup white wine vinegar
1½ tbsp. lemon juice
¾ tsp. garlic powder

½ tsp. dried basil
½ tsp. dried parsley
½ tsp. dried thyme
Pepper to taste
1 cup plain nonfat yogurt

Combine cucumbers and onion in medium bowl. Combine remaining ingredients in blender; puree until smooth and creamy. Pour mixture over cucumbers and onion; toss until coated. Cover and refrigerate several hours or overnight; toss before serving.

Shopping List:

PRODUCE	DAIRY	SPICES
3 large cucumbers	8 oz. nonfat plain yogurt	Garlic powder
1 large red onion		Dried basil
Lemon juice	CONDIMENTS	Dried parsley
	White wine vinegar	Dried thyme
		Pepper

NUTRITION PER SERVING Calories 54 • Fat .3 g • Carbohydrates 11 g • Protein 3 g • Cholesterol <1 mg • Dietary Fiber 2 g • Sodium 33 mg
EXCHANGES 2 vegetable
CARB CHOICES 1

Cucumbers are one of the oldest cultivated vegetables; they've been growing around human dwellings since at least 7750 B.C., coming originally from India and Burma to Europe.

SIMPLE SIDES

Holiday Cranberry Sauce

Prep—Cook—Chill   • Serves: 12

4 cups fresh cranberries, washed and drained
1½ cups port wine
2½ cups sugar
1½ tsp. ground cinnamon
1½ tsp. ground allspice

Combine all ingredients in large saucepan and cook, stirring frequently, over medium heat until berries pop. Cool to room temperature; pour mixture into airtight containers and refrigerate at least 3 days before serving. Cranberry sauce will keep several months in refrigerator.

Shopping List:

PRODUCE	SPICES
2 (12-oz.) pkgs. fresh cranberries	Ground cinnamon
	Ground allspice
PACKAGED	OTHER
1 lb. sugar	12 oz. port wine

NUTRITION PER SERVING Calories 214 • Fat 0 g • Carbohydrates 49 g • Protein 0 g • Cholesterol 0 mg • Dietary Fiber 0 g • Sodium 2 mg EXCHANGES 2½ fruit • ½ other carb CARB CHOICES 3

USDA researchers have found that a single spoonful of cinnamon (¼ to 1 teaspoon) helps the body metabolize sugar 20 times better.

SIMPLE SIDES

Honey Mustard Fries

Prep—Bake—Refrigerate or Freeze   • Serves: 8

6 medium potatoes, cut into wedges
1½ tbsp. garlic powder
½ cup nonfat garlic honey mustard salad dressing

Preheat oven to 450°F. Line baking sheet(s) with foil and spray with cook-ing spray. Arrange potato wedges on baking sheet(s) and sprinkle with garlic powder. Brush potatoes with salad dressing. Bake 20 to 25 minutes, until potatoes are cooked through. Turn broiler on high heat; broil potato wedges 3 to 5 minutes, until browned and crisp. Potatoes can be refriger-ated or frozen; reheat in 350°F oven when ready to serve.

Shopping List:

PRODUCE	CONDIMENTS	SPICES
6 medium potatoes	Nonfat garlic honey mustard salad dressing	Garlic powder

NUTRITION PER SERVING Calories 131 • Fat .1 g • Carbohydrates 30 g • Protein 3 g • Cholesterol 0 mg • Dietary Fiber 3 g • Sodium 71 mg
EXCHANGES 1½ starch • ½ other carb
CARB CHOICES 2

Democritus, an ancient Greek philosopher, partially attributed his long life (109 years) to honey, a highly valued food with healing and restorative properties.

SIMPLE SIDES

Lemon-Pepper Asparagus Spears

Prep—Cook—Chill or Prep—Chill—Cook   • Serves: 6

1½ lbs. fresh or frozen asparagus
1 tbsp. lemon juice
3 tbsp. grated nonfat Parmesan cheese
¼ to ½ tsp. lemon pepper

Spray microwave-safe dish with cooking spray. Snap off ends of fresh asparagus and place in dish. Drizzle asparagus with lemon juice; sprinkle with
Parmesan cheese and lemon pepper. Cover with plastic wrap, leaving one
corner slightly opened. Microwave fresh asparagus on High 10 to 15
minutes, until crisp-tender. For best results, turn dish every 5 minutes
unless microwave has rotating dish. This dish can be prepared, refrigerated
and microwaved just before serving or microwaved, refrigerated and reheated in microwave 1 to 2 minutes until heated through. If using frozen
asparagus, do not assemble until ready to heat.

Shopping List:

PRODUCE	DAIRY	SPICES
1½ lbs. asparagus	Grated nonfat	Lemon pepper
Lemon juice	Parmesan cheese	

NUTRITION PER SERVING Calories 36 • Fat .3 g • Carbohydrates 6 g •
Protein 4 g • Cholesterol 0 mg • Dietary Fiber 1 g • Sodium 27 mg
EXCHANGES 1 vegetable
CARB CHOICES 0

*Asparagus is a good source of saponins, compounds associated with killing
cancer cells and lowering blood cholesterol levels.*

SIMPLE SIDES

196

Minted Baby Carrots

Prep—Cook—Chill   ♦ Serves: 4

4 cups baby carrots
2 tbsp. nonfat chicken broth
¼ cup fresh mint leaves, minced
1 tsp. ground ginger

Steam carrots in boiling water or microwave just until crisp-tender, 3 to 5 minutes. Remove carrots from heat (they can be refrigerated at this point). Prepare sauce: Combine broth, mint and ginger and mix well. Just before serving, reheat carrots 1 to 2 minutes in microwave on High. Heat sauce in microwave-safe cup 30 to 45 seconds. Drizzle sauce over carrots and serve. Recipe can also be fully prepared and refrigerated; reheat in microwave on High 1 to 3 minutes, until heated through.

Shopping List:

PRODUCE	CANNED	SPICES
1¼ to 1½ lb. baby carrots	Nonfat chicken broth	Ground ginger
Fresh mint		

NUTRITION PER SERVING Calories 57 • Fat .3 g • Carbohydrates 13 g • Protein 2 g • Cholesterol 0 mg • Dietary Fiber 6 g • Sodium 112 mg
EXCHANGES 2 vegetable
CARB CHOICES 1

Baby carrots are actually full-size carrots peeled and polished down to size; about 25 percent of California's fresh carrot crop is turned into "babies."

SIMPLE SIDES

Mixed Greens with Balsamic Vinaigrette

Prep—Chill   • Serves: 4

4 cups mixed salad greens	2 tbsp. sugar
1 cup grape tomatoes	½ cup chopped green onions
2 tbsp. orange juice	1 tsp. garlic powder
2 tsp. Dijon mustard	¼ cup dried parsley
½ cup balsamic vinegar	¼ tsp. pepper
½ cup nonfat chicken broth	

Combine mixed greens and tomatoes in large bowl. Cover and refrigerate. Combine remaining ingredients in blender and process until blended. Pour into sealed jar and refrigerate several hours or up to 2 weeks. Serve over mixed greens.

Shopping List:

PRODUCE	PACKAGED/CANNED	SPICES
¾ to 1 lb. mixed salad greens	Nonfat chicken broth	Garlic powder
1 cup grape tomatoes	Sugar	Dried parsley
1 small bunch green onions	Orange juice	Pepper
	CONDIMENTS	
	Dijon mustard	
	Balsamic vinegar	

NUTRITION PER SERVING Calories 111 • Fat 1.3 g • Carbohydrates 24 g • Protein 2 g • Cholesterol 0 mg • Dietary Fiber 1 g • Sodium 322 mg
EXCHANGES 3 vegetable • ½ other carb
CARB CHOICES 2

To keep baby greens fresher longer, sort, wash and dry them. Wrap in paper towels and place them in a resealable plastic bag in the refrigerator.

SIMPLE SIDES

Not-Just-for-Breakfast Hash Browns

Prep—Chill—Bake or Prep—Bake—Freeze ◆ Serves: 4

16-oz. pkg. precooked, diced potatoes with rosemary and garlic
1 cup chopped onion
1½ tsp. Mrs. Dash seasoning
1½ tsp. dried parsley

Line baking sheet with foil; spray with cooking spray. Spread potatoes and onion across baking sheet; sprinkle with Mrs. Dash seasoning and parsley. Cover and refrigerate until ready to serve (up to 1 day ahead). Preheat oven to 450°F. Bake potatoes and onions 20 to 25 minutes, until browned and crisp. For best results, toss potatoes and onion several times while baking.

Shopping List:

PRODUCE	SPICES
16-oz. pkg. precooked, diced potatoes with rosemary and garlic or plain precooked, diced potatoes	Mrs. Dash seasoning Dried parsley

NUTRITION PER SERVING Calories 113 • Fat .2 g • Carbohydrates 26 g • Protein 2 g • Cholesterol 0 mg • Dietary Fiber 2 g • Sodium 7 mg
EXCHANGES 1½ starch
CARB CHOICES 2

Onions have been touted as protectors against disease due to their association with fighting cancer, building bone, reducing asthmatic symptoms and preventing heart disease.

SIMPLE SIDES

Parmesan Potato Crisps

Prep—Bake—Refrigerate   ◆ Serves: 6

1 cup cornflake crumbs
½ cup grated nonfat Parmesan cheese
1½ tsp. Mrs. Dash seasoning
½ tsp. garlic powder
¾ cup egg substitute

3 medium baking potatoes, sliced
½-inch thick
3 medium sweet potatoes, sliced
½-inch thick

Preheat oven to 400°F. Line baking sheet(s) with foil and coat with cooking
spray. Combine cornflake crumbs, Parmesan cheese, Mrs. Dash seasoning
and garlic powder in plastic bag; shake until mixed and pour onto paper
plate. Dip potato slices in egg substitute; roll in crumb mixture. Arrange
potato slices in single layer on baking sheet(s); spray lightly with cooking
spray. Bake 20 minutes; turn potatoes and bake 15 to 20 minutes, until
lightly browned and crisp. Serve with nonfat ranch salad dressing, ketchup
or barbecue sauce. Potatoes can be refrigerated and reheated in 350°F oven
10 to 12 minutes.

Shopping List:

PRODUCE	DAIRY	PACKAGED
3 medium baking potatoes	6 oz. egg substitute	21-oz. pkg. cornflake crumbs
3 medium sweet potatoes	Grated nonfat Parmesan cheese	
		SPICES
		Mrs. Dash seasoning
		Garlic powder

NUTRITION PER SERVING Calories 218 • Fat .1 g • Carbohydrates 45 g •
Protein 9 g • Cholesterol • 0 mg • Dietary Fiber 4 g • Sodium 270 mg
EXCHANGES 3 starch
CARB CHOICES 3

As reported in Bottom Line/Health *(March 2002), food cravings vary by
gender. About 25 percent of women have cravings, but only 13 percent of
men do. Women experience cravings when depressed or bored, while men
tend to get them when they're happy.*

Perfect Picnic Salad

2 large cucumbers, peeled and thinly
sliced
1 large red bell pepper, thinly sliced
1 large Vidalia onion, peeled and
thinly sliced

1 cup water
½ cup white wine vinegar
⅓ cup sugar
½ tsp. celery seeds
½ tsp. mustard seeds

Combine cucumbers, bell pepper and onion in large bowl. Combine remaining ingredients in small saucepan; cook, stirring constantly, until sugar is dissolved. Pour mixture over vegetables; toss until coated. Cover and refrigerate up to 3 days.

Shopping List:

PRODUCE	PACKAGED	SPICES
2 large cucumbers	Sugar	Celery seeds
1 large red bell pepper		Mustard seeds
1 large Vidalia onion	CONDIMENTS	
	White wine vinegar	

NUTRITION PER SERVING Calories 126 • Fat .6 g • Carbohydrates 31 g • Protein 2 g • Cholesterol 0 mg • Dietary Fiber 4 g • Sodium 8 mg
EXCHANGES 3 vegetable • 1 other carb
CARB CHOICES 2

Vinegar has been rated as one of the most versatile condiments. From Hippocrates, who recommended vinegar and honey to ease breathing to hand-washing in the tenth century and wound disinfectant during World War I, vinegar is an excellent low-calorie flavor enhancer.

SIMPLE SIDES

Popeye's Barley

Prep—Cook—Refrigerate or Freeze   • Serves: 4

1¼ cups nonfat chicken broth
1¼ cups water
1 tsp. onion powder
½ tsp. garlic powder

10-oz. pkg. frozen chopped spinach,
   partially thawed
¾ cup barley

Combine all ingredients in medium saucepan; bring to a boil over medium-high heat, stirring occasionally. Reduce heat to low, cover and simmer 40 to 45 minutes, until liquid is absorbed. Barley can be covered and refrigerated; reheat in microwave. If mixture is too dry, add a little chicken broth to moisten before heating. Barley can also be cooked and frozen; thaw in refrigerator or microwave, heat and serve.

Shopping List:

PACKAGED/CANNED	SPICES	FROZEN
14½-oz. nonfat chicken broth	Onion powder	10-oz. pkg. frozen chopped spinach
Barley (not instant)	Garlic powder	

NUTRITION PER SERVING Calories 167 • Fat 1 g • Carbohydrates 34 g • Protein 8 g • Cholesterol 0 mg • Dietary Fiber 7 g • Sodium 307 mg
EXCHANGES 2 starch
CARB CHOICES 2

One-third cup cooked barley provides 3 grams beta-glucan, a fiber that helps reduce cholesterol levels.

SIMPLE SIDES

Ratatouille for Pizza, Pasta or Potatoes

Prep—Cook—Refrigerate or Freeze   ♦ Serves: 8

¼ cup vegetable broth
1½ cups chopped onions
1 tsp. minced garlic
1 large eggplant, cut into ½-inch
  cubes
2 medium zucchinis, sliced ¼-inch
  thick
1 medium yellow squash, sliced
  ¼-inch thick

2 large bell peppers, cut into thin
  strips
1 tbsp. sugar
1½ tbsp. Italian seasoning
28-oz. can diced tomatoes, undrained
¼ cup dried parsley
Pepper to taste

Spray large nonstick skillet with cooking spray; add vegetable broth and heat over medium-high heat. Add onions and garlic; cook, stirring occasionally, until softened, about 5 minutes. Stir in eggplant, zucchinis, yellow squash, bell peppers, sugar, Italian seasoning and tomatoes with juice. Bring to a boil over high heat; reduce heat to low, cover and simmer 25 to 30 minutes. Stir in parsley and pepper. Cool to room temperature and freeze in freezer-safe containers for up to 3 months. Ratatouille can be thawed in refrigerator overnight or in microwave on Low. Reheat in microwave or on stovetop over medium heat, stirring frequently.

Shopping List:

PRODUCE	PACKAGED/CANNED	SPICES
2 onions	Vegetable broth	Italian seasoning
1 large eggplant	28-oz. can diced	Dried parsley
2 medium zucchinis	tomatoes	Pepper
1 medium yellow	Sugar	
squash		
2 large bell peppers		
Minced garlic		

NUTRITION PER SERVING Calories 67 • Fat .7 g • Carbohydrates 15 g • Protein 3 g • Cholesterol 0 mg • Dietary Fiber 3 g • Sodium 191 mg
EXCHANGES 3 vegetable
CARB CHOICES 1

Ratatouille can be served hot or cold. It can be served as a side dish or as topping for cooked pasta or baked potatoes, or baked on a premade pizza crust for 12 to 15 minutes in 400°F oven.

SIMPLE SIDES

Red, White and Green Veggie Ensemble

Prep—Cook—Refrigerate ◆ Serves: 8

2 tbsp. nonfat chicken broth
2 tbsp. chopped green onions
2 small onions, cut into chunks
4 cups celery, cut into 1-inch pieces
1 tsp. garlic powder
28-oz. can stewed tomatoes, undrained
2 (6-oz.) cans tomato paste
1 cup water

¼ tsp. pepper
½ tsp. Mrs. Dash seasoning
1 tsp. sugar
¾ tsp. Italian seasoning
1½ tsp. dried parsley
2 large bell peppers, cut into chunks
4 small zucchinis, cut into ¾-inch slices
2 cups mushrooms, cut in half

Spray Dutch oven with cooking spray; add broth to pan and heat over medium-high heat. Add green onions, onion chunks and celery to pan; sprinkle with garlic powder, toss to coat and cook over medium heat, stirring frequently, until onions are transparent and celery is tender. Combine tomatoes, tomato paste, water, pepper, Mrs. Dash seasoning, sugar, Italian seasoning and parsley in medium bowl; stir until ingredients are blended. Pour tomato mixture over vegetables and bring to a boil over high heat. Reduce heat to low, cover and simmer 12 to 15 minutes. Add bell peppers, zucchinis and mushrooms; cover and simmer 15 to 20 minutes. Vegetable mixture can be stored in refrigerator 2 to 3 days and reheated on stovetop over low temperature until heated through, 15 to 20 minutes.

Shopping List:

PRODUCE	PACKAGED/CANNED	SPICES
1 lb. mushrooms	Nonfat chicken broth	Italian seasoning
2 large bell peppers	28-oz. can stewed	Dried parsley
2 small onions	tomatoes	Mrs. Dash seasoning
1 large bunch celery	2 (6-oz.) cans tomato	Pepper
4 small zucchinis	paste	Garlic powder
1 bunch small green	Sugar	
onions		

NUTRITION PER SERVING Calories 116 • Fat 1 g • Carbohydrates 26 g • Protein 5 g • Cholesterol 0 mg • Dietary Fiber 6 g • Sodium 752 mg
EXCHANGES 5 vegetable
CARB CHOICES 2

Zucchini supplies 2 grams fiber per serving, 10 percent of the recommended daily allowance, which may contribute to lowering blood pressure.

SIMPLE SIDES

Red Potato Salad with Chicken

Prep—Cook—Refrigerate   • Serves: 6

3 cups diced red potatoes
½ cup nonfat sour cream
¼ cup nonfat mayonnaise
1½ tsp. cider vinegar
1 tsp. Dijon mustard
2 tbsp. sweet pickle relish
1 tsp. dried parsley

¾ cup chopped celery
½ cup chopped green onions
Celery seeds to taste
Pepper to taste
1½ cups cubed, cooked low-fat
    chicken breast

Place diced potatoes in saucepan; cover with water. Bring water to a boil; reduce heat to low, cover and simmer just until potatoes are tender, 4 to 5 minutes. Drain and cool. Combine sour cream, mayonnaise, vinegar, mustard and pickle relish in medium bowl; mix well. Add remaining ingredients and potatoes; toss carefully until ingredients are well mixed. Cover and refrigerate at least several hours before serving. Store in refrigerator up to 1 week.

Shopping List:

PRODUCE	MEAT	Cider vinegar
1½ lbs. red potatoes	6-oz. pkg. cooked	Sweet pickle relish
1 bunch celery	chicken breast cuts	
1 bunch green onions		SPICES
	CONDIMENTS	Dried parsley
DAIRY	Nonfat mayonnaise	Celery seeds
4 oz. nonfat sour cream	Dijon mustard	Pepper

NUTRITION PER SERVING Calories 196 • Fat 1.7 g • Carbohydrates 31 g • Protein 13 g • Cholesterol 26 mg • Dietary Fiber 3 g • Sodium 176 mg EXCHANGES 1½ starch • 1 vegetable • 1 very lean meat CARB CHOICES 2

Did you know that about 27 billion potatoes are grown each year in Idaho?

SIMPLE SIDES

Roasted Red Potatoes

Prep—Bake—Refrigerate or Prep—Chill—Bake   ◆ Serves: 8

Olive oil cooking spray
2 lbs. red potatoes
1 tbsp. Mrs. Dash seasoning
1 tbsp. sugar
2 tsp. pepper

Line baking sheet or roasting pan with foil and spray with olive oil cooking spray. Wash potatoes and place on paper towel to drain but do not dry completely. Combine Mrs. Dash seasoning, sugar and pepper in large plastic bag and shake until blended. Add potatoes to plastic bag and shake until completely coated. Arrange on baking sheet or in roasting pan; spray lightly with cooking spray. Preheat oven to 400°F. Bake potatoes 45 to 60 minutes, until tender. Potatoes can be prepared, refrigerated and baked later or baked and reheated in microwave or oven.

Shopping List:

PRODUCE	SPICES
2 lbs. red potatoes	Mrs. Dash seasoning
	Pepper
PACKAGED	Olive oil cooking spray
Sugar	

NUTRITION PER SERVING Calories 118 • Fat 0 g • Carbohydrates 28 g • Protein 2 g • Cholesterol 0 mg • Dietary Fiber 0 g • Sodium 8 mg
EXCHANGES 2 starch
CARB CHOICES 0

Skip the fries—without the fat, you'd have to eat 11 pounds of potatoes to gain 1 pound—a potato has no more calories than an apple.

Romaine Salad with Honey-Vinegar Dressing

Prep—Chill • Serves: 6

⅜ cup honey
⅜ cup balsamic vinegar
Pepper to taste
1 lb. romaine lettuce, washed, dried
and separated

3 navel oranges, peeled and
segmented
3 tbsp. chopped walnuts

Combine honey, balsamic vinegar and pepper in blender; blend until creamy and smooth. Pour into covered container and refrigerate up to 1 week. When ready to serve: Arrange whole lettuce leaves on salad plates. Top each with orange segments (½ orange per plate), and sprinkle with chopped walnuts. Drizzle salad dressing over top and serve.

Shopping List:

PRODUCE	CONDIMENTS
1 lb. romaine lettuce	Honey
3 navel oranges	Balsamic vinegar
PACKAGED	SPICES
Chopped walnuts	Pepper

NUTRITION PER SERVING Calories 147 • Fat 2 g • Carbohydrates 30 g • Protein 3 g • Cholesterol 0 mg • Dietary Fiber 3 g • Sodium 10 mg
EXCHANGES 3 vegetable • 1 other carb
CARB CHOICES 2

Walnuts are rich in alpha-linolenic acid, an omega-3 fatty acid that has been shown to lower the risk of heart disease. They also contain ellagic acid, a compound that reduces the risk of heart disease by reducing the formation of artery-clogging plaque.

SIMPLE SIDES

Sandwich Sliced Pickles

Prep—Chill ◆ Serves: 24

1⅓ lbs. pickling cucumbers, sliced
2⅔ cups sliced onions
1⅓ tbsp. salt

⅓ to ½ cup water
1⅓ cups sugar
⅔ cup cider vinegar

Combine cucumbers, onions, salt and water in large bowl; let stand at room temperature 2 to 2½ hours. Add sugar and vinegar; stir until sugar is completely dissolved. Divide pickles among 3 to 4 (2-cup) containers, leaving 1-inch space on top. Tightly seal with lid and freeze up to 1 month. Thaw at room temperature 4 to 5 hours or overnight in refrigerator before serving.

Shopping List:

PRODUCE	PACKAGED	SPICES
1⅓ lbs. pickling cucumbers	Sugar	Salt
3 onions	**CONDIMENTS**	
	Cider vinegar	

NUTRITION PER SERVING Calories 49 • Fat 0 g • Carbohydrates 14 g • Protein <1 g • Cholesterol 0 mg • Dietary Fiber <1 g • Sodium 357 mg
EXCHANGES 2½ vegetable
CARB CHOICES 1

The USDA reports that the average American consumes 8½ pounds of pickles each year; dill pickles are twice as popular as sweet.

SIMPLE SIDES

Sweet and Spicy Green Beans

Prep—Chill

½ cup sugar
½ cup white wine vinegar
¼ tsp. crushed red pepper flakes

¼ tsp. garlic powder
1 lb. green beans, blanched
1 tbsp. slivered almonds

Combine sugar, vinegar, pepper flakes and garlic powder in a small bowl; mix until sugar is dissolved and ingredients are blended. Cover and refrigerate at least 4 hours or overnight. Combine green beans and dressing mixture 30 to 45 minutes before serving. Refrigerate at least 30 minutes before serving. Sprinkle with slivered almonds just before serving.

Shopping List:

PRODUCE	CONDIMENTS
1 lb. green beans	White wine vinegar
PACKAGED	**SPICES**
Sugar	Crushed red pepper
Slivered almonds	flakes
	Garlic powder

NUTRITION PER SERVING Calories 146 • Fat 1.3 g • Carbohydrates 35 g • Protein 3 g • Cholesterol 0 mg • Dietary Fiber 2 g • Sodium 5 mg
EXCHANGES 4 vegetable • 1 other carb
CARB CHOICES 2

Green beans are high in antioxidant vitamins A and C, contributing to healthy, clear skin.

SIMPLE SIDES

Sweet Car-tato Bake

Prep—Freeze—Bake or Prep—Bake—Refrigerate or Freeze   • Serves: 6

8 cups water
12-oz. pkg. frozen crinkle-cut carrot
  slices
3 medium sweet potatoes, peeled and
  cubed
¼ cup egg substitute

2 tbsp. nonfat sour cream
¾ tsp. onion powder
¼ tsp. pepper
⅔ cup shredded nonfat cheddar
  cheese

Pour water into Dutch oven; bring to a boil over high heat. Add carrots and potatoes to boiling water and cook 8 to 10 minutes until crisp-tender. Reduce heat to medium-high and cook, covered, until carrots and potatoes are softened. Drain well; mash carrots and potatoes until smooth. Stir in egg substitute, sour cream, onion powder and pepper; mix well. Stir in cheese and mix until blended. Transfer to casserole; dish can be covered, frozen and baked later (after complete thawing) or baked in preheated 350°F oven 40 to 45 minutes.

Shopping List:

PRODUCE	3 oz. shredded nonfat	FROZEN
3 sweet potatoes	cheddar cheese	12-oz. pkg. frozen
		crinkle-cut carrot
DAIRY	SPICES	slices
4 oz. egg substitute	Onion powder	
Nonfat sour cream	Pepper	

NUTRITION PER SERVING Calories 101 • Fat .6 g • Carbohydrates 18 g •
Protein 6 g • Cholesterol 1 mg • Dietary Fiber 3 g • Sodium 332 mg
EXCHANGES 1 starch • 1 vegetable
CARB CHOICES 1

Beta-carotene–rich sweet potatoes protect DNA in the cell nucleus from cancer-causing compounds.

SIMPLE SIDES

Twice-Baked Mini Red Potatoes

Prep—Chill—Bake   ◆ Serves: 8

2 lbs. red potatoes, washed and dried   ½ cup skim milk
¼ tsp. garlic powder   2 tsp. Butter Buds
1 tbsp. nonfat chicken broth
2 tbsp. chopped green onion plus
  extra for garnish

Preheat oven to 400°F. Pierce potatoes with fork; bake 30 to 45 minutes, until tender. Remove potatoes from oven and cool at room temperature 10 to 15 minutes. Line baking sheet with foil and spray with cooking spray. Cut potatoes in half; scoop out pulp and place in medium bowl. Add remaining ingredients; mash potatoes until mixture is smooth and ingredients are well mixed. Divide mixture among potato shells. Potatoes can be covered and refrigerated overnight if desired. When ready to serve: Preheat oven to 400°F. Bake potatoes 10 to 15 minutes, until lightly browned. Garnish with additional chopped green onions.

Shopping List:

PRODUCE	CANNED
1 bunch green onions	Nonfat chicken broth
2 lbs. red potatoes	
	SPICES
DAIRY	Butter Buds
4 oz. skim milk	Garlic powder

NUTRITION PER SERVING Calories 125 • Fat 0 g • Carbohydrates 28 g • Protein 4 g • Cholesterol 0 mg • Dietary Fiber .5 g • Sodium 23 mg
EXCHANGES 1¾ starch
CARB CHOICES 2

Research shows that eating a diet high in complex carbohydrates can help reduce symptoms of PMS, stress and depression.

SIMPLE SIDES

Wild Rice with Mushrooms

Prep—Cook—Refrigerate or Freeze ◆ Serves: 6

½ cup wild rice
1 cup brown rice
3¼ cups nonfat chicken broth,
  divided
1½ cups chopped onions

2 tsp. minced garlic
2 cups chopped mushrooms
2 cups diced red bell pepper
¼ cup low-sodium soy sauce

Combine wild rice, brown rice and 3 cups chicken broth in medium saucepan; bring to a boil over high heat. Reduce heat to low, cover and simmer until liquid is absorbed, 40 to 45 minutes. Spray nonstick skillet with cooking spray; add 1 to 2 tablespoons chicken broth to skillet and heat over medium-high heat. Add onions and garlic; cook, stirring frequently, until onions are softened. Add mushrooms and bell pepper; cook, stirring frequently, until vegetables are tender. Pour soy sauce over vegetables and mix well. Add vegetable mixture to rice and mix well. Spoon rice mixture into microwave-safe bowl; cover with plastic wrap and refrigerate until ready to serve. Allow rice to stand at room temperature 15 to 20 minutes before reheating. If mixture seems a bit dry, add a little chicken broth. Microwave on High 4 to 5 minutes, until heated through.

Shopping List:

PRODUCE	PACKAGED/CANNED	CONDIMENTS
2 onions	Wild rice	Low-sodium soy sauce
¾ to 1 lb. mushrooms	Brown rice	
2 red bell peppers	2 (14½-oz.) cans nonfat	
	chicken broth	SPICES
		Minced garlic

NUTRITION PER SERVING Calories 200 • Fat 1 g • Carbohydrates 42 g • Protein 7 g • Cholesterol 0 mg • Dietary Fiber 1 g • Sodium 873 mg EXCHANGES 2 starch • 2 vegetable CARB CHOICES 3

Red bell peppers are an excellent source of vitamin C and beta-carotene, as well as beta-cryptoxanthin, another antioxidant carotenoid.

FINISHING TOUCHES

Safe Food-Handling and Storage

- Thoroughly cool baked goods before freezing, or they will become soggy. For best results, place baked goods on wire cooling rack so air can circulate and promote faster cooling.
- Perishable baked goods (i.e., cheesecakes) should not be left at room temperature longer than 2 hours. Foods will complete cooling in the refrigerator.
- Keep flour in the refrigerator or freezer. Use within 3 months of purchase and warm to room temperature before using.

To Freeze or Not to Freeze

- The lower the moisture level in baked goods, the more successfully they will freeze.
- Well-wrapped breads will maintain quality for 4 to 5 months when frozen.
- Cookies can be prepared, baked, cooled and packed with freezer or waxed paper between layers. Prepared cookie dough can be frozen, thawed and baked as directed.
- Muffins can be prepared, baked, cooled, packaged, frozen and re-heated in the oven (300°F for 20 minutes) or microwaved on High 1 minute.
- Store crumb and nut crust mixtures in plastic freezer bags or FoodSaver® bags in the freezer. Thaw and pat into pie pans as needed.
- Toast coconut and/or chopped nuts in a shallow baking pan (5 to 10 minutes at 350°F); cool and freeze in plastic bags.
- Frozen fruit: If used in a cooked dish (muffins, cakes, bread), frozen fruit can be used directly from freezer. For uncooked dishes, thaw frozen fruit at room temperature.
- Store yeast in the refrigerator or freezer. It will last longer than its use-by date; bring to room temperature before adding to dough ingredients.
- Store marshmallows in the freezer to preserve freshness. Thaw at room temperature.
- Freeze peeled or unpeeled ginger. Freezing releases the juices and makes it easier to crush.
- Foods that freeze well:
  - Unbaked pie crusts

- Unbaked fruit- and meat-filled pies
- Unfrosted cakes
- Butter cream (or other high-fat frosting) frosted cake
- Baked goods low in moisture (breads, rolls, cakes, cookies, pie crusts)
- Foods that *don't* freeze well:
  - Cream fillings
  - Cake frostings made with egg whites
  - Meringues
  - Custards
  - Unbaked biscuits or muffins
  - Seasonings: cloves, cinnamon, nutmeg, vanilla or other extracts, rosemary, basil, and dill

Freezing does *not* freshen baked goods. It can only maintain the quality the food had before freezing.

From Oven to Refrigerator or Freezer and Back Again

- Frozen unbaked goods can go directly from freezer to oven.
- Previously baked goods low in moisture content (breads, cakes, cookies) should be kept covered and thawed at room temperature.
- Previously baked goods that are higher in moisture content or contain eggs or dairy products (i.e., cheesecakes) should be thawed in the refrigerator.
- Required thawing time for baked goods:
  - Refrigerator: 12 to 24 hours
  - Room temperature: 1 to 2 hours
- Quick or yeast breads (coffee cake, fruit and/or nut breads): Prepare, bake, cool, package, freeze, thaw at room temperature in original wrapping. Slice fruit and nut breads while partially frozen to prevent crumbling. Suggested freezer time: 2 to 3 months or store up to 1 year in a FoodSaver® bag.
- Yeast breads (coffee cake, bread, sweet rolls): Prepare, bake, cool, package, freeze, thaw at room temperature in original wrap. To reheat, wrap in foil or place in foil-covered container and bake in preheated 300°F oven 15 to 20 minutes, 5 to 10 minutes for yeast rolls. Suggested freezer time: 3 to 6 months
- Cakes and cupcakes:
  - Slice cakes before freezing for faster defrosting.
  - Unfrosted cakes should be wrapped *before* freezing and thawed at room temperature in original wrapping.
  - Frosted cakes should be frozen *before* packaging to prevent wrapping

from sticking to frosting. Thaw frosted cakes unwrapped in the refrigerator.

• Suggested freezer time for all cakes: 2 to 3 months.

■ Cookies: Prepare, bake, cool, pack in sturdy container with freezer wrapping or waxed paper between layers. Fill in empty spaces with crumpled waxed paper; too much air in the container will diminish the quality of the food. Suggested freezer time: 3 to 6 months.

■ Pies: For best taste and quality, freeze pies *before* baking. Do not freeze custard or cream-filled pies.

■ Reheat previously baked goods or unbaked frozen foods in *preheated* oven; this prevents foods from overbrowning and/or drying out.

Shortcuts with the Same Results (in Less Time)

■ Quick thawing: Prevent condensation by thawing previously baked goods on wire cooling rack; air can circulate around the frozen food for even thawing.

■ Packaged cake, cookie, muffin and brownie mixes: For low-fat versions, use egg substitute instead of whole eggs and applesauce instead of oil.

■ Cut clean-up time:
   • Line pans with foil when preparing bar cookies. Once bars have cooled, you can lift the foil out and cut the bars.
   • Line cookie sheets, loaf pans and layer cake pans with waxed or parchment paper.

■ Eliminate sticky dried fruit mess: Freeze dried fruits before chopping them in a food processor.

■ If a recipe calls for sifting, combine all the dry ingredients in a bowl and stir with a wire whisk.

■ Quick and ready-to-serve: Scoop ice cream into paper-lined muffin pans and refreeze.

■ If you need eggs at room temperature but forgot to take them out of the refrigerator in time, you can place them in warm water for 10 minutes.

Always Room for Improvement

■ When baking cakes in glass dishes, reduce oven temperature 25°F.

■ Optimize juice output of citrus fruits: Bring them to room temperature and roll them under your palm against a hard surface before squeezing or microwave on High power for 10 seconds.

■ Eliminate a sticky mess: When measuring corn syrup, molasses or honey, dip the cup or spoon in hot water or spray with cooking spray before measuring.

- To easily unmold gelatin salads or desserts: Lightly spray mold with cooking spray before adding gelatin mixture.
- To help gelatin hold its shape when unmolded, add a teaspoon of white vinegar to the recipe.
- Add a pinch of baking powder to powdered sugar when preparing frosting to prevent it from hardening and cracking.
- For maximum flavor and best results, toast nuts before adding them to batter or other mixtures. Toasting nuts intensifies their flavor and adds crunch.
- Always beat eggs at room temperature for maximum volume.
- Never beat egg whites in an aluminum or plastic bowl.

Everything Old Is New Again!

- Restore honey that has crystallized by placing the jar in a bowl of boiling water or microwave without lid. To prevent crystallization, store honey in a cool, dry place.
- Give leftover fruit pies a "just-baked" taste by wrapping in foil and reheating 10 minutes at 350°F.

Selecting the Right Pan

Type of Pan	Pan Size	Batter Amount	Estimated Baking Time @350°F
Rectangular or square	8 × 8 × 1¼" deep	4 cups	30–35 minutes
	8 × 8 × 2" deep	6 cups	25–35 minutes
	9 × 9 × 1½" deep	8 cups	25–35 minutes
	9 × 9 × 2" deep	10 cups	25–35 minutes
	11¾ × 7½ × 1¾" deep	10 cups	25–30 minutes
	13 × 9 × 2" deep	12–14 cups	30–35 minutes
Jelly roll	15 × 10 × 1" deep	10 cups	25–30 minutes
Roaster	14 × 10½ × 2½" deep	12 cups	35–40 minutes
Round	8 × 1½" deep	4 cups	35–40 minutes
	9 × 1½" deep	6 cups	30–35 minutes

Type of Pan	Pan Size	Batter Amount
Pie plates	8 × 1¼" deep	3 cups filling level or 4–4½ cups filling mounded
	9 × ½" deep	4 cups level or 5–6 cups filling mounded
Loaf	7⅜ × 3⅝ × 2¼" deep	4 cups
	8½ × 4½ × 2½" deep	6 cups
	9 × 5 × 3" deep	8 cups
Bundt	7½ × 3"	6 cups
	9 × 3½" deep	9 cups
Angel food	9 × 3½" deep	12 cups
	10 × 4 " deep	18 cups
Fancy tube mold	9 × 3½" deep	12 cups
	10 × 4" deep	16 cups
Springform	8 × 3"	12 cups
	9 × 3"	16 cups
Ring molds	8½ × 2¼" mold	4½ cups
	9¼ × 2¾" mold	8 cups

Almond Biscotti

2¼ cups all-purpose flour
1¼ cups sugar
2 tsp. baking powder
½ cup egg substitute
2 large egg whites

1 tbsp. canola oil
¼ tsp. almond extract
2 tbsp. chopped almonds
Cinnamon-sugar, for topping

Preheat oven to 350°F. Line baking sheet with foil and spray with cooking spray. Combine flour, sugar and baking powder in large bowl; mix well. Combine egg substitute, egg whites, canola oil and almond extract in small bowl and beat until smooth and creamy. Gradually add egg mixture to flour mixture until completely blended. Fold in chopped almonds. Divide dough in half; shape each half into 8-inch-long log (about 1-inch thick × 2½ inches wide). Bake 30 to 35 minutes. Remove from oven and cool 10 to 15 minutes. Cut logs into ¾-inch slices and place cut side down on baking sheet. Sprinkle tops with cinnamon-sugar. Return to oven and bake 7 to 8 minutes; turn biscotti and bake 5 to 6 minutes, until lightly browned on both sides. Cool to room temperature and store in airtight container for up to 2 weeks or freeze in plastic freezer bags. Thaw at room temperature before serving.

Shopping List:

DAIRY	Baking powder
2 eggs	Canola oil
4 oz. egg substitute	Almond extract
	Ground cinnamon
BAKING	Chopped almonds
All-purpose flour	
Sugar	

NUTRITION PER SERVING Calories 140 • Fat 1.6 g • Carbohydrates 29 g • Protein 3 g • Cholesterol 0 mg • Dietary Fiber 1 g • Sodium 59 mg
EXCHANGES 2 other carbs
CARB CHOICES 2

One ounce almonds contains as much calcium as ¼ cup milk.

Banana Cream Pie

Prep—Chill

½ cup nonfat cream cheese, softened
1½ cups cold skim milk
2 (4-serving) pkgs. instant banana
  pudding mix
8-oz. container nonfat Cool Whip,
  thawed

1 banana, thinly sliced
9-inch low-fat graham cracker pie
  crust
1 cup sliced strawberries

Combine cream cheese and skim milk in large bowl; beat with electric mixer until creamy and smooth. Add pudding mix; beat until blended, 1 to 2 minutes. Fold in 1 cup Cool Whip and mix lightly. Arrange banana slices on crust. Spoon pudding mixture on top of banana slices; top with remaining Cool Whip. Cover carefully and refrigerate 4 to 5 hours or overnight. Just before serving, top with slices strawberries (or other berries of choice).

Shopping List:

PRODUCE	PACKAGED	FROZEN
1 banana	2 (4-serving) pkgs.	8-oz. container nonfat
½ pint strawberries	instant banana	Cool Whip or other
	pudding mix	frozen whipped
DAIRY		topping
12 oz. skim milk	**BAKING**	
4 oz. nonfat cream	9-inch low-fat graham	
cheese	cracker pie crust	

NUTRITION PER SERVING Calories 269 • Fat .8 g • Carbohydrates 60 g • Protein 6 g • Cholesterol <1 mg • Dietary Fiber 4 g • Sodium 284 mg
EXCHANGES 4 other carbs
CARB CHOICES 4

One banana supplies 20 percent of the recommended daily allowance for vitamin B₆, a vitamin that helps the body use proteins and fats.

FINISHING
TOUCHES

Cherry-Almond-Cheese Tart

Prep—Chill ◆ Serves: 8

8-oz. pkg. nonfat cream cheese,
  softened
⅓ cup powdered sugar
¼ tsp. vanilla extract
¼ tsp. almond extract

8-oz. container nonfat Cool Whip,
  thawed
9-inch low-fat graham cracker pie
  crust
1 cup light cherry pie filling

Combine cream cheese, powdered sugar, vanilla extract and almond extract in medium bowl; beat with electric mixer until creamy and smooth. Fold in whipped topping and mix lightly. Spoon mixture into prepared crust; cover and refrigerate at least 2 hours. Top with cherry pie filling; pie can be refrigerated overnight or served immediately.

Shopping List:

DAIRY	BAKING	9-inch low-fat graham
8-oz. pkg. nonfat cream cheese	20-oz. can light cherry pie filling	cracker pie crust
	Powdered sugar	FROZEN
	Vanilla extract	8-oz. container nonfat
	Almond extract	Cool Whip

NUTRITION PER SERVING Calories 156 • Fat .6 g • Carbohydrates 32 g • Protein 6 g • Cholesterol 0 mg • Dietary Fiber 2 g • Sodium 267 mg
EXCHANGES 2 other carb
CARB CHOICES 2

In the 1820s, the average American consumed about 10 pounds of sugar a year. Today, we eat about 420 pounds annually, the equivalent of eating 6 candy bars a day.

Berry Sorbet Pie

Prep—Freeze

• Serves: 8

2 cups vanilla or strawberry nonfat
  sorbet, softened
8-oz. container Cool Whip, divided
¾ cup frozen strawberries or
  raspberries, chopped

9-inch low-fat graham cracker pie
  crust
1¼ cups cold skim milk
2 (4-serving) pkgs. vanilla or banana
  instant pudding mix

Combine sorbet and ½ cup Cool Whip in medium bowl; fold in strawberries or raspberries and mix until completely blended. Spoon sorbet mixture into crust. Place in freezer 15 to 20 minutes, until hardened. Pour cold skim milk into large bowl; add pudding mix and beat vigorously with wire whisk until blended and smooth. Fold in ½ cup Cool Whip just until ingredients are mixed. Spoon pudding mixture over sorbet; cover and freeze overnight. Remove pie from freezer 10 to 15 minutes before serving. Serve with additional whipped topping, if desired.

Shopping List:

DAIRY	BAKING	1 pint nonfat sorbet
10 oz. skim milk	9-inch low-fat graham cracker pie crust	10-oz. pkg. frozen strawberries or raspberries
PACKAGED		
2 (4-serving) pkgs. vanilla or banana instant pudding mix	FROZEN 8-oz. container nonfat Cool Whip	

NUTRITION PER SERVING Calories 242 • Fat .7 g • Carbohydrates 57 g • Protein 6 g • Cholesterol <1 mg • Dietary Fiber 3 g • Sodium 315 mg
EXCHANGES 4 other carbs
CARB CHOICES 4

We all know milk does a body good—the question is, just how good? One glass of milk provides 30 percent of the RDA for calcium; 25 percent of the RDA for vitamin D; 20 percent of the RDA for riboflavin; 16 percent of the RDA for protein; 13 percent of the RDA for vitamin B$_{12}$ and 11 percent of the RDA for potassium.

FINISHING
TOUCHES

Chocolate-Chip Honey Cake

Prep—Bake—Freeze   ◆ Serves: 12

1 cup all-purpose flour	¾ cup egg substitute
1 cup whole-wheat flour	1 cup honey
1½ tbsp. baking powder	1 cup applesauce
½ tsp. baking soda	1 tsp. vanilla extract
1 tsp. ground cinnamon	½ cup miniature chocolate chips

Preheat oven to 350°F. Spray 2 (9 × 5-inch) loaf pans with cooking spray. Combine flours, baking powder, baking soda and cinnamon in large bowl; mix well. Combine egg substitute, honey, applesauce and vanilla extract in separate bowl; blend with electric mixer until creamy and smooth. Pour liquid mixture into flour mixture; blend well. Fold in chocolate chips. Divide batter among loaf pans; bake 50 to 60 minutes, until toothpick inserted in centers comes out clean. Cool 10 to 15 minutes; remove from loaf pans. Cool completely; wrap loaves in plastic wrap and aluminum foil. Place in plastic freezer bag. Thaw cakes at room temperature before serving.

Shopping List:

DAIRY	BAKING	Miniature chocolate
Egg substitute	All-purpose flour	chips
	Whole-wheat flour	
PACKAGED	Baking powder	SPICES
8 oz. applesauce	Baking soda	Ground cinnamon
8 oz. honey		Vanilla extract

NUTRITION PER SERVING Calories 242 • Fat 2 g • Carbohydrates 54 g • Protein 3 g • Cholesterol 0 mg • Dietary Fiber 2 g • Sodium 174 mg
EXCHANGES 4 other carbs
CARB CHOICES 4

Whole-wheat flour is a unmilled version of white flour, whole-wheat flour makes hearty pasta and deeply flavored breads. To convert a regular bread recipe into a whole-wheat recipe, substitute half of the white flour with whole-wheat flour.

Chocolate Marshmallow Crème Cake

Prep—Bake—Freeze   • Serves: 8

4 large egg whites	¾ cup flour
¼ cup egg substitute	⅓ cup unsweetened cocoa powder
2 tsp. vanilla extract	½ tsp. baking powder
¾ cup granulated sugar	½ tsp. baking soda
¼ cup packed brown sugar	Powdered sugar for topping
1½ cups marshmallow crème	

Preheat oven to 325°F. Spray 8-inch-square baking dish with cooking spray. Combine egg whites, egg substitute, vanilla extract, sugars and marshmallow crème in large bowl; mix with electric mixer until creamy and smooth. Combine flour, cocoa powder, baking powder and baking soda in plastic bag; shake until ingredients are blended. Pour flour mixture into sugar mixture; mix until smooth and creamy. Pour mixture into prepared baking dish; bake 25 to 30 minutes, until toothpick inserted in center comes out clean. Cool completely; sprinkle with powdered sugar and cut into squares. Cake can be frozen in pieces or whole; thaw at room temperature before serving.

Shopping List:

DAIRY	BAKING	
4 eggs or egg whites only	Vanilla extract	Baking powder
	All-purpose flour	Baking soda
Egg substitute	Unsweetened cocoa powder	7-oz. jar marshmallow crème
	Granulated sugar	Powdered sugar
	Brown sugar	

NUTRITION PER SERVING Calories 193 • Fat .5 g • Carbohydrates 45 g • Protein 4 g • Cholesterol 0 mg • Dietary Fiber <1 g • Sodium 119 mg
EXCHANGES 3 other carbs
CARB CHOICES 3

Egg whites, with no fat or cholesterol, are the purest form of protein.

Chocolate Cupcakes

Prep—Bake—Refrigerate or Freeze •Serves: 24

3 cups all-purpose flour
1 cup granulated sugar
¾ cup packed brown sugar
⅔ cup unsweetened cocoa powder
1½ tsp. baking powder
½ tsp. baking soda

1½ cups skim milk
¼ cup egg substitute
2 large egg whites
2 tsp. vanilla extract
Low-fat frosting or powdered sugar
  (optional)

Preheat oven to 350°F. Line 24 muffin cups with fluted paper liners or spray with cooking spray. Combine flour, sugars, cocoa powder, baking powder and baking soda in large bowl; mix until ingredients are blended. Add remaining ingredients and mix with electric mixer until creamy and smooth. Spoon batter into muffin cups, filling each two-thirds full. Bake 22 to 25 minutes, until toothpick inserted in centers come out clean. Remove cupcakes from pan and cool to room temperature. Freeze in individual-size plastic freezer bags; thaw at room temperature several hours before serving. After thawing, top with low-fat frosting or sprinkle with powdered sugar, if desired.

Shopping List:

DAIRY	BAKING	
12 oz. skim milk	Unsweetened cocoa	Brown sugar
Egg substitute	powder	Baking powder
2 large eggs	All-purpose flour	Baking soda
	Sugar	Vanilla extract

NUTRITION PER SERVING Calories 144 • Fat 1.3 g • Carbohydrates 28 g • Protein 5 g • Cholesterol <1 mg • Dietary Fiber <1 g • Sodium 58 mg
EXCHANGES 2 other carbs
CARB CHOICES 2

Cocoa powder provides the flavor and cancer-fighting flavonoids of regular chocolate, but 1 tablespoon has a mere 20 calories and ½ gram fat compared to 140 calories and 10 grams fat in 1 ounce semisweet chocolate.

Cinnamon Apple Strudel

Prep—Bake—Freeze   ◆ Serves: 8

½ cup dried apricots   ½ tsp. ground cinnamon
¼ cup dried dates   ¼ tsp. ground nutmeg
20-oz. can sliced apples, drained   8 sheets phyllo dough
½ cup corn syrup   Butter-flavored cooking spray
1 tbsp. lemon juice   Cinnamon-sugar mixture

Preheat oven to 350°F. Line baking sheet(s) with foil and spray with cooking spray. Combine apricots and dates in small saucepan; cover with water and cook over medium heat until fruits are softened, 10 to 15 minutes. Remove fruits from water and chop into small pieces. Combine dates, apricots, apples, corn syrup, lemon juice, cinnamon and nutmeg in medium bowl; mix well.

Keep phyllo dough moist by covering lightly with a damp (not wet) towel. Lay one sheet of phyllo dough on dry, flat surface; spray lightly with cooking spray. Top with another sheet of phyllo dough and brush lightly with water. Repeat the process with remaining phyllo sheets alternating with cooking spray and water. Spoon fruit mixture onto dough; leave a 1-inch border on the sides. Fold in sides and spray lightly with cooking spray to seal. Roll strudel from the bottom up and spray lightly to seal. Place strudel on baking sheet seam side down; brush top lightly with water and sprinkle with cinnamon-sugar mixture. Bake 30 to 35 minutes, until golden brown. Cool slightly before slicing into 1-inch pieces. Strudel can be frozen up to 6 months. Thaw at room temperature before serving.

Shopping List:

PRODUCE	Butter-flavored cooking	SPICES
Dried apricots	spray	Ground cinnamon
Dried dates	Cinnamon-sugar (or	Ground nutmeg
Lemon juice	sugar to make your	
	own)	FROZEN
BAKING		Phyllo dough
20-oz. can sliced apples		
Corn syrup		

NUTRITION PER SERVING Calories 173 • Fat 1 g • Carbohydrates 40 g • Protein 2 g • Cholesterol 0 mg • Dietary Fiber 2 g • Sodium 1 mg
EXCHANGES 3 other carbs
CARB CHOICES 3

Three apricots, naturally low in calories and fat, provide 55 percent of the daily value for vitamin A in the form of beta-carotene.

Cinnamon Bread Pudding

Prep—Bake—Refrigerate

◆ Serves: 4

2 cups day-old bread cubes
½ cup egg substitute
¼ cup granulated sugar
¼ cup packed brown sugar
1¾ cups evaporated skim milk

½ cup boiling water
1½ tsp. ground cinnamon
½ tsp. ground nutmeg
½ cup golden raisins
2 tsp. vanilla extract

Preheat oven to 350°F. Spray 1½-quart baking dish with cooking spray. Place bread cubes in dish. Combine egg substitute, sugars and evaporated skim milk in a medium bowl; mix well. Add boiling water, cinnamon, nutmeg, raisins and vanilla extract; mix until all ingredients are blended. Pour mixture over bread cubes. Bake 40 to 45 minutes. Bread pudding can be covered and refrigerated until ready to serve. Serve warm (heat in oven or microwave) or cold.

Shopping List:

DAIRY	5-oz. can evaporated	Ground cinnamon
Egg substitute	skim milk	Ground nutmeg
	6 oz. golden raisins	Vanilla extract
PACKAGED/CANNED		
Bread	BAKING	
12-oz. can evaporated	Sugar	
skim milk	Brown sugar	

NUTRITION PER SERVING Calories 291 • Fat 1.4 g • Carbohydrates 62 g • Protein 9 g • Cholesterol 2 mg • Dietary Fiber 1 g • Sodium 245 mg
EXCHANGES 4 other carbs
CARB CHOICES 4

According to USDA research, cinnamon helps to control blood sugar levels. Ground cinnamon stimulates the production of glucose-burning enzymes and boosts insulin's effectiveness.

Cranberry Oatmeal Cake

Prep—Bake—Refrigerate or Freeze   • Serves: 12

1 cup rolled oats	1 cup all-purpose flour
1¼ cups boiling water	1 cup packed brown sugar
½ cup applesauce	¾ tsp. baking soda
¼ cup skim milk	¼ tsp. baking powder
¼ tsp. lemon juice	1 tsp. ground cinnamon
4 large egg whites	¼ tsp. ground nutmeg
1 tsp. vanilla extract	¾ cup dried cranberries
1 cup granulated sugar	¾ cup nonfat Cool Whip
½ cup whole-wheat flour	3 to 6 tsp. cinnamon-sugar mixture

Preheat oven to 350°F. Spray 9-inch baking dish with cooking spray. Place oats in medium bowl; pour boiling water on top. Cover bowl and let stand until oats are softened, 20 minutes. Combine applesauce, skim milk, lemon juice, egg whites, vanilla extract and granulated sugar in large mixing bowl; beat with electric mixer until creamy and smooth. Combine flours, brown sugar, baking soda, baking powder, cinnamon and nutmeg in plastic bag; shake until ingredients are well mixed. Gradually add to applesauce mixture, stirring until ingredients are moistened and blended. Stir in oats and cranberries; mix lightly. Spoon batter into prepared baking dish and bake 40 to 50 minutes, until toothpick inserted in center comes out clean. Cool slightly before cutting into squares. Just before serving, top with 1 tablespoon whipped topping and sprinkle with ¼ to ½ teaspoon cinnamon-sugar mixture. Oatmeal cake can be cut in squares and frozen; thaw completely before serving. If freezing, add whipped topping and cinnamon-sugar mixture just before serving.

Shopping List:

DAIRY	BAKING	Ground nutmeg
Skim milk	All-purpose flour	Vanilla extract
4 large eggs	Whole-wheat flour	Rolled oats
	Sugar	
PACKAGED	Brown sugar	FROZEN
Dried cranberries	Baking soda	Nonfat Cool Whip
Lemon juice	Baking powder	
Applesauce	Ground cinnamon	

NUTRITION PER SERVING Calories 272 • Fat 1.1 g • Carbohydrates 62 g • Protein 5 g • Cholesterol <1 g • Dietary Fiber 3 g • Sodium 86 mg
EXCHANGES 4 other carbs
CARB CHOICES 4

During the fifteenth century, nutmeg was so rare that people traded 3 sheep for 1 pound mace, the thin outer covering of nutmeg.

Freezer Pineapple Pudding Mold

Prep—Freeze

◆ Serves: 8

3-oz. pkg. instant vanilla pudding mix
16-oz. can crushed pineapple in juice, undrained
4½ cups nonfat Cool Whip, thawed

Combine pudding mix and pineapple (with juice) in medium bowl; mix well. Fold in Cool Whip and mix until ingredients are blended. Pour mixture into freezer-safe mold; cover and freeze up to 3 months. When ready to serve: Place pudding mold in refrigerator at least 2 hours before serving. Remove from mold, slice and serve.

Shopping List:

PACKAGED/CANNED	FROZEN
3-oz. instant vanilla pudding mix	16-oz. container nonfat Cool Whip (or other frozen whipped topping)
16-oz. can crushed pineapple in juice	

NUTRITION PER SERVING Calories 137 • Fat 0 g • Carbohydrates 32 g • Protein 0 g • Cholesterol 0 mg • Dietary Fiber <1 g • Sodium 101 mg
EXCHANGES 2 other carbs
CARB CHOICES 2

The perfect dessert for company, pineapple is a symbol of hospitality.

Fresh Apricot Berry Crisp

Prep—Chill
• Serves: 8

8 to 10 apricots, peeled and pitted
2 cups blueberries
¼ cup + 1 tbsp. sugar
⅓ cup apricot nectar
½ cup + 2 tbsp. flour
1 tbsp. lemon juice
¼ cup rolled oats

1 tbsp. powdered sugar
2 tbsp. brown sugar
¾ tsp. ground cinnamon
2 tbsp. Butter Buds, reconstituted
Nonfat frozen yogurt or whipped
    topping (optional)

Preheat oven to 375°F. Spray 9-inch-square baking dish with cooking spray. In medium bowl, combine apricots, blueberries, ¼ cup sugar, apricot nectar, 2 tablespoons flour and lemon juice; mix well and spoon into baking dish. Wipe bowl with paper towel; combine remaining flour, 1 tablespoon sugar, oats, powdered sugar, brown sugar and cinnamon; toss until ingredients are mixed. Gradually sprinkle Butter Buds over mixture and toss with hands until mixture is crumbly. Sprinkle over fruit; bake 45 to 50 minutes, until lightly browned. Serve immediately or cool to room temperature and refrigerate until ready to serve. To reheat, place in ovenproof dish and bake 10 to 15 minutes in 350°F oven or microwave on high 1 to 2 minutes, until heated. If desired, serve with nonfat frozen yogurt or whipped topping.

Shopping List:

PRODUCE	BAKING	Butter Buds
8 to 10 apricots	All-purpose flour	Rolled oats
1 pt. blueberries	Sugar	
	Brown sugar	BEVERAGES
	Powdered sugar	Apricot nectar
	Ground cinnamon	Lemon juice

NUTRITION PER SERVING Calories 160 • Fat .8 g • Carbohydrates 37 g • Protein 3 g • Cholesterol 0 mg • Dietary Fiber 4 g • Sodium 8 mg
EXCHANGES 2 other carbs
CARB CHOICES 2

Apricots, rich in potassium, help balance sodium levels in the blood, lower blood pressure and reduce the risk of heart disease.

FINISHING TOUCHES

231

Fresh Berries and Pineapple with Papaya Dip

Prep—Chill   • Serves: 6

⅓ cup nonfat sour cream   ½ tsp. vanilla extract
⅓ cup vanilla nonfat yogurt   18 large strawberries with stems
½ cup diced papaya   2 cups cubed fresh pineapple

Combine sour cream, yogurt, papaya and vanilla extract in food processor or blender; process until smooth and creamy. Cover and refrigerate several hours before serving or store in refrigerator up to 3 days. Serve with strawberries and pineapple.

Shopping List:

PRODUCE	DAIRY
1 papaya	Nonfat sour cream
18 large strawberries with stems	Vanilla nonfat yogurt
1 fresh pineapple or pineapple cubes	BAKING
	Vanilla extract

NUTRITION PER SERVING Calories 69 • Fat .5 g • Carbohydrates 15 g • Protein 2 g • Cholesterol <1 mg • Dietary Fiber 2 g • Sodium 18 mg
EXCHANGES 1 fruit
CARB CHOICES 1

Nutrient-rich and fat-free papayas aid in digestion. One medium papaya boasts 250 percent of your daily allowance for vitamin C, 29 percent for folate and 16 percent for fiber.

Frosted Carrot Bars

Prep—Bake—Refrigerate or Freeze   • Makes 48 pieces

¾ cup egg substitute
2 large egg whites
1 cup granulated sugar
1 cup packed brown sugar
1¼ cups crushed pineapple in juice,
   undrained, divided
1 cup all-purpose flour
1 cup whole-wheat flour

2 tsp. baking soda
1 tbsp. ground cinnamon
3 cups shredded carrots
½ cup raisins
1 cup nonfat cream cheese, softened
2 tbsp. skim milk
5 cups powdered sugar
2 tbsp. vanilla extract

Preheat oven to 350°F. Spray 2 (9 × 13-inch) baking pans with cooking spray. Combine egg substitute, egg whites and sugars in large bowl; beat with electric mixer until creamy and fluffy. Add ½ cup crushed pineapple to egg mixture and mix well. Combine flours, baking soda and cinnamon in plastic bag; seal tightly and shake to mix ingredients. Gradually add flour mixture to egg mixture, alternating with remaining crushed pineapple; mix until ingredients are combined. Fold in carrots and raisins. Divide batter between baking pans; bake 25 to 30 minutes, until knife inserted in centers comes out clean. Cool completely. Combine cream cheese, skim milk, powdered sugar and vanilla extract in small bowl; mix with electric mixer until creamy and smooth. When carrot bars are completely cooled, spread frosting on top. Cover and refrigerate several hours. Cut into squares; wrap in freezer wrap and store in freezer up to 2 months. Thaw at room temperature before serving.

Shopping List:

PRODUCE
12-oz. pkg. shredded
  carrots or 1 lb.
  carrots

DAIRY
6 oz. egg substitute
2 large eggs

8-oz. pkg. nonfat cream
  cheese
Skim milk

PACKAGED CANNED
16-oz. crushed
  pineapple in juice
6-oz. pkg. raisins

BAKING
All-purpose flour
Whole-wheat flour
Sugar
Brown sugar
2-lb. pkg. powdered
  sugar
Baking soda
Ground cinnamon
Vanilla extract

NUTRITION PER SERVING Calories 108 • Fat .1 g • Carbohydrates 26 g •
Protein 2 g • Cholesterol 0 mg • Dietary Fiber 1 g • Sodium 80 mg
EXCHANGES 1½ other carb
CARB CHOICES 2

*One medium carrot provides more than 200 percent of your vitamin A
needs as beta-carotene, a powerful antioxidant.*

FINISHING TOUCHES

No-Cheat Chocolate Pie

Prep—Freeze

2 cups nonfat chocolate sorbet, softened
1½ cups nonfat Cool Whip, thawed
9-inch low-fat graham cracker crust

3 tbsp. nonfat chocolate syrup
1¼ cups cold skim milk
2 (4-serving-size) pkgs. instant chocolate pudding mix

Combine sorbet and 1 cup Cool Whip in large bowl; mix until creamy and smooth. Spoon into crust; freeze 15 to 20 minutes, until slightly hardened. Drizzle with chocolate syrup and freeze while preparing pudding layer. Pour cold skim milk into large bowl; add pudding mix and beat with wire whisk until smooth; stir in ½ cup Cool Whip and mix well. Carefully spoon pudding mixture over chocolate layer; cover and freeze 6 hours or overnight. Remove from freezer and let stand in refrigerator or at room temperature until softened, about 10 minutes. Slice and serve with whipped topping and a little drizzle of chocolate syrup, if desired.

Shopping List:

DAIRY	BAKING	FROZEN
10 oz. skim milk	9-inch low-fat graham cracker crust	1 pint nonfat chocolate sorbet
PACKAGED	Nonfat chocolate syrup	8-oz. container nonfat Cool Whip
2 (4-serving-size) pkgs. instant chocolate pudding		

NUTRITION PER SERVING Calories 258 • Fat .7 g • Carbohydrates 62 g • Protein 3 g • Cholesterol <1 mg • Dietary Fiber 2 g • Sodium 276 mg
EXCHANGES 4 other carbs
CARB CHOICES 4

Chocolate raises levels of the soothing brain chemical serotonin and releases mood-boosting endorphins into the blood.

Peanut Butter Brownie Sandwiches

Prep—Bake—Freeze   • Serves: 12

2 (18-oz.) pkgs. fat-free Krusteaz   1 tbsp. powdered sugar
  brownie mix   Nonfat vanilla frozen yogurt
2 tbsp. reduced-fat peanut butter   (optional)

Prepare brownies according to package directions (prepare both packages together in 9 × 13-inch baking dish). Cool to room temperature; cut brownies into 24 squares. Spread each square with ¼ to ½ teaspoon peanut butter, and top with another brownie square; sprinkle with powdered sugar. Wrap brownies individually in freezer wrap and store in plastic freezer bag. Defrost at room temperature before serving. For a peanut-butter-brownie sundae, top with nonfat vanilla frozen yogurt.

Shopping List:

PACKAGED	BAKING
Reduced fat peanut butter	2 pkgs. fat-free Krusteaz brownie mix
	Powdered sugar

NUTRITION PER SERVING Calories 322 • Fat 1.2 g • Carbohydrates 76 g • Protein 3 g • Cholesterol 0 mg • Dietary Fiber <1 g • Sodium 480 mg
EXCHANGES 5 other carbs
CARB CHOICES 5

Ever heard of arachibutyrophobia? It's a fear of peanut butter sticking to the roof of your mouth!

Piña-Colada Carrot Squares

Prep—Bake—Refrigerate or Freeze   • Serves: 12

2 cups all-purpose flour	½ cup packed brown sugar
1 tsp. baking soda	½ cup granulated sugar
½ tsp. baking powder	8-oz. can crushed pineapple in juice,
1½ tsp. ground cinnamon	undrained
½ tsp. ground ginger	¾ cup shredded carrots
¼ cup egg substitute	¼ cup flaked coconut
3 large egg whites	½ cup raisins
¾ tsp. vanilla extract	¼ cup slivered almonds

Preheat oven to 350°F. Spray 9 × 13-inch baking dish with cooking spray. Combine flour, baking soda, baking powder, cinnamon and ginger in medium bowl; mix well. Combine egg substitute, egg whites, vanilla extract and sugars in large bowl; beat with electric mixer until creamy and smooth. Stir in crushed pineapple, carrots and coconut; mix well. Gradually add flour mixture, mixing just until ingredients are moistened. Do not overmix. Fold in raisins and almonds. Spread batter in prepared baking dish; bake 25 to 30 minutes until toothpick inserted in center comes out clean. Cool 10 to 15 minutes before cutting into squares. Serve immediately, store in refrigerator up to 1 week or cut in squares and freeze. Thaw and eat at room temperature or heat in microwave 10 to 15 seconds, just until warm.

Shopping List:

PRODUCE	PACKAGED/CANNED	BAKING
1 to 2 large carrots	8-oz. can crushed	All-purpose flour
	pineapple in juice	Sugar
DAIRY	6-oz. pkg. raisins	Brown sugar
Egg substitute	Slivered almonds	Baking powder
3 large eggs	Flaked coconut	Baking soda
		Ground cinnamon
		Ground ginger
		Vanilla extract

NUTRITION PER SERVING Calories 202 • Fat 2.2 g • Carbohydrates 43 g • Protein 4 g • Cholesterol 0 mg • Dietary Fiber 2 g • Sodium 110 mg
EXCHANGES ½ fat • 3 other carbs
CARB CHOICES 3

Don't go nuts over nut nutrition! Almonds, Mother Nature's heart-protecting nut, provide fiber, zinc, magnesium and a healthy dose of vitamin E.

Royalty-Rich Cannoli Cream

Prep—Chill

15-oz. carton nonfat ricotta cheese
1 cup powdered sugar
½ tsp. orange extract

2 tbsp. miniature chocolate chips
1 cup sliced strawberries
Nonfat chocolate syrup, for topping
(optional)

Combine ricotta cheese and powdered sugar in medium bowl; beat with electric mixer until creamy and smooth. Stir in orange extract and mix well; fold in chocolate chips. Cover and refrigerate several hours before serving. Divide cream among 4 individual dessert dishes; top each with ¼ cup sliced strawberries and drizzle with chocolate syrup, if desired.

Shopping List:

PRODUCE	BAKING
½ pint strawberries	½ lb. powdered sugar
	Orange extract
DAIRY	Miniature chocolate
15-oz. carton nonfat	chips
ricotta cheese	Nonfat chocolate syrup

NUTRITION PER SERVING Calories 251 • Fat 1.4 g • Carbohydrates 48 g • Protein 16 g • Cholesterol 18 mg • Dietary Fiber 1 g • Sodium 239 mg
EXCHANGES 3 other carbs
CARB CHOICES 3

Enjoying a slice of your favorite dessert now and then might help you maintain healthy eating habits and discourage deprivation or overeating.

Strawberries with Cream Sauce

Prep—Chill   • Serves: 4

2 pints fresh strawberries with stems	1 tbsp. sugar
2 cups frozen strawberries	2 tsp. vanilla extract
1 cup vanilla nonfat yogurt	1 tbsp. orange juice

Wash fresh strawberries but keep whole with stems; dry well. Place frozen strawberries in food processor or blender and puree until smooth. Transfer to medium bowl; add remaining ingredients, except whole strawberries, and mix until blended. Cover and refrigerate until ready to serve. Just before serving, place sauce in small bowl and arrange whole strawberries around the dish.

Shopping List

PRODUCE	BAKING	FROZEN
2 pints strawberries	Sugar	16-oz. pkg. frozen
	Vanilla extract	strawberries
DAIRY		
8-oz. carton vanilla		BEVERAGES
nonfat yogurt		Orange juice

NUTRITION PER SERVING Calories 232 • Fat .7 g • Carbohydrates 56 g • Protein 4 g • Cholesterol 1 mg • Dietary Fiber 14 g • Sodium 40 mg
EXCHANGES 3 fruit • 1 other carb
CARB CHOICES 4

Strawberries, an excellent source of vitamin C, are incredible collagen boosters and promote healthy-looking skin.

Tantalizing Trifle Treat

Prep—Chill   • Serves: 12

1 angel food cake, torn into bite-size pieces
1½ cups nonfat custard-style yogurt
2 cups nonfat Cool Whip, thawed
2 cups sliced berries of choice
3 kiwifruit, peeled and sliced

Arrange half the cake pieces in a 2-quart glass serving bowl. Combine yo-gurt and Cool Whip in medium bowl; mix lightly. Spoon half the yogurt mixture over cake pieces; top with half the berries and kiwifruit. Repeat layering, ending with fruit on top. Cover and refrigerate at least 2 to 3 hours before serving. Serve with additional Cool Whip if desired.

Shopping List:

PRODUCE	on the bottom), fruit	FROZEN
1 pint berries of choice	flavor of choice	8-oz. container nonfat
3 kiwifruit		Cool Whip (or other
	BAKING	frozen whipped
DAIRY	Angel food cake or mix	topping)
12 oz. nonfat custard-	to prepare	
style yogurt (not fruit		

NUTRITION PER SERVING Calories 204 • Fat .3 g • Carbohydrates 44 g • Protein 6 g • Cholesterol <1 mg • Dietary Fiber 1 g • Sodium 163 mg
EXCHANGES 3 other carbs
CARB CHOICES 3

One kiwifruit contains more vitamin C than an orange; it is also a good source of potassium and vitamin E.

FINISHING
TOUCHES

Tropical Sorbet

Prep—Freeze

• Serves: 6

2 (16-oz.) pkgs. frozen tropical fruit mix
½ cup orange juice
1 tbsp. sugar

Thaw tropical fruit mix at room temperature until slightly defrosted, 5 to 10 minutes. Combine all ingredients in food processor or blender and process until smooth and creamy. Spoon mixture into plastic container; cover and freeze up to 2 days. Thaw slightly before serving; top with fresh fruit if desired.

Shopping List:

BAKING	BEVERAGES
Sugar	4 oz. orange juice

FROZEN
2 (16-oz.) pkgs. frozen
  tropical fruit mix

NUTRITION PER SERVING Calories 180 • Fat .3 g • Carbohydrates 45 g • Protein 3 g • Cholesterol 0 mg • Dietary Fiber 2 g • Sodium 5 mg
EXCHANGES 3 fruit
CARB CHOICES 3

Sleep better and boost your mood! About eight strawberries provide 20 percent of the RDA for the folic acid your body needs to produce serotonin, a neurotransmitter that may prevent insomnia and depression.

Vanilla Cupcakes

Prep—Bake—Freeze

• Serves: 24

2¼ cups all-purpose flour	¼ cup applesauce
1 cup sugar	¾ cup skim milk
½ cup powdered sugar	1½ tsp. vanilla extract
1 tbsp. baking powder	¾ cup egg substitute

Preheat oven to 350°F. Spray 24 muffin cups with cooking spray or line with fluted paper liners. In a large bowl, combine flour, sugars and baking powder; mix until ingredients are blended. Add applesauce, skim milk, vanilla extract and egg substitute to flour mixture; beat with electric mixer until smooth and creamy. Spoon batter into muffin cups, filling half to two-thirds full; bake 22 to 25 minutes, until toothpick inserted in centers comes out clean. Cool 10 minutes; remove from pan and cool completely. Cupcakes can be frozen at this point. Top cupcakes with low-fat frosting or powdered sugar, or decorate with a variety of sprinkles if desired, before or after freezing.

Shopping List:

DAIRY	BAKING
6 oz. skim milk	All-purpose flour
6 oz. egg substitute	Sugar
	Powdered sugar
PACKAGED	Vanilla extract
4 oz. applesauce	Baking powder

NUTRITION PER SERVING Calories 90 • Fat .1 g • Carbohydrates 20 g • Protein 2 g • Cholesterol <1 mg • Dietary Fiber <1 g • Sodium 55 mg
EXCHANGES 1 other carb
CARB CHOICE 1

Did you forget the powdered sugar? No problem. Blend ½ cup sugar with 1½ teaspoons cornstarch for a simple substitute for each ½ cup powdered sugar.

Walnut-Apple Cake

Prep—Bake—Refrigerate or Freeze   • Serves: 8

4 large Granny Smith apples, peeled,
   quartered and divided
½ tsp. lemon juice
1¼ cups granulated sugar, divided
1½ tsp. cinnamon, divided
1 cup all-purpose flour
½ tsp. baking powder

½ cup packed brown sugar
¼ cup egg substitute
2 large egg whites
¾ tsp. vanilla extract
⅓ cup cinnamon-flavored applesauce
¼ cup chopped walnuts
½ cup nonfat Cool Whip, thawed

Preheat oven to 325°F. Line 8- or 9-inch-square cake pan with parchment or waxed paper and spray with cooking spray. Slice 2 apples into thin slices and set aside in medium bowl. Sprinkle with lemon juice to prevent browning; add ¼ cup sugar and ½ teaspoon cinnamon to apples and mix lightly. Spread over bottom of cake pan. Place remaining apples in food processor, grate or shred apples into matchsticks. Combine flour, baking powder, baking soda, brown sugar and remaining 1 teaspoon cinnamon in large bowl and mix well. Combine egg substitute, egg whites, remaining 1 cup sugar, vanilla extract and applesauce in separate bowl and mix with electric mixer until creamy and smooth. Gradually add to flour mixture; stir in grated apples and walnuts. Spoon batter over apple slices; spread evenly. Bake cake 45 to 50 minutes, until knife inserted in center comes out clean. Cool cake 15 minutes; run knife around edge of pan and turn onto plate. Serve with Cool Whip. Cake can be prepared, baked and refrigerated or frozen for later use.

Shopping List:

PRODUCE	PACKAGED	Brown sugar
4 large Granny Smith apples	Cinnamon-flavored applesauce	Baking powder
Lemon juice	Chopped walnuts	Baking soda
		Ground cinnamon
		Vanilla extract
DAIRY	BAKING	
Egg substitute	All-purpose flour	FROZEN
2 large eggs	Sugar	Nonfat Cool Whip

NUTRITION PER SERVING Calories 286 • Fat 2.8 g • Carbohydrates 64 g • Protein 4 g • Cholesterol 0 mg • Dietary Fiber 3 g • Sodium 102 mg
EXCHANGES ½ fat • 4 other carbs
CARB CHOICES 4

Apples are a good source of thiamin (vitamin B_1), needed for healthy brain functioning.

Yogurt-Berry Dessert

Prep—Chill   • Serves: 6

.3-oz. pkg. sugar-free strawberry-
  flavored gelatin mix
1 cup boiling water
¾ cup cold water
½ cup vanilla nonfat yogurt

1 cup diced strawberries
6 tbsp. nonfat Cool Whip, thawed
6 whole strawberries, stemmed and
  hulled

Place gelatin mix in medium bowl; pour boiling water over top. Stir mixture until gelatin mix is completely dissolved. Add cold water; stir until mixed. Refrigerate gelatin mixture 1 hour, until it begins to thicken. Add yogurt and mix with electric mixer until fluffy; fold in strawberries. Divide gelatin mixture into individual serving dishes. Just before serving, top each dish with 1 tablespoon Cool Whip. Garnish with whole strawberry.

Shopping List:

PRODUCE	PACKAGED
1 to 1½ pints strawberries	.3-oz. pkg. sugar-free strawberry Jell-O
DAIRY	FROZEN
4 oz. vanilla nonfat yogurt	Nonfat Cool Whip

NUTRITION PER SERVING Calories 35 • Fat .2 g • Carbohydrates 6 g • Protein 2 g • Cholesterol <1 mg • Dietary Fiber 1 g • Sodium 53 mg
EXCHANGES ½ fruit
CARB CHOICES 0

Strawberries are a good source of pectin, a fiber that helps the body eliminate cholesterol, reducing the risk of coronary artery disease.

FINISHING
TOUCHES

MIX-AND-MATCH MENUS

BREAKFAST	LUNCH	DINNER
Cinnamon Whole-Wheat Pancakes with Chunky Applesauce (p. 41) ¾ cup calcium-fortified orange juice or 1 cup skim milk	Turkey Rollups (p. 59) ½ cup grapes	Honey Dijon Salmon (p. 109) Mushroom rice (from package) Lemon Pepper Asparagus Spears (p. 196)
Egg White Frittata (p. 44) ½ bagel with 1 tbsp. preserves ¾ cup calcium-fortified orange juice or 1 cup skim milk	Crustless Vegetable Quiche (p. 73) Tossed salad with mixed veggies and 2 tbsp. nonfat salad dressing	Barbecue Meat Loaf Muffins (p. 126) Honey Mustard Fries (p. 195) Cut-up fresh veggies
Smoothie made with ¾ cup fruit juice, 8 oz. nonfat yogurt, ½ banana and ¾ cup fresh or frozen fruit	Layered Taco Salad (p. 133)	Superfoods Vegetable Stew (p. 174) French, sourdough or Italian bread
Banana Bran Bread (p. 36) ½ cup scrambled egg substitute with 1 oz. nonfat cheese ¾ cup calcium-fortified orange juice or 1 cup skim milk	Baked Seafood Sandwich (p. 98) Sliced tomatoes drizzled with nonfat salad dressing or balsamic vinegar	Chick 'n' Artichoke Casserole (p. 128) ½ cup cooked rice, pasta or couscous Tossed salad with mixed veggies and 2 tbsp. nonfat salad dressing
Orange Almond Granola (p. 52) 8 oz. nonfat yogurt ¼ cantaloupe or honeydew melon	Chicken and Rice Soup (p. 155) Tossed salad with 2 tbsp. nonfat salad dressing Sourdough bread roll	Cajun Style Orange Roughy (p. 102) ½ cup cooked rice Creole Mixed Salad Greens (p. 192)
Cheese and egg white omelet made with 4 egg whites and 1 oz. nonfat cheese Not Just for Breakfast Hash Browns (p. 199) ¾ cup fruit juice	Bow Tie Chicken 'n' Bean Pasta Salad (p. 38) Apple	Chili 'n' Noodles (p. 129) Cornbread (p. 71)

BREAKFAST	LUNCH	DINNER
Peanut Butter 'n' Raisin Muffins (p. 53) Banana milkshake (¾ cup skim milk, ½ cup vanilla nonfat yogurt, 1 banana)	Pocket Full of Veggies (p. 54) 1 oz. nonfat or low-fat cheese ½ cup grapes	Cheese Ravioli (p. 187) Romaine Salad with Honey Vinegar Dressing (p. 207)
Sausage Egg Muffin (p. 56) Orange or fruit of choice 1 cup skim milk	Chicken and Broccoli Quiche Muffin (p. 40) Make-Ahead 'n' Marinate Garden Vegetable Salad (p. 48)	Baked-in-Bun Sloppy Joes (p. 125) Baked Beans (p. 186) ½ cup chunky-style applesauce
Freeze and Serve Oatmeal (p. 45) 2 tbsp. raisins ¾ cup calcium-fortified orange juice	Crab Pasta Salad (p. 104) 1 serving whole-wheat crackers or flatbread Melon slices (equivalent to ¼ melon)	Southwest Chicken Stew (p. 173) French bread or sourdough bread roll
Cranberry Scones (p. 42) 1 cup nonfat cottage cheese mixed with ½ cup pineapple tidbits	Spinach-Feta Stuffed Potato (p. 85) ½ cup red grapes	10-Minute Teriyaki Fish (p. 117) Wild Rice with Mushrooms (p. 212) Steamed broccoli
Whole-Wheat Raisin Bars (p. 60) 6 oz. nonfat yogurt (flavor of choice) Fresh fruit	Fruit 'n' Chicken Salad Stuffed Pita (p. 46) Baby carrots and celery sticks with nonfat ranch salad dressing	Cook It Later Lasagna (p. 70) Mixed Greens with Balsamic Vinaigrette (p. 198) Garlic bread (made with Butter Buds and garlic powder)
½ cup mini shredded wheat or high-fiber cereal of choice ½ cup skim milk ½ bagel with 1 tbsp. nonfat cream cheese 1 banana	Chunky Gazpacho (p. 160) 1 oz. baked tortilla chips with 1 oz. nonfat cheese	Turkey Enchiladas (p. 144) ½ cup canned nonfat refried beans
Yogurt parfait (8 oz. nonfat yogurt, 1 cup berries and 1 tbsp. granola or sliced almonds)	Dress It Up Caesar Salad (p. 43) with romaine lettuce; tomatoes; 3 oz. cooked chicken breast cuts, water-packed canned tuna or salmon Rye crisp crackers	Veggie Packed Lentil Stew (p. 179) Whole-wheat bread roll

| --- | --- | --- |
| Baked French Toast (p. 35)
2 tbsp. maple syrup
¾ cup fruit juice | Rice and Black Bean
Burritos (p. 80)
1 oz. baked tortilla chips
with salsa | Seafood Rice Casserole
(p. 115)
Tossed salad with mixed
veggies and 2 tbsp.
nonfat salad dressing |

SUBSTITUTION CHART

❖ ❖ ❖

FOOD	AMOUNT	EQUALS	SUBSTITUTIONS
Allspice	1 tsp.		½ tsp. cinnamon + ½ tsp. ground cloves **OR** ½ tsp. cinnamon + ¼ tsp. nutmeg + ¼ tsp. ground cloves
Almonds	1 serving 3 oz. whole 3 oz. sliced 3 oz. slivered 1 lb.	⅓ cup ½ cup = 65 almonds 1 cup sliced ⅔ cup 3 cups chopped	hazelnuts (baking) **OR** Brazil nuts, cashews or pistachios (unsalted)
—in shell	1 lb.	1¾ cups nutmeats	
—shelled	1 lb.	3 cups blanched whole	
Almond butter	1 cup		2 cups blanched and toasted almonds + ¾– 1 tsp. salt processed in food processor until smooth **OR** 1 cup peanut butter
Almond extract	½ tsp.		¾–1 tsp. vanilla extract **OR** 2–4 tsp. almond liqueur
Amaretto	2 tbsp.		¼–½ tsp. almond extract
Angel hair pasta	1 lb. dried	1½ lb. fresh	capellini, spaghetti or vermicelli
Anise extract, pure	1 tsp.	1½ tsp. anise seed	
Anise seed	1 tsp.		1 tsp. fennel seed
Apples	1 serving 1 lb.	1 apple 3 medium 2¾–3 cups sliced	pears

FOOD	AMOUNT	EQUALS	SUBSTITUTIONS
Apples (cont.)	1 medium	1 cup sliced or chopped	
Apple pie spice	1 tsp.		½ tsp. cinnamon + ¼ tsp. nutmeg + ⅛ tsp. cardamom
Applesauce	1 serving 1 cup	½ cup unsweetened	1 cup pumpkin or plum puree (for baking)
Apricots	1 serving	2 apricots (fresh or dried)	1 peach or nectarine
Arrowroot starch	1½ tsp.		1 tbsp. flour **OR** 1½ tsp. cornstarch
	1 tbsp.	thickens 1 cup liquid	2 tbsp. flour **OR** 1 tbsp. cornstarch
Artichokes, Jerusalem	1 lb.	2 cups slices	
Arugula	1 oz.	1 cup	watercress, Belgian endive, escarole or radicchio
Asian fish sauce	1 tbsp.		2 tsp. soy sauce + 2 mashed anchovies
Asparagus	1 lb.	16–20 spears = 2 cups pieces = 3 cups trimmed and peeled pieces	
	½ lb.	1 serving	
Avocado	1 serving 1 large	⅓ avocado 1 cup mashed	chayote squash (cooked and mashed); peas, asparagus or broccoli (pureed in blender for guacamole); artichoke hearts (in salads)
Bacon	8 slices 1 slice	½ cup crumbled 1 tbsp. cooked and crumbled	½ cup bacon bits 1 tbsp. bacon bits
Bagel	½	1 serving	English muffin or bialy

FOOD	AMOUNT	EQUALS	SUBSTITUTIONS
Baking mix	2 cups		1¾ cup all-purpose flour + 2½ tsp. baking powder + ¾ tsp. salt; cut in ⅓ cup shortening until mixture becomes the texture of fine crumbs 1 tbsp. flour + 1½ tsp. cornstarch
Baking powder	1 tsp.		½ tsp. cream of tartar + ¼ tsp. baking soda **OR** ¼ tsp. baking soda + ½ cup buttermilk (decrease liquid by ½ cup) **OR** ¼ tsp. baking soda + ¼–½ cup molasses
Baking soda			no adequate substitute
Banana	1 serving 1 medium 1 lb.	½ banana ⅓ cup mashed 3 medium 1 cup mashed	plantain or mango
Barley —**pearled**	1 cup uncooked	4 cups cooked	Arborio rice or orzo
—**quick cooking**	1 cup uncooked	3 cups cooked	pearled
Basil	1 tsp.		½–¾ tsp. oregano or thyme
Bay leaf	1 whole	¼ tsp. crushed	
Beans dry	1 lb. dried	2 cups dried 4–5 cups cooked	2½ cups cooked or canned Great Northern beans 1 cup pinto or red kidney beans
—**black** *(turtle)*	1 serving 1 lb. dried	½ cup cooked 6 cups cooked	pinto or chili bean
—**cannellini** *(white kidney)*	1 cup dried	2½ cups cooked	fava beans

FOOD	AMOUNT	EQUALS	SUBSTITUTIONS
—chili *(pink)*	1 cup 1 serving 1 cup uncooked	½ cup 2½–3 cups cooked	1 cup cooked Great Northern beans or cannelloni
—kidney	1 lb. uncooked	1½ cups uncooked	chili or red kidney beans
—lima, dry shelled	1 lb. uncooked	9 cups cooked	
—navy	3 cups uncooked	1 cup cooked	
—pinto	2 cups dried	6 cups cooked	
—refried	1 serving 2 cups	½ cup	2 cups pinto or chili beans cooked until tender; mashed with enough water until smooth and creamy and fried in ½ cup fat **OR** canned refried beans (regular, low fat or nonfat)
Beans, snap	1 serving	½ cup	
—Chinese pea pod *(snow pea, Chinese snow pea, sugar pea)*	2 cups fresh	6 oz. frozen	sugar-snap peas or asparagus
—edamame *(vegetable soybean)*	1 lb.	3–3½ cups 1-inch pieces	garden pea or fresh black-eyed pea
—French green bean	1 lb.	3–3½ cups pieces	string beans
—string bean *(green bean or snap bean)*			1 lb. wax beans, asparagus or broccoli
—sugar snap pea			Chinese pea pod or asparagus
Beau Monde Seasoning	1 tsp.		1 tsp. seasoned salt **OR** ½ tsp. salt **OR** ½ tsp. Mei Yen seasoning
Beef, ground	1 serving	4 oz. uncooked 3 oz. cooked	ground chicken, ground turkey, TSP or TVP

FOOD	AMOUNT	EQUALS	SUBSTITUTIONS
Beets	1 lb.	3–5 medium beets 2–2¾ cup cubes 2 cups sliced 2½ cups cooked	
Belgian endive			arugula, radicchio or watercress
Bell pepper	1 serving 1 tbsp. dried	1 medium 3 tbsp. chopped fresh	
Berries	1 serving	1 cup	
Bialy	1	1 serving	½ bagel or whole English muffin
Blackberries	1 serving 1¼ lb.	1⅓ cups 3–4 cups	raspberries
Blueberries	1 serving 1 pint 1 lb.	⅔ cup 2–3 cups 2 cups	raspberries **OR** raisins or dates (in baked goods)
Bok choy			napa cabbage (for stir-fry), broccoli, celery, Swiss chard (substitute either in amount called for in recipe)
Boullion	1 cube	1 tsp. powdered	
Brandy	1 tsp.		1 tsp. brandy extract **OR** water, white grape juice, apple cider, apple juice, diluted peach or apricot syrups
Brandy extract	1 tbsp.		5 tbsp. brandy
Bread	1 serving —1 slice, soft —1 slice, dry —1 lb. loaf —1 slice —2 slices (white)	1 slice ½–¾ cup crumbs ¼–⅓ cup crumbs 14–20 slices ¾ cup soft crumbs 1 cup soft crumbs	
Bread crumbs	¼ cup dry	¾ cup soft	¼ cup cracker crumbs ¼ cup cornmeal ⅔ cup rolled oats

FOOD	AMOUNT	EQUALS	SUBSTITUTIONS
Bread crumbs (cont.)			¼ cup cornflake crumbs ¾ cup soft bread crumbs
	⅓ cup dry	1 slice bread	
	¼ cup soft	1 slice bread	
	1 cup fine dry	4 slices bread	¾ cup cracker crumbs, crushed croutons, crushed stuffing, cornflake crumbs or matzo meal
	1 cup fresh	3 slices bread	
Brioche *(rich sweet yeast bread made with eggs and butter)*			croissant
Broccoflower			cauliflower or broccoli
Broccoli	1 serving	¾ cup cooked 3 cups florets	broccoflower, cauliflower or broccoli raab
	¾ lb.	2 cups	
	1 lb.	5 cups florets	
	1½ lb.		
Broccolini *(baby broccoli)*			asparagus
Broth: beef, chicken or vegetable	1 cup		1 bouillon cube dissolved in 1 cup boiling water **OR** 1 envelope (1½ tsp.) powdered broth base dissolved in 1 cup boiling water
Brown sugar	1 lb.	2¼ cups firmly packed	
	1 cup		1 cup sugar + 1 tsp. molasses
Brussels sprouts	1 lb.	4 cups	broccoli florets
Bulgur	1 cup dry	3 cups cooked	
Butter	¼ lb.	8 tbsp.	
	1 lb.	2 cups = 4 sticks	
	1 cup		1 cup margarine + ½ tsp. salt
—whipped	1 lb.	3 cups	

FOOD	AMOUNT	EQUALS	SUBSTITUTIONS
Buttermilk	1 cup	1 cup milk + 1¾ tsp. cream of tartar **OR** 1 tbsp. lemon juice or vinegar + enough milk to measure 1 cup (let stand 5 minutes)	1 cup nonfat plain yogurt
Cabbage	1 lb. 3½–4½ shredded 1 lb. cooked	2 cups	
—green	1 head	8 cups shredded	red, napa or savoy (in slaws)
—napa			bok choy or cabbage
—red	1 head	8 cups shredded	green, napa or savoy (in slaws)
Cantaloupe	1 serving	¼	⅛ honeydew or casaba melon
Capellini			angel hair pasta, spaghettini or vermicelli
Capers	1 tbsp.		1 tbsp. chopped green olives
Cardamom	1 tsp.		½ tsp. ginger **OR** ½ tsp. ground nutmeg + ½ tsp. cinnamon **OR** ½ tsp. ground cloves + ½ tsp. cinnamon
	1 pod	⅙ tsp. cardamom	
Carob	3 tbsp.		3 tbsp. unsweetened cocoa powder + 1 tbsp. shortening
Carrots	1 serving 1 lb. 1 large (¼ lb.)	1 medium 3 cups shredded 3 cups sliced ¾–1 cup shredded	parsnip (cooked only), jicama, celery, turnip, kohlrabi, or cauliflower
—baby carrots	1 lb	3½ cups	
Cashews	1 serving	⅓ cup	

FOOD	AMOUNT	EQUALS	SUBSTITUTIONS
Catsup	1 cup (for cooking)		1 cup tomato sauce + ½ cup sugar + 2 tbsp. vinegar
Cauliflower	1 serving 1½ lb. head	½ cup 4 cups florets	broccoflower or broccoli
Cayenne pepper	1 pepper	⅛ tsp. ground cayenne	
Celery	1 serving 1 rib or stalk 1 bunch ½ cup	2 ribs ½ cup sliced or chopped 10–12 ribs 5–6 cups sliced or chopped	carrot, bok choy or jicama 1 tbsp. celery flakes
Celery salt			ground celery seed OR ground celery seed + salt OR Beau Monde seasoning
Celery seed	½ tsp.	1 tbsp. finely chopped celery leaves	
Cereal —ready to eat	1 serving	1 oz.	
—cooked	1 serving	½ cup	
Challah (Jewish yeast bread made with eggs and butter)			brioche or croissant
Champagne (for cooking)	1 cup		1 cup ginger ale
Chapati (Indian flat bread)			flour tortilla, pita bread or naan
Cheese	1 serving	1½ oz.	
—Asiago	1 cup		1 cup Parmesan
—cottage	16 oz.	2 cups	2 cups ricotta cheese or crumbled tofu
—cream cheese	8 oz.	1 cup	

256

FOOD	AMOUNT	EQUALS	SUBSTITUTIONS
—mozzarella	¼ lb.	1 cup shredded	jack or brick
—Parmesan/ Romano	1 serving 4 oz.	2 tbsp. 1–1¼ cup grated	2 tbsp. asiago
—ricotta	1 cup		1 cup cottage cheese
—Swiss or cheddar	1 lb.	4–5 cups shredded 2⅔ cups cubed	
—soy cheese			similar variety of regular cheese (cheddar, Parmesan, mozzarella, jack, Swiss)
Cherries	1 serving 4 cups unpitted	⅔ cup pitted fresh 2 cups pitted	
Cherry flavoring	1 tbsp.		2½ tsp. cherry juice from maraschino cherries + ½ tsp. vanilla
Cherry pepper			pepperoncini
Chervil	1 tsp.		1 tsp. dried parsley flakes + ⅛ tsp. dried sage
Chicken	1 serving 1 lb. boneless	3 oz. 3 cups cubed meat	turkey, extra-firm tofu, scallops or shrimp
Chick pea (garbanzo beans)	1 cup		1 cup Great Northern beans (for hummus) OR lima beans
Chili powder	1 tsp.		dash bottled hot pepper sauce + ⅛ tsp. oregano + ⅛ tsp. cumin
Chili sauce	1 cup		1 cup tomato sauce + ¼ cup brown sugar + 2 tbsp. vinegar + ¼ tsp. cinnamon + dash cloves + dash allspice OR 1 cup catsup + ¼ tsp. cinnamon + dashes of ground cloves and allspice OR 1 cup catsup

SUBSTITUTION CHART

FOOD	AMOUNT	EQUALS	SUBSTITUTIONS
Chili sauce (cont.)			+ ¼ cup horseradish + ¼ cup lemon juice
Chili seasoning mix	1 tbsp.		2 tsp. chili powder + 1 tsp. paprika
Chinese five-spice powder	5 tsp.		1 tsp. each: cinnamon, cloves, fennel seed, star anise, Szechwan peppercorns or black pepper
Chives	2 tsp. finely chopped		2 tsp. green onion tops, onion or leek
Chocolate —chips, semisweet	1 oz.		1 oz. sweet cooking chocolate, chopped **OR** 1 oz. carob chips
—semisweet	1 oz. 1⅔ oz. 6 oz. pkg.		1 oz. unsweetened chocolate + 1 tbsp. sugar **OR** 1 tbsp. unsweetened cocoa + 1 tbsp. sugar + 1 tsp. vegetable oil
	6 oz., melted	1 cup	1 oz. unsweetened chocolate + 4 tsp. sugar **OR** 2 squares unsweetened chocolate + 2 tbsp. shortening + ½ cup sugar
—unsweetened	6 oz. chips 1 oz. or square	1 cup chips	3 tbsp. cocoa + 1 tbsp. cooking oil or shortening, melted
—sweet baking	4 oz.		¼ cup unsweetened cocoa powder + ⅓ cup sugar + 3 tbsp. shortening
—bittersweet			semisweet chocolate
—milk			sweet or semisweet
—chocolate chips			equivalent amount of chocolate bars chopped into pieces; M & M

258

FOOD	AMOUNT	EQUALS	SUBSTITUTIONS
Chocolate (cont.)			candies; carob chips; raisins; chocolate-covered raisins; peanut butter or butterscotch chips; or white chocolate chips
Ciabatta *(rustic bread with heavy crust)*			Italian or French bread
Cilantro	1 tsp.		½–¾ tsp. parsley **OR** 1 tsp. Italian parsley + dash coriander **OR** ½ tsp. parsley + ½ tsp. mint
Cinnamon	1 tsp. 1 stick	½ tsp. ground cinnamon	¼–½ tsp. nutmeg or allspice
Cinnamon-sugar mixture	1 cup	⅞ cup sugar + 2 tbsp. ground cinnamon	
Clam juice	1 cup		1 cup fish broth **OR** ½ cup chicken broth + ½ cup water
Cloves	1 tsp.		½ tsp. allspice, cinnamon or nutmeg
Coating for fish or chicken *(i.e. Shake 'N Bake)*	1 cup		1 cup cornflake crumbs, bread crumbs or cracker crumbs, seasoned to taste
Cocktail sauce	1 cup		1 cup catsup + 2 tbsp. horseradish **OR** 1 cup catsup + ¼ cup prepared horseradish + 1 tbsp. lemon juice
Cocoa powder, unsweetened	1 oz.	¼ cup	1 oz. square unsweetened baking chocolate (decrease fat in recipe by ½ tbsp.) **OR** ¼ cup carob powder

FOOD	AMOUNT	EQUALS	SUBSTITUTIONS
Cocoa mix (hot chocolate)	1 lb.	4 cups	2 cups powdered milk + 1½ cups powdered sugar + ½ cup cocoa powder + ½ cup powdered nondairy creamer; mix 1 part with 3 parts boiling water
Coconut	1 lb. 1½ tbsp., grated 1 cup grated	6 cups grated 1 tbsp. grated dry 1⅓ cup flaked	
Coconut cream	1 cup		1 cup whipping cream OR 1 cup cream + ¼ tsp. coconut extract
Coconut milk	1 cup		1 cup milk + ½ tsp. coconut extract OR 1 cup whole or 2% milk
Cod	1 serving	3 oz.	
Coffee	1 lb.	80 tbsp. 40–50 servings (brewed)	
Cognac *(for cooking)*	1 cup		1 cup juice from peaches, apricots or pears
Cointreau *(for cooking)*	1 cup		1 cup orange juice or frozen orange juice concentrate
Collard greens	1 serving	½ cup cooked	kale, kohlrabi leaves, bok choy or mustard greens
Cookies —chocolate wafer			gingersnaps
—chocolate sandwiches *(e.g., Oreo)*			chocolate or vanilla wafer
—gingersnap			graham crackers, chocolate or vanilla wafers
—ladyfingers			sponge cake or pound cake

FOOD	AMOUNT	EQUALS	SUBSTITUTIONS
—vanilla wafers	22	1 cup fine crumbs	chocolate wafers or gingersnaps
Cool Whip	4 oz.	1¾ cups	
Coriander seeds	1½ tbsp. whole seeds	1 tbsp. ground	1 tbsp. cumin
Corn	1 serving 1 ear fresh 1 dozen ears	1 medium ear ⅔–¾ cup kernels 2½ cups cooked	
Cornmeal	1 serving 1 lb. 1 cup uncooked	½ cup 3–3¼ cups dry 4 cups cooked mush thickens 1 cup liquid	polenta or corn flour
Cornstarch	1 tbsp. (¼ oz.) 1½ tsp.		2 tbsp. granular tapioca OR 2 tbsp. flour (for thickening) 1 tbsp. flour
Corn syrup	1 cup (light) 1 cup (dark)		1 cup sugar dissolved in ¼ cup hot water OR ⅞–1 cup honey or molasses OR 1 cup dark corn syrup ¾ cup light corn syrup + ¼ cup molasses OR 1 cup light corn syrup
Couscous			rice
Cracked wheat			bulgur (cooks quicker)
Crackers —buttery round	12 crackers	½ cup finely crushed	
—graham	14 square	1 cup fine crumbs	ginger snaps, vanilla or chocolate wafers
—saltines	28 crackers	1 cup fine crumbs	
—soda	16 crackers	1 cup fine crumbs	
Cracker crumbs	¾ cup		1 cup dry bread crumbs, matzo meal or cornflake crumbs

FOOD	AMOUNT	EQUALS	SUBSTITUTIONS
Cracker crumbs (cont.)	12 oz.-pkg.	3 cups	
Cranberries	1 lb. fresh uncooked	4 cups cooked	
	1 cup dried		Craisins, raisins, dried cherries or currants
Cream			
—heavy	1 cup	2–2½ cups whipped	¾ cup milk + ⅓ cup butter
—half and half	1 cup	⅞ cup milk + 1½ tsp. butter or margarine	1 cup evaporated milk, undiluted
—whipped *(also see whipping cream)*			12-oz. can evaporated milk chilled until ice crystals form; add 1 tsp. lemon juice and whip until stiff
Cream of tartar	1 tsp.		1 tbsp. lemon juice or vinegar
Croissant *(rich crescent-shaped rolls)*			brioche or challah
Crostini *(small slice of toasted bread often used for appetizers)*			baguette cut into slices melba toast or water crackers
Crumpet *(low-fat yeast muffins)*			English muffin
Cucumber	1 serving	⅓ medium	
	1 lb	2 medium	
		2 cups sliced	
Cumin	1 tsp.		½ tsp. chili powder **OR** ½ tsp. caraway seeds
	1 oz. or 4½ tbsp. whole seed	4 tbsp. ground	
Currants, Zante	1 cup		1 cup dark raisins
Dates	1 serving	5 medium dried dates	dried figs, raisins or fresh dates

FOOD	AMOUNT	EQUALS	SUBSTITUTIONS
Dates (cont.)	1 lb. whole	1½ cups pitted and cut	
	1 lb. pitted and cut up	2½ cups	
Dill (fresh or dried	3 heads	1 tbsp dill seed	1 tbsp. celery seed
Eggs	1 serving 1 whole	1 egg 1 tbsp. egg yolk + 2 tbsp. egg white	2 egg whites **OR** 2 egg yolks **OR** ¼ cup egg substitute **OR** 2½ tbsp. sifted dry whole egg powder **OR** 3 tbsp. mayonnaise (cakes recipes) **OR** ½ tsp. baking powder + 1 tbsp. vinegar + 1 tbsp. liquid (baking) **OR** 2 egg yolks + 1 tbsp. water (cookie recipes) **OR** 2 egg yolks (custard recipes) **OR** 3 tbsp. beaten egg **OR** 2 tbsp. ground flaxmeal + ⅛ tsp. baking powder + 3 tbsp. water per egg (called for in recipe) **OR** 1 mashed ripe banana + ½ tsp. baking powder per 2 eggs
	2 large 1 cup	3 small 4–5 eggs **OR** 7–9 egg whites **OR** 12–14 egg yolks	
—for scrambling and omelets			extra-firm or firm tofu
Egg noodles	1 serving	½ cup	fettuccine or linguine
Eggplant	1 lb. (medium)	4–5 cups peeled and diced or cubed	
	1 American (or globe) eggplant		3 Japanese eggplants
Egg white	1	2 tbsp.	2 tbsp. frozen egg white, thawed **OR** 2 tsp. dry egg white powder + 2 tbsp. lukewarm water

FOOD	AMOUNT	EQUALS	SUBSTITUTIONS
Egg yolk	1	1½ tbsp.	
	1 cup	12 large egg yolks	
Fish **—white meat; light** **delicate flavor;** **flaky tender texture** *(best microwaved,* *baked, poached,* *sautéed or steamed)*			cod Dover sole haddock flounder
—white meat; **moderate flavor;** **flaky, tender** **texture** *(best* *microwaved, baked,* *broiled, poached,* *sautéed, steamed or* *deep-fried)*			catfish English sole rock sole
—light meat; **moderate flavor;** **moderately firm** **texture** *(best* *microwaved, baked,* *grilled, broiled,* *poached or deep-* *fried)*			Alaskan pollock giant sea bass grouper mahi-mahi orange roughy Pacific Ocean perch rainbow trout red snapper striped bass
—darker meat; **moderate flavor;** **moderately firm** **texture** *(best* *microwaved, baked* *grilled, broiled,* *sautéed, steamed or* *poached)*			Atlantic salmon king salmon (chinook) monkfish perch pink salmon pollock silver salmon (coho) striped bass
—dark meat; **moderate flavor;** **firm texture** *(best* *grilled, broiled,* *microwaved sautéed,* *poached, steamed,* *pickled or stewed)*			Atlantic mackerel tuna (all varieties) shark (all varieties) sockeye salmon (red)
Fish—best **substitute for:** **—anchovies**			anchovy paste (½ tsp. per fillet) **OR** sardines

FOOD	AMOUNT	EQUALS	SUBSTITUTIONS
—catfish			mahi-mahi, grouper or whitefish
—cod			halibut, sole, flounder, orange roughy or haddock
—flounder			sole, orange roughy, cod or haddock
—grouper			striped bass, mahi-mahi or catfish
—haddock			cod, flounder or sole
—halibut			sea bass
—mahi-mahi			monkfish, shark, swordfish or tuna
—monkfish			lobster, mahi-mahi, shark or red snapper
—orange roughy			flounder, sole, red snapper, ocean perch or grouper
—pollock			cod
—red snapper			sea bass, rockfish, grouper, halibut, sole, flounder, cod, orange roughy or catfish
—rockfish			red snapper, sea bass, halibut, perch or cod
—salmon			swordfish, mahi-mahi, albacore, marlin, striped bass or trout
—salmon, canned			canned tuna
—salmon, Chinook			coho salmon (smaller)
—salmon, coho			Chinook salmon (larger)
—sardines			anchovies or small herring

FOOD	AMOUNT	EQUALS	SUBSTITUTIONS
—shark			swordfish, mahi-mahi, tuna or halibut
—sole			flounder, cod, orange roughy or haddock
—striped bass			grouper, sea bass, halibut or salmon
—surimi (imitation seafood)			crabmeat
—swordfish			shark, tuna, halibut or mahi-mahi
—trout			whitefish, salmon or perch
—tuna			swordfish, halibut or salmon
—whitefish			catfish or trout
Fish sauce	1 tbsp.		1 tbsp. Worcestershire sauce
Fish stock	1 cup		½ cup clam juice + ½ cup water
Flour —all purpose	1 cup	½ cup whole wheat + ½ cup all purpose	1 cup + 2 tbsp. cake flour OR 1 cup rolled oats, crushed OR
	1 lb.	4 cups	½ cup cornmeal, bran, rice flour or whole wheat + ⅔ cup all-purpose flour OR ¾ cup whole-wheat flour or bran flour + ¼ cup all-purpose flour OR 1 cup rye or rice flour OR ¼ cup soybean flour + ¾ cup all-purpose flour
	1 tbsp. (for thickening)		1½ tsp. cornstarch, arrowroot starch, potato starch or rice starch OR 1 tbsp. granular tapioca OR 1½ tbsp. whole-wheat flour OR 1 tbsp. quick-cooking tapioca

FOOD	AMOUNT	EQUALS	SUBSTITUTIONS
—cake	1 lb. 1 cup	4¾ cups	1 cup minus 2 tbsp. all-purpose flour
—corn	2 lbs.	8 cups	
—low-fat soy			
—self rising	2 lbs. 1 cup	11 cups	1 cup all-purpose flour + 1 tsp. baking powder + ½ tsp. salt + ¼ tsp. baking soda **OR** 1 cup minus 2 tsp. all-purpose flour + 1½ tsp. baking powder + ½ tsp. salt 1 cup bleached flour
—quinoa	1 cup	¾ cup whole quinoa ground in blender	
—unbleached	1 cup		graham flour or all-purpose flour
—whole wheat	1 lb.	3¾ cups	**For best results, do not substitute more than ¼ of white flour in a cake recipe, as it will result in a heavier product. In other recipes, whole-wheat flour can be substituted for ¼–½ of the white flour called for.**
Focaccia (*Italian flatbread*)			baked pizza crust or bread dough
French bread			Italian bread
Fruit	1 serving	1 medium piece ½ cup mixed fruit ¾ cup fruit juice	
Fruit liqueur	1 tbsp.		1 tbsp. fruit juice
Garbanzo beans (*see chick peas*)			
Garlic	1 head or bulb		about 10 cloves

FOOD	AMOUNT	EQUALS	SUBSTITUTIONS
Garlic (cont.)	1 clove, medium	1 tsp. chopped garlic	⅛–¼ tsp. garlic powder **OR** ¼ tsp. garlic salt (reduce salt in recipe) **OR** ½ tsp. instant minced garlic **OR** ¼ tsp. granulated garlic **OR** ½ tsp. garlic juice
—granulated garlic	1 tsp.		½ tsp. garlic powder
Garlic salt	1 tsp.		¼ tsp. garlic powder + ¾ tsp. salt
Gelatin **—unflavored**	1 envelope (¼ oz.)	1 tbsp. (will gel 2 cups liquid)	
—flavored	3 oz.		1 tbsp. plain gelatin + 2 cups fruit juice
Ginger	1 tbsp. raw fresh 1 tsp. fresh chopped ½ cup candied ginger	¼ tsp. powdered ½ tsp. ground	½ tsp. allspice, cinnamon, mace or nutmeg 1 tsp. ground ginger **OR** ½ cup chopped nuts
Ginger root	1 tsp.	¼ tsp. ground ginger	
Gordita *(similar to corn tortilla but smaller and thicker)*			corn tortilla, flour tortilla or pita bread
Graham cracker crumbs	1 cup	15 graham crackers ground in blender or food processor	1 cup vanilla wafer, zwieback or chocolate wafer crumbs **OR** 1½ cup chopped nuts + ⅛ cup sugar
Grapefruit	1 serving	½	½ cup grapefruit juice
Grapes	1 serving 1 lb.	½ cup 2 cup seeded 2½ cup seedless	kiwifruit or blueberries
Greens, cooked	1 lb.	4–6 cups	
Green onions	¼ lb. bunch	½ cup sliced	leeks, shallots or chives

FOOD	AMOUNT	EQUALS	SUBSTITUTIONS
Guava	1	½ cup pulp	pineapple or strawberries
Half-and-half	1 cup		½ cup cream + ½ cup milk **OR** ⅞ cup milk + 1½ tbsp. butter or margarine **OR** fat-free half-and-half
Hazelnuts	1 cup		1 cup walnuts or pecans
Hazelnut butter	1 cup		1 cup roasted and skinned hazelnuts + 1–2 tbsp. vegetable oil + salt + sugar to taste in food processor or blender
Hearts of palm	146 grams	1 cup	artichoke hearts
Herbs, fresh	1 tbsp., chopped	½ tsp. dried crushed herbs	
Honey	1 cup		1¼ cup sugar + ¼ cup water, milk or apple juice
	1 lb.	1⅓	
Horseradish	1 tbsp.	2 tbsp. bottled fresh	
Hot pepper sauce	2–3 drops		dash crushed red pepper flakes or cayenne pepper
Italian bread			French bread
Italian seasoning	1 tsp.		¼ tsp. each: oregano, basil, thyme, rosemary + dash cayenne **OR** ¼ tsp. each: dried marjoram, oregano, basil + ⅛ tsp. sage
	2 tbsp.		1 tsp. each: oregano, marjoram, thyme, basil, rosemary, sage
Jicama	1 medium (10 oz.)	2 cups cubed	water chestnuts, tart apples or turnips

FOOD	AMOUNT	EQUALS	SUBSTITUTIONS
Juice			
—apple cider	1 serving	¾ cup	apple juice
—apple			apple cider
—grapefruit			orange or pineapple
—lemon	2–3 tbsp.	1 whole lemon squeezed	
	1 cup		¾ cup lime juice **OR** ½ cup vinegar
—lime	2 tbsp. ¾ cup	1 lime squeezed	1 cup lemon juice
—orange	1 serving	¾ cup	grapefruit or pineapple
—pineapple			grapefruit or orange
—tomato	1 cup		½ cup tomato sauce or puree + ½ cup water
Kahlua *(or other coffee-favored liqueur)*	2 tbsp.		½–1 tsp. instant coffee dissolved in 2 tbsp. hot water **OR** ½–1 tsp. chocolate extract
Kale	1 serving	⅓ cup cooked	collard greens, Swiss chard or spinach
Ketchup *(see catsup)*			
Kirsch	1 tbsp.		1 tbsp. syrup or juices from cherries, raspberries, boysenberries, currants or cider
Kiwifruit	1 serving	1 kiwi	strawberry or papaya
Kohlrabi —greens	1 lb.	3 cups strips	collard greens, kale or Swiss chard
Lahvosh *(Armenian cracker bread)*			matzo or flour tortilla (baked until crisp)
Leeks	1½ lb. ½ cup sliced	3 cups slices	½ cup sliced shallots or green onions

FOOD	AMOUNT	EQUALS	SUBSTITUTIONS
Lemon	1 medium	1–3 tbsp. juice 1–2 tsp. grated peel	2–3 tbsp. bottled lemon juice
Lemon extract	1 tsp.		2 tsp. lemon zest **OR** 1–2 tbsp. lemon-flavored liqueur
Lemon juice	1 tsp.		½ tsp. vinegar ½ tsp. lemon extract
Lemon peel dried	1 tsp.	1–2 tsp. grated fresh lemon peel	
Lemon pepper			combine lemon zest, black pepper and a pinch of salt
Lettuce —bibb	1 serving	1½ cups	Boston
—Boston			bibb, leaf or iceberg
—Belgian endive	1 serving 1 lb.	1½ cups 4¼ cups	arugula, radicchio or watercress
—curly endive			escarole, radicchio or mustard greens curly endive
—escarole	1 serving	1½ cups	arugula, curly endive, radicchio or spinach
—green-leaf —head (iceberg) —leaf —radicchio —romaine —spring salad mix	1 lb. 1 lb. 1 lb.	6¼ cups 6¼ cups 6 cups	red leaf or bibb romaine or leaf butterhead or romaine Belgian endive, escarole or red-leaf iceberg or Boston arugula, frisee, oakleaf, red chard, radicchio, mustard greens and mizuna
Lime	1 medium	1½–2 tsp. juice	
Linguine			fettuccine or spaghetti
Liquors (rum, bourbon, whiskey)	½ cup		¼ cup unsweetened fruit juice or broth

FOOD	AMOUNT	EQUALS	SUBSTITUTIONS
Lobster	1 serving	3 oz	
Macaroni, 1-inch pieces	½ lb. uncooked	2 cups uncooked 4 cups cooked	2 cups spaghetti, uncooked **OR** 4 cups noodles, uncooked **OR** 8 oz. any pasta
	1 cup (3½ oz.) uncooked	2½ cups cooked	
Mace	1 tsp.		1 tsp. cinnamon, nutmeg or allspice
Mango	1 serving	½ medium ¾ cup diced 1 cup puree	peaches, nectarines or papayas
Maple syrup	1 tbsp.		1 tbsp. pancake syrup or berry syrup (for pancakes, waffles, etc.) **OR** 1 tbsp. brown sugar (on hot cereal) **OR** 1 tbsp. light molasses
Marjoram	1 tsp.		½–¾ tsp. basil, thyme or savory
Marshmallows	1 cup miniature	10 large	
Marshmallow crème			Cook over low heat: 16 oz. marshmallows quarter cup corn syrup (stir constantly until melted)
Matzo *(unleavened bread served during Passover)*	3 whole	1 cup matzo meal	cracker bread bread crumbs or cracker crumbs
Matzo meal	1 cup	3 matzos	1 cup bread crumbs or cracker crumbs
Mayonnaise	1 cup		½ cup yogurt + ½ cup mayonnaise **OR** 1 cup sour cream **OR** 1 cup cottage cheese pureed in blender
Melba toast			crostini, flatbread crackers or water crackers

FOOD	AMOUNT	EQUALS	SUBSTITUTIONS
Melon	1 serving 1 lb.	⅛ melon 1 cup cubed	
Milk	1 serving	1 cup	
—buttermilk	1 cup		1 cup plain yogurt **OR** 1 cup whole milk + 1 tbsp. lemon juice or vinegar (stand 20 minutes at room temperature)
—skim milk	1 cup		4–5 tbsp. nonfat dry milk powder + water to make 1 cup **OR** ½ cup evaporated skim milk + ½ cup water
—sweetened condensed	1 can (1⅓ cup)		⅓ cup + 2 tbsp. evaporated milk + 1 cup sugar + 3 tbsp. butter or margarine (cook in saucepan over medium heat) **OR** 1 cup + 2 tbsp. dry milk + ½ cup warm water; mix well; add ¾ cup sugar + 3 tbsp. melted butter or margarine (stir until smooth)
—whole	1 cup		1 cup reconstituted nonfat dry milk **OR** ½ cup evaporated milk + ½ cup water **OR** 1 cup fruit juice or 1 cup potato water (for baking)
Mint	1 tsp. 1 tbsp. fresh	1 tsp. dried	½–¾ tsp. basil, marjoram or rosemary 1 tbsp. fresh parsley + pinch of dried mint **OR** 1 tsp. dried basil
Miso *(soybean paste)*	1 tbsp. 8 oz.	1 cup	1 tsp. soy sauce 1 cup honey
Molasses			1 cup dark corn syrup **OR** 1½ cups brown sugar

FOOD	AMOUNT	EQUALS	SUBSTITUTIONS
Mrs. Dash seasoning	1 tsp.		1 tsp. Spike or seasoned salt
Mushrooms	1 serving	5 medium	
—fresh	1 lb.	2–3 cup whole 3 oz. dried 6 cups sliced	eggplant, asparagus, bell peppers or zucchini
	1 cup cooked, sliced		4 oz. can mushroom stems and pieces, drained
	crimini mushrooms		white, portabello or shiitake
	enoki mushrooms 1 lb. morels oyster mushrooms 1 lb. fresh porcini Portobello 1 lb. shiitake	2–3 oz. dried 3 oz. dried 3 oz. dried	oyster or white shiitake or chanterelles Portobello or oyster cremini or porcini crimini, enoki, straw, porcini, white or oyster
	straw white		enoki or white cremini or oyster
—canned	4 oz.	2 cup sliced fresh 6 tbsp. whole dried	
Mustard			mayonnaise or prepared horseradish
—dry	1 tsp.	1 tbsp. prepared	
—prepared Naan *(Indian flatbread made with wheat flour)*	1 tbsp.	1 tsp dry	½ tsp. dry mustard + 2 tsp. vinegar chapati, flour tortilla or pita bread
Nectarine			peach or apricot
Noodles, 1-inch pieces	1 lb. 3 cups uncooked 1 cup uncooked	6–8 cups uncooked = 8 cups cooked 4 cup cooked 1¾ cup cooked	
Nutmeg	1 tsp.		½ tsp. cinnamon, ginger or mace
Nuts *(see also almonds, pecans, walnuts, peanuts)*	3¾ oz. ground nuts	1 cup	equal amount of browned rolled oats

FOOD	AMOUNT	EQUALS	SUBSTITUTIONS
Nuts (cont.)	1 lb. pecan halves	4½ cups chopped	walnuts
	1 lb. pecans in shell	½ lb. shelled = 2 cups	
	1 serving walnuts	⅓ cup	pecans, hazelnuts or pine nuts (in pesto)
	1 lb. walnuts unshelled	1½ cups shelled walnuts	
	4½ oz. chopped walnuts	1 cup chopped walnuts	
	3½ oz. walnut halves	1 cup walnut halves	
	2 lbs. unshelled Brazil nuts	1 lb. shelled	macadamia nuts, almonds or pecans
	1 serving	⅓ cup cashews	⅓ cup peanuts, pine nuts, almonds, pecans or water chestnuts (stir-fry dishes)
	1 lb. chestnuts (in shell)	2½ cups shelled whole nuts	hazel nuts or pecans (for stuffing)
	2 cups pistachios in shell	1 cup shelled nutmeats	pine nuts or blanched almonds
	pine nuts		walnuts, almonds or hazelnuts (for pesto sauce) **OR** raw, unsalted cashews **OR** unsalted peanuts **OR** sunflower seeds
	peanuts		cashews or almonds
	hazelnut (filbert)	almonds, walnuts,	pecans, Brazil nuts or macadamia nuts
Oat bran	1 tbsp.		1 tbsp. wheat bran
Oat flour	1 cup	1¼ cups rolled oats blended to consistency of flour	whole-wheat flour
Oats	1 serving	½ cup cooked	
—instant			quick-cooking oats rolled or instant oats
—quick-cooking			
—rolled	1 cup uncooked	1¾ cups cooked	steel-cut, quick-cooking, or instant
	1 oz. uncooked	⅓ cup uncooked	
—steel-cut *(Irish oats)*			rolled

FOOD	AMOUNT	EQUALS	SUBSTITUTIONS
Oil *(for baking cakes and cookies)*	1 cup		1 cup applesauce
—canola			corn oil, safflower, oil, soybean oil, olive oil (may affect flavor) or vegetable oil
Okra	1 lb.	2¼ cups cooked	
Onion fresh	1 serving	½ cup chopped	1 tbsp. instant minced onion **OR** 1 tsp. onion powder
	1 small	⅓ cup chopped	1 tbsp. onion powder
	1 medium	½–⅔ cup chopped	
	1 large	1 cup chopped	
	1 lb.	3 large or 5 medium 2–2½ cups chopped 3 cups sliced	
—boiling	½ lb.	10–12	
—pearl	½ lb.	20–24 (2 cups)	
—red			
—sweet *(Vidalia, Walla Walla Maui)*	1 whole 1 whole		Spanish, sweet or white Bermuda, red or Spanish
—white	1 whole		Spanish, sweet or yellow
—yellow	1 whole		Spanish or white
Onion flakes, dehydrated *(instant minced)*	1 tbsp.		1 tsp. onion powder **OR** ⅓ cup chopped fresh onion
Onion powder	1 tsp. 1 tbsp.		1 tbsp. onion flakes **OR** ⅓ cup chopped fresh onion 1 medium onion, chopped or ¼ cup chopped onion
Onion soup mix	1⅜ oz. package		¼ cup instant minced onion + 2 tbsp. bouillon

FOOD	AMOUNT	EQUALS	SUBSTITUTIONS
Onion soup mix (cont.)			(beef, chicken or vegetable) + ½ tsp. onion powder
Orange	1 serving 1 medium	1 orange ⅓–½ cup juice 2–3 tbsp. grated peel	1 tbsp. dried orange peel **OR** grated peel of 1 medium orange **OR** 1 tsp. orange extract
—extract	1 tsp.		1 tbsp. orange liqueur
—juice	1 cup	3 medium oranges	
—peel dried	2 tsp.		
—rind	1 tsp.	½ orange	
Oregano	1 tsp.		½–¾ tsp. thyme or basil **OR** 1 tsp. marjoram
Oyster sauce	1 tbsp.		1 tbsp. soy sauce
Papaya	1 serving 1 cup	1 cup cubed	2 cups mango, peaches, nectarines **OR** 1 cup cantaloupe, honeydew melon or pineapple chunks
Parsley fresh	1 tbsp. chopped 1 tsp.	1 tsp. dried	½–¾ tsp. chervil or cilantro
Parsnips	1 lb.	4 medium 2 cups slices 2 cups cooked	carrots, turnips or sweet potatoes
Passion fruit	12 whole	1 cup puree	guava or pineapple
Pasta *(also see individual listings)*	1 lb. dried pasta 4 cups cooked	1½ lbs. fresh pasta	8 oz. uncooked elbow macaroni, medium shells, rotini, twists, spirals, wagon wheels, bow ties, mostaccioli, penne, radiatore, rigatoni, spaghetti, angel hair, linguine, vermicelli and fettuccine

FOOD	AMOUNT	EQUALS	SUBSTITUTIONS
Pasta (cont.)	8 oz. uncooked 8 oz. uncooked egg noodles		4 cups cooked 2½ cups cooked egg noodles
—pasta salads			cavatelli, fusilli, macaroni, penne or rotini
—with heavy sauces			fettuccine, fusilli or linguine
—with light sauces			spaghetti or vermicelli
—with butter or cream sauces			fettuccine, penne or spaghetti
—with primavera or other chunky sauces			cavatelli, farfalle, fusilli, macaroni, penne, rigatoni or ziti
—in soups			ditalini, orzo or tubettini
—in baked casseroles			fusilli, macaroni or rigatoni
Peaches	1 serving 1 lb.	1 medium 4 medium 2 cups sliced	nectarine, apricot, papaya or mango
Peanuts	1 serving	⅓ cup dry roasted	
—in shell	1 lb.	2–2¼ cups nut meats	
—shelled	1 lb.	3–3¼ cups nut meats	
Peanut butter	1 serving 1 cup	2 tbsp.	2 cups roasted peanuts + 1–2 tbsp. peanut oil processed in food processor
Pears	1 serving 1 lb.	1 pear 3–4 medium 2⅓ cups sliced	1 apple
Peas	1 serving	½ cup	
—pods	1 lb.		

FOOD	AMOUNT	EQUALS	SUBSTITUTIONS
—black-eyed	1 lb. 2 cups fresh	4 cups 2⅓ cups cooked 1 cup dried	split peas or lentils
—garden (fresh pea)	1 lb. unshelled	1 cup shelled	edamame or lima beans
Pecans —in shell	1 lb.	2¼ cups nut meats	
—shelled	1 lb.	4–4½ cups halves 3–3¾ cups chopped	
Peppers —bell	1 medium ¼ cup chopped fresh	¾ cup chopped or diced	1 tbsp. dried sweet pepper flakes
—red	1 tbsp. dried	3 tbsp. chopped fresh	2 tbsp. chopped pimento
Peppermint dried	1 tbsp.	¼ cup chopped fresh mint	
Persimmon	1 serving	¼ medium	plums or mashed pumpkin
Pimiento	2 tbsp. dried		1 tbsp. dried red bell peppers, rehydrated OR 3 tbsp. fresh red bell pepper, chopped
Pineapple	1 serving 3 lb. (1 medium)	½ cup or 1 slice 3 cups cubed	papaya
Pine nuts	1 cup		1 cup walnuts or almonds
Pita bread (Middle Eastern flatbread)	1 serving	½ whole pita	flour tortilla
Pizza crust, baked (i.e., Boboli)			focaccia bread or frozen bread dough (thawed)
Pizza spice	1 tsp.		1 tsp. Italian seasoning

FOOD	AMOUNT	EQUALS	SUBSTITUTIONS
Plums	1 serving 1 lb.	2 plums 8–20 whole (depending on size) 2 cups sliced	
Polenta meal			coarsely ground yellow cornmeal, ready-made polenta (in refrigerator section) or hominy grits
Popcorn	1 serving ¼ cup kernels ⅓ cup kernels	1 cup 8 cups popped 12 cups popped	
Poppy seeds	2 oz.	1 cup ground poppy seeds	sesame seeds poppy seeds
Pork	1 serving	3 oz.	turkey or chicken tenders
Potatoes —sweet	1 serving 1 lb. whole	1 medium 3 medium 4 cups diced	yams or mashed cooked pumpkin
—white	1 lb. whole	3 medium 2¾ cups cubes 1½–2¼ cups cooked diced or sliced 1¾–2 cups mashed	
Poultry seasoning	1 tsp.		¼ tsp. ground thyme + ¾ tsp. ground sage
Pretzel	1 serving	1 oz.	
Prunes, dried, whole and pitted	1 serving 1 lb.	2¼ cup pitted	2 tbsp. raisins
Pumpernickel bread			Sourdough rye or Russian black bread
Pumpkin mashed, and cooked	1 lb.	1 cup	1 cup canned pumpkin
Pumpkin seeds			sesame, squash or sunflower seeds

FOOD	AMOUNT	EQUALS	SUBSTITUTIONS
Pumpkin pie spice	1 tsp.		½ tsp. cinnamon + ⅛ tsp. ginger + ⅛ tsp. nutmeg + ⅛ tsp. mace + ⅛ tsp. ground cloves **OR** ½ tsp. cinnamon + ¼ tsp. nutmeg + ⅛ tsp. allspice + ⅛ tsp. cardamom
Radishes	6 oz.	1¼ cups sliced	jicama
Raisins	15 oz. 1 lb.	3 cups 3¼ cups	dried dates, figs, apricots, cherries or cranberries
—golden	1 cup		raisins, currants or dried apricots
Ramen noodles			lo mein or soba noodles
Raspberry	1 serving	1⅓ cups	boysenberry or strawberry
Ravioli wrappers			eggroll, wonton or dumpling wrappers
Red pepper	3–4 drops		⅛ tsp. ground red cayenne pepper **OR** dash bottled hot pepper sauce **OR** black pepper
Rhubarb fresh	1 lb.	4–8 pieces 2 cups cooked	
Rice	1 serving	½ cup cooked	
—basmati	1 cup dried	3 cups cooked	
—brown			
—converted			
—instant	1 cup uncooked	2 cups cooked	
—long-grain			
—medium-grain			

FOOD	AMOUNT	EQUALS	SUBSTITUTIONS
—regular	1 lb.	2 cups uncooked 6 cups cooked 3 cups cooked	
	½ lb. whole grain	1 cup whole grain 1 qt. cooked rice	
	1 cup uncooked		
—short-grain			
—Spanish (paella)			
—white			
—wild (is not really rice but a grass seed with a nutty flavor)			
Rice cake	1 serving	1 piece	
Rosemary	1 tsp.		
Rum	¼ cup		1 tbsp. rum extract + 3 tbsp. water OR ¼ cup water, white grape juice, pineapple juice, apple juice or apple cider
	1 tbsp.		1 tsp. rum extract OR ¾ tsp. orange extract
Rutabagas	1 lb. ⅛ tsp.	2¾ cups cubes	
Saffron	1 tsp. threads	⅛ tsp. powder	½ tsp. turmeric
Sage	1 tsp.		½–¾ tsp. poultry seasoning, savory, marjoram or rosemary
Sake	1 cup		1 cup dry sherry or dry vermouth
Salmon	1 serving	3 oz.	
Salsa	1 serving	2 tbsp.	
Salt, seasoned	1–1¼ cup		1 cup salt + 2½ tsp. paprika + 2 tsp. dry mustard + 1½ tsp. dried oregano + 1 tsp.

FOOD	AMOUNT	EQUALS	SUBSTITUTIONS
Salt, seasoned (cont.)			garlic powder + ½ tsp. onion powder
Savory	1 tsp.		½–¾ tsp. thyme, marjoram or sage
Scone			English muffin or shortcake
Sesame seeds	1 tbsp.		1 tbsp. finely chopped blanched almonds **OR** pumpkin seeds
Shallots	3 whole	⅓ cup chopped 1 small onion	⅓ cup chopped green onions (whites only) **OR** ¾ tsp. minced onion + ½ tsp. minced garlic
Sherry, sweet	2 tbsp.		1–2 tsp. vanilla extract, orange juice, apple juice or port wine
Shortening—melted	1 cup		1 cup cooking oil (only if recipe calls for melted shortening)
—solid (for baking)	1 cup		⅞ cup lard **OR** 1⅛ cups butter minus ½ tsp. salt (called for in recipe) **OR** ¾ cup applesauce, ¾ cup pureed prunes, ¾ cup apple butter or 1 cup mashed bananas (in baked goods only)
Shrimp, fresh	1 serving	¾ lb. raw in shell 7 oz. package, frozen, peeled, cooked 4½–5 oz. can	
Snap beans *(see string beans)*			
Sour cream	1 cup		¾ cup buttermilk + ⅓ cup butter or margarine **OR** ⅓ cup buttermilk + 1 tbsp. lemon juice + 1 cup cottage cheese **OR**

FOOD	AMOUNT	EQUALS	SUBSTITUTIONS
Sour cream (cont.)			1 cup plain yogurt **OR** ¾ cup milk + ¾ tsp. lemon juice + ⅓ cup butter or margarine
Sourdough bread			French bread
Soy—cheese	1 cup		1 cup regular, low-fat, or nonfat variety cheese
—mayonnaise	1 tbsp.		regular, low-fat or nonfat mayonnaise **OR** hummus **OR** sour cream
—milk	1 cup		1 cup milk or rice milk
—soynut butter			soy yogurt or soy mayonnaise
—yogurt	1 tbsp. 1 cup	1 tbsp. peanut butter	1 cup regular, low-fat or nonfat yogurt **OR** regular or soy sour cream
Soy sauce	½ cup		3 tbsp. Worcestershire sauce + 1 tbsp. water 1 tbsp. teriyaki sauce
Spaghetti	1 serving 1 lb.	½ cup 4–5 cups 2-inch pieces 8–10 cups cooked	angel hair pasta, fettuccine, spaghetti squash or vermicelli
Spaghettini			angel hair pasta or vermicelli
Spinach	1 serving 1 lb. fresh	½ cup 4 cups fresh 12 cups torn stems removed 1–1½ cups cooked	5 oz. package frozen chopped spinach Swiss chard or kale
Sprouts —alfalfa			mung bean or soybean
—broccoli			alfalfa
—buckwheat			alfalfa

FOOD	AMOUNT	EQUALS	SUBSTITUTIONS
—mung bean			snow peas or soybean sprouts
—soybean			mung bean
Squash—summer (yellow or zucchini)	1 lb.	1⅔ cup cooked and mashed	cooked eggplant, bok choy (stir-fry), cucumbers (raw)
—winter	1 lb.	1 cup cooked and mashed 2 servings	
—acorn			butternut, buttercup or banana
—banana			butternut, buttercup, acorn, Hubbard or pumpkin
—buttercup			butternut, acorn, Hubbard or pumpkin
—butternut			buttercup, acorn or Hubbard
—pumpkin			Hubbard, butternut, buttercup, acorn or sweet potatoes (for pies)
—spaghetti			spaghetti pasta, butternut or banana squash
Strawberries	1 serving 1 qt. 1 pint	8 whole 4 cups sliced 3½ cups whole	raspberry or kiwifruit
Stuffing croutons			bread sliced into ¼-inch cubes and baked in 300°F oven 20–30 minutes until crisp **OR** coarse breadcrumbs
Sugar—brown	1 lb. 1 cup (firmly packed)	2¼ cup firmly packed	1 cup granulated sugar

FOOD	AMOUNT	EQUALS	SUBSTITUTIONS
—light brown	1 lb. 1 cup	2¼ cups	⅔ cup dark brown sugar + ⅓ cup granulated sugar
—granulated	1 cup		1½ cups corn syrup (decrease liquid in recipe by ¼ cup) OR 1⅓ cup molasses (decrease liquid by ⅓ cup) OR 1 cup powdered sugar OR 1 cup brown sugar, firmly packed OR ¾ cup honey (decrease liquid in recipe by ¼ cup; for each cup of honey in baked goods, add ½ tsp. baking soda)
	¼ cup (for baking)		1 tsp. (3 packets) artificial sweetener
—maple	½ cup		1 cup maple syrup OR 1 cup brown sugar
—powdered	1 lb. 1 cup	2¾ cups 3½ cups sifted	 1 cup granulated sugar + 1 tbsp. cornstarch (processed until blended and powdery)
Sun-dried tomatoes			tomato paste (in sauces)
Sunflower seeds	1 serving	⅓ cup	pine nuts or pumpkin seeds
Sweet pepper (bell pepper)	3 tbsp. fresh	1 tbsp. dried	
Swiss chard	1 serving	⅓ cup cooked	escarole, bok choy or spinach
Tabasco sauce	dash		red pepper flakes or ground red pepper
Taco seasoning	1¼ pkg. ½ cup	7 tsp.	6 tsp. chili powder + 5 tsp. paprika + 4½ tsp. cumin + 3 tsp. onion powder + 2½ tsp. garlic powder + ⅛ tsp. cayenne pepper

FOOD	AMOUNT	EQUALS	SUBSTITUTIONS
Tamarind paste	1 tbsp.		1 tsp. dates + 1 tsp. prunes + 1 tsp. dried apricots + 1 tsp. lemon juice
Tangerine	1 serving	2 small	
Tapioca—granular	1 tbsp. 2 tsp.	2 tbsp. pearl tapioca	1½ tbsp. all-purpose flour 1 tbsp. flour
—instant (*quick cooking*)	1 tbsp.		2 tbsp. regular tapioca **OR** 1½ tsp. cornstarch
Tarragon	1 tsp.		½–¾ tsp. chervil, **OR** dash fennel seed **OR** dash aniseed
Tartar sauce	½ cup		6 tbsp. mayonnaise or salad dressing + 2 tbsp. sweet relish
Tea loose	1 lb.	200 cups	
Tempeh	1 lb.		1 lb. tofu, ground beef or textured vegetable protein (TVP)
TSP or TVP (*textured soy protein or textured vegetable protein*)	1 lb.		1 lb. tofu, ground beef or tempeh
Thyme	1 tsp.		½–¾ tsp. basil, marjoram, oregano or savory
Tofu	1 serving	3 oz.	
—extra firm		firm	
—firm			extra-firm, regular or pressed; beef or chicken (in stir-fries); feta cheese (in salads)
—regular			ricotta cheese; firm or soft tofu

FOOD	AMOUNT	EQUALS	SUBSTITUTIONS
—silken			soft tofu; sour cream (dressings, dips, sauces); mayonnaise (dressings, dips, sauces); yogurt (smoothies)
—soft			silken; sour cream or mayonnaise (in dressings, dips, sauces) or yogurt (smoothies)
Tomatoes	1 serving	1 medium	
—fresh	1 lb. 1 large	3 medium 1–1½ cup chopped ¾ cup sliced	reconstituted sun-dried tomatoes OR 1½ tbsp. tomato paste
—canned	16 oz. can 1 cup	2 cups chopped	1⅓ cups cut-up fresh, simmered 10 minutes
Tomato juice	1 cup		½ cup tomato sauce + ½ cup water
Tomato paste	1 tbsp.		1 tbsp. ketchup
Tomato sauce	1 cup		⅜ cup (6 tbsp.) tomato paste + ½ cup water
Tomato soup	10¾-oz. can		1 cup tomato sauce + ¼ cup water
Tortilla—corn			flour tortilla, taco or tostada shell
—flour			pita bread, chapatti or naan
Tuna—fresh	1 serving	3 oz.	
—canned in water	1 serving	3 oz.	3 oz. canned salmon
Turkey	1 serving 1 lb. boneless	3 oz. 3 cups cubed	chicken
—ground	1 serving	3 oz.	3 oz. ground chicken, beef or TSP
Turmeric ground	1 tsp.	1 piece fresh	1 tsp. mustard powder

FOOD	AMOUNT	EQUALS	SUBSTITUTIONS
Turnips	1 lb.	3 medium turnips, 2 cups cooked	
Udon noodles (*Japanese thick noodles*)			soba noodles, whole-wheat linguine or whole-wheat spaghetti
Vanilla bean	1-inch		1 tsp. vanilla extract
Vanilla extract, pure	1 tsp.	1 tsp. vanilla powder	
Vermicelli			capellini or spaghettini
Vinegar—balsamic	1 tbsp.		1 tbsp. sherry, cider or fruit vinegar
—cider			malt, white or wine
—raspberry			apple cider, balsamic, red wine, rice or sherry
—red wine			apple cider, balsamic, rice, sherry or white wine
—rice	1 tbsp.		apple cider + pinch of sugar **OR** 2 tsp. white vinegar + 1 tsp. water **OR** 1 tbsp. white vinegar + ½ tsp. sugar + ⅛ tsp. salt **OR** 1 tbsp. dry sherry **OR** 1 tbsp. white wine vinegar
—seasoned rice	1 cup		¾ cup white rice vinegar + ¼ cup sugar + 2 tsp. salt
—sherry			balsamic, red wine + pinch of sugar or rice
—tarragon	1 cup		1 cup vinegar (white wine or apple cider) + 1 tbsp. fresh tarragon leaves **OR** 1 cup vinegar (white wine or apple cider) + 1 tsp. dried tarragon

FOOD	AMOUNT	EQUALS	SUBSTITUTIONS
—white distilled			cider or malt
—white wine			cider, red wine or rice
Walnuts —in shell	1 lb.	1⅔ cups nutmeats	
—shelled	1 lb.	1½–1¾ cup shelled 4½ cups halves 3⅔ cups chopped	
Water chestnuts	1 cup sliced 1 serving	2 cups	1 cup sliced jicama
Watermelon			
Wheat berries			cracked wheat or bulgur
Wheat bran	1 tbsp.		1 tbsp. oat bran or wheat germ
Wheat germ	1 tbsp.		1 tbsp. wheat bran or ground sunflower seeds
Whipping cream	1 cup		1 cup frozen (thawed) whipped topping **OR** 1 cup prepared whipped topping mix
Wine —red	1 cup ¼ cup		1 cup grape juice **OR** cranberry juice **OR** 1 cup apple cider or beef broth 1 tbsp. balsamic or red wine vinegar
—White	1 cup		1 cup apple juice **OR** white grape juice **OR** vermouth (for cooking) **OR** 1 cup apple cider or chicken broth
—for marinade	½ cup		¼ cup vinegar + ¼ cup water + 1 tbsp. sugar
—Marsala	¼ cup		¼ cup dry wine + 1 tsp. brandy

FOOD	AMOUNT	EQUALS	SUBSTITUTIONS
Wonton wrappers			eggroll skins cut into fourths, dumpling skins or potsticker wrappers
Worcestershire sauce	1 tsp.		1 tsp. bottled steak sauce
Yeast, active dry	1 pkg. (¼ oz.) active dry yeast 1 cake compressed (3/5 oz.)	1½ tsp.	1 cake compressed yeast ¼ oz. (1 pkg.) active dry yeast 2¼–2½ tsp. loose active dry yeast
	1 tbsp. baker's yeast (bread yeast) 1 pkg. bread machine yeast ¼ oz. pkg. instant yeast	1 pkg. or 1 cake 2¼ tsp. bread machine yeast 2¼ tsp. instant yeast	instant yeast, active dry yeast or compressed yeast (1 cake per pkg. or 2¼ tsp. dry yeast) bread machine yeast, active dry yeast (substitute equivalent amounts)
Yogurt plain	1 serving 1 cup	1 cup	1 cup buttermilk, 1 cup cottage cheese blended until smooth, 1 cup sour cream or silky tofu blended
Zucchini	1 serving 1 medium (5–6 oz.)	¼ cup 1 cup loosely packed grated 1 cup sliced	yellow squash, eggplant or grated carrots (in breads or cakes)

BASIC MEASURES AND EQUIVALENTS

BASIC MEASURES	EQUALS
¼ teaspoon	1 ml
½ teaspoon	2 ml
¾ teaspoon	4 ml
1 teaspoon	5 ml
pinch or dash	¹⁄₁₆ teaspoon
¼ tablespoon	¾ teaspoon
⅓ tablespoon	1 teaspoon
⅜ tablespoon	1⅛ teaspoons
½ tablespoon	1½ teaspoons
⅝ tablespoon	1⅞ teaspoons
⅔ tablespoon	2 teaspoons
¾ tablespoon	2¼ teaspoons
⅞ tablespoon	2½ teaspoons
1 tablespoon	3 teaspoons = 15 ml
1 tablespoon	½ ounce
2 tablespoons	1 ounce = 30 grams
1 jigger	1½ ounces
¹⁄₁₆ cup	1 tablespoon = ½ ounce
⅛ cup	2 tablespoons = 1 ounce = 30 gm
¼ cup	4 tablespoons = 2 ounces
⅓ cup	5 tablespoons + 1 teaspoon
⅜ cup	6 tablespoons = 3 ounces
½ cup	8 tablespoons = 4 ounces = 125 ml
⅝ cup	½ cup + 2 tablespoons
⅔ cup	10 tablespoons + 2 teaspoons
¾ cup	12 tablespoons

BASIC MEASURES	EQUALS
⅞ cup	¾ cup + 2 tablespoons
1 cup	16 tablespoons = 8 ounces = 250 ml = 225 g
2 cups	1 pint = 16 ounces = 1 lb
2 pints	1 quart = 32 ounces = 1 liter
4 quarts	1 gallon = 128 ounces
8 quarts	1 peck
4 pecks	1 bushel
1 ounce	2 tablespoons = 30 grams
4 ounces	¼ cup
8 ounces	1 cup
10 ounces	280 grams
10½ ounces	294 grams
12 ounces	¾ cup
16 ounces	2 cups or 1lb.
1 liter	4 cups + 3½ tablespoons
1 lb. 24 oz.	850 grams

WHICH CAN IS WHICH?

Can Size	Weight	Cups	Products
6 oz.	6 oz.	¾	seafood
8 oz.	8 oz.	1	fruits, vegetables
#1	10½–12 oz.	1¼	condensed soups
12 oz. vacuum	12 oz.	1½	vacuum-packed corn
#300	14–16 oz. (1 lb.)	1¾	pork and beans, baked beans, meat products, cranberry sauce, blueberries
#303	16–17 oz. (1 lb.–1 lb. 1 oz.)	2	fruits/vegetables, ready-to-serve soups
#2	20 oz. (1 lb. 4 oz.) 18 fl. oz. (1 pt. 2 fl. oz.)	2½	juices, ready-to-serve soups
#2½	27–29 oz. (1 lb. 11 oz. to 1 lb. 13 oz.)	3½	vegetables
#3 cylinder or 46 fl. oz.	51 oz. (3 lb. 3 oz.) or 46 fl. oz. (1 qt. 14 fl. oz.)	5¾	fruit/vegetable juice, pork and beans
#10	6½ lb.–7 lb. 5 oz.	12–13	food-service size for fruits, vegetables, sauces, soups

METRIC CONVERSION GUIDE

U.S. UNITS	CANADIAN METRIC	AUSTRALIAN METRIC
Volume		
¼ teaspoon	1 mL	1 ml
½ teaspoon	2 mL	2 ml
1 teaspoon	5 mL	5 ml
1 tablespoon	15 mL	20 ml
¼ cup	50 mL	60 ml
⅓ cup	75 mL	80 ml
½ cup	125 mL	125 ml
⅔ cup	150 mL	170 ml
¾ cup	175 mL	190 ml
1 cup	250 mL	250 ml
1 quart	1 liter	1 liter
1½ quarts	1.5 liters	1.5 liters
2 quarts	2 liters	2 liters
2½ quarts	2.5 liters	2.5 liters
3 quarts	3 liters	3 liters
4 quarts	4 liters	4 liters
Weight		
1 ounce	30 grams	30 grams
2 ounces	55 grams	60 grams
3 ounces	85 grams	90 grams
4 ounces (¼ pound)	115 grams	125 grams
8 ounces (½ pound)	225 grams	225 grams
16 ounces (1 pound)	445 grams	500 grams
1 pound	455 grams	½ kilogram

MEASUREMENTS		TEMPERATURES	
Inches	Centimeters	Fahrenheit	Celsius
1	2.5	32°	0°
2	5.0	212°	100°
3	7.5	250°	120°
4	10.0	275°	140°
5	12.5	300°	150°
6	15.0	325°	160°
7	17.5	350°	180°
8	20.5	375°	190°
9	23.0	400°	200°
10	25.5	425°	220°
11	28.0	450°	230°
12	30.5	475°	240°
13	33.0	500°	260°
14	35.5		
15	38.0		

REFERENCES

Applegate, Liz. *101 Miracle Foods That Heal Your Heart*. New York: Prentice Hall, 2000.

The Essential Women's Health Guide 2001. New York: Time, Inc., Health, 2001.

"How Cancer Researcher Dr. Ritva Butrum Eats to Prevent Cancer." *Bottom Line Health*, April 2001.

Natow, Annette B., and Jo-Ann Heslin. *The Most Complete Food Counter*. New York: Pocket Books, 1999.

Prevention: Food Cures. Emmaus, PA: Rodale, Inc. 2001.

Vegetarian Times: Vegetarian Beginner's Guide. New York: MacMillan, 1996.

Websites
www.bottomlinesecrets.com
www.cdc.gov
www.eatright.org
www.findarticles.com
www.foodfit.com
www.healthharvard.edu
www.homefoodsafety.org
www.navigator.tufts.edu
www.nutrio.com
www.nutritionfocus.com
www.vegweb.com

INDEX

INDEX

INDEX

INDEX

INDEX

INDEX